VULCAN BOYS

PREVIOUS BOOKS BY TONY BLACKMAN

Vulcan Test Pilot
ISBN 978-1-906502-30-0
Published Grub Street 2007

Tony Blackman Test Pilot
ISBN 978-1-906502-28-7
Published Grub Street 2009

Nimrod Rise and Fall
ISBN 978-1-90811779-3
Published Grub Street 2011

Victor Boys
ISBN 978-1908117-4-58
Published Grub Street 2012

FICTION

A Flight Too Far
ISBN 978-0-9553856-3-6, 0-9553856-3-6
Published Blackman Associates

The Final Flight
ISBN 978-0-9553856-0-5, 0-9553856-0-1
Published Blackman Associates

The Right Choice
ISBN 978-0-9553856-2-9, 0-9553856-2-8
Published Blackman Associates

Flight to St Antony
ISBN 978-0-9553856-6-7 0-9553856-6-0
Published Blackman Associates

Now You See It
ISBN 978-0-9553856-7-4, 0-9553856-7-9
Published Blackman Associates

Dire Strait
ISBN 978-0-9553856-8-1
Published Blackman Associates

VULCAN BOYS

From the Cold War to the Falklands:
True Tales of the Iconic
Delta V Bomber

TONY BLACKMAN

Grub Street • London

Published by
Grub Street
4 Rainham Close
London
SW11 6SS

Reprinted 2015, 2016 (twice), 2017, 2018 (twice)

A CIP record for this title is available from the British Library

ISBN-13: 978-1-909808-08-9

Cover design by Sarah Driver

Printed and bound in India by Replika Press Pvt. Ltd.

AUTHOR'S NOTE
The reader will note that there are two styles to the
text layout in the book. Indented and full out.
All indented text is my commentary. TB.

CONTENTS

Foreword *7*

Acknowledgements *9*

Preface *10*

Chapter One   11
Test Flying the Vulcans

Chapter Two   27
Navigating the Test Pilots

Chapter Three   33
Engine Test Bed

Chapter Four   38
Piloting the Vulcan

Chapter Five   52
Nav Radar and H2S

Chapter Six   67
'Down Under' Navigator

Chapter Seven   80
An AEO's Story

Chapter Eight   89
Blue Steel

Chapter Nine   95
Taceval – on Being Combat Ready

Chapter Ten   100
Vulcan Crew Training in North America

Chapter Eleven   115
North American Support

Chapter Twelve   127
Operation Corporate

Chapter Thirteen   151
Wideawake and Port Stanley

Chapter Fourteen   171
Shriking, Rio and Return

Chapter Fifteen   195
The Vulcan K2 Tanker

Chapter Sixteen   204
Those that are left

Epilogue *215*

Appendix 1
Acronyms and Explanations
216

Appendix 2
Black Buck Raids of Falkland Islands by Vulcans 1982
217

Index *220*

DEDICATION

To the many Vulcan aircrews and ground crews, some
sadly no longer with us, who operated the aircraft for over
thirty years helping to guard the United Kingdom
through many troubled times.

FOREWORD

When Tony asked me to write the foreword to *Vulcan Boys* I was delighted to be associated with this book telling the whole story of the aircraft from its design concept, through the Cold War when, along with the other V bombers, it played out its most important role as Britain's nuclear deterrent–before unbelievably, at the end of its service life, also playing a significant role both with bombs and missiles, in liberating the Falkland Islands, for which it (and I) gained much celebrity.

As chief test pilot of Avros Tony helped develop the Nimrod, the Victor K2 tanker and the Vulcan and so he is probably in a unique position to write books about these aircraft and compare their capabilities. Despite being in competition with Handley Page during the early days of the V bombers, he clearly recognised what a wonderful tanker the Victor became with its very large bomb bay and underwing tanks though always preferring to fly the Vulcan with its greater strength and delightful handling qualities.

While the well documented Black Buck missions certainly were not 'Britain's most daring raids' in the conflict (as depicted in a *Channel 4* documentary), they were possibly the most complex and imaginative since the Second World War.

Today, Typhoon pilots have questioned why we were congratulated and even decorated for pressing on to the target, risking losing aircraft by running out of fuel, when they could expect to face a court martial for doing the same! However, this story has made the Vulcan well known, and the last flying example, XH558, is now extremely popular at air shows and a great success with the ladies, who particularly seem to like the famous 'howl'. However, had the Argentinians waited another six months before invading the islands, Britain would have scrapped our two aircraft carriers and disbanded all the Vulcan squadrons. There would have been no Vulcan tanker, possibly no Vulcan Display Flight and most likely not enough public interest to fund a Vulcan 'returning to flight', and for me to become the oldest V bomber pilot in history (or has that title already gone to Bob Prothero?).

For my part, I first saw a Vulcan, near Woodford, when I was about ten years old and have always admired it. When I was not streamed to fly 'fast jets' at the end of my basic flying training it was the only aircraft I wanted to fly.

The Vulcan, particularly at low level and in practice intercepts, with its low wing-loading and massive flying controls could roll rapidly into tight turns, and being able to slow down or accelerate rapidly, could easily evade any fighter of its era including the Lightning, F104, Voodoo or MiG. I can assure you that it was (and still is) a real pilot's aeroplane and a joy to fly.

As a bomber, given the antiquated system which it shared with the Victor, it was little better than a Lancaster, but getting to the target was all important, and in its nuclear strike role when a 'Bucket of Sunshine' (as we called an H bomb) didn't actually require pinpoint accuracy!

When it was no longer viable to attack the USSR from high altitudes, the Vulcan unlike the Victor was able to adapt to the low-level role and thereafter remained a viable part of NATO's Strike Force right up to 1982 when it was replaced in that role by the Tornado.

So indisputably, though the Victor was a great aircraft and the best tanker, the Vulcan has to be accredited with the title of 'The Best Bomber'.

Martin Withers
December 2013

ACKNOWLEDGEMENTS

When I was asked to write this book I realised I would need to search far and wide to get contributions. As a test pilot I did not know the actual operators of the aircraft or the methods of operation and the only people I was in touch with were Martin Withers, who kindly agreed to write the foreword, and Barry Masefield, both of whom were flying XH558. However, John Reeve, 44 Squadron and Black Buck 2, very kindly invited me as a guest to the squadron reunion and that made this book possible. In fact, I have been very lucky to have had so much help and encouragement that it is difficult to know where to begin but I feel I must give special mention to my long suffering crewmen Ted Hartley and Bob Pogson who put up with my idiosyncrasies through my Avro years.

For the main RAF part of the book I would like to mention Anthony Wright who has not only supplied material and been a constant source of information but has also read through the draft of the book to help remove errors. In addition I would like to give many thanks to Charles Brimson, David Bourne, David Castle, David Griffiths, Mel James, Ken Kendrick, John Laycock, Ray Leach, Phil Leckenby, Chris Lumb, Ted Marmont, 'Monty' Montgomery, Harry Pollitt, Mike Pollitt, Chris Reid, Adrian Sumner, Jim Vinales and Peter West. Sadly there was not enough room in the book for all the contributions I received but I have saved them all and hopefully they will be available at a later date. Would those I have inadvertently left out or whose contributions I have had to defer because of space limitations please accept my apologies.

With regard to photographs, hopefully I have acknowledged all the ones that I have received including Bill Perrins who clearly had the best camera on Ascension.

I would also like to thank my publisher for all his support, with his suggestions, superb editing and his efforts in turning the draft into a book of which we can be proud.

Finally, I would like to thank my wife Margaret Blackman for her meticulous editing and for giving me so many ideas and so much encouragement. Inevitably there will be errors and omissions for which I apologise and take full responsibility.

Tony Blackman
December 2013

PREFACE

This book is about the second of the three V bombers which were built to guard the United Kingdom during the Cold War. The Vulcan has become an aviation icon like the Spitfire and it is probably true to say that most people, whatever their age, will recognise the aircraft notwithstanding the fact that the RAF stopped flying it over thirty years ago. Its delta shape makes it instantly identifiable as does its noise when the engines are opened up for take-off. Thanks to Robert Pleming and his Vulcan to the Sky charity, Vulcan Mk 2 XH558 is still flying, making its howling noise and wowing the crowds all over the UK.

The objective in producing this book is to put on record all the things the aircraft did alongside memories written by the operators themselves. Wherever necessary I introduce the writer and pass comments on various issues raised but the book is mainly composed of first-hand accounts and personal opinions which give an authenticity that is impossible to match just by relating conversations third hand; David Castle's account of his Black Buck sorties is a first class prime example.

One cannot help but be impressed when reading the book of the long hours spent by the crews, ground as well as flight, sitting by the aircraft at the readiness platforms waiting to be scrambled to defend the country in the event of a third world war. Thankfully it never happened but it might well have done if the crews had not been sitting there in constant vigilance. The tedium was relieved by occasional Lone Rangers flying to the States and westward round the world and, most importantly, by taking part in Giant Voice and Red Flag exercises, honing the crews' aggressive skills in competition with United States Strategic Air Command.

The last throw of the dice for the Vulcan proved to be the Falklands campaign and again it is fascinating to read what had to be done on the ground and in the air at very short notice to enable the Vulcan to support the ground troops. There have been numerous accounts of the operations from Ascension attacking Port Stanley but in this book there are first-hand accounts from the people concerned. The attacks with Shrike missiles are described properly for the first time including the landing at Rio de Janeiro. In addition Black Buck 3 is explained in Appendix 2.

One has to admire the RAF commanders who took the decision to launch the Black Buck sorties; I've always felt that any Staff College student who had proposed such an operation would have been sent off his course.

Thanks again to all the people who helped write this book and making it such a fascinating read, reminding us about the Cold War, how it was fought and the considerable effort required to which we all contributed.

Tony Blackman
December 2013

Chapter One

TEST FLYING THE VULCANS

XA899 pre-flight. From left, Johnny Baker, Jack Haddock, Ted Hartley,
Eric Burgess 16th February 1957. (*Ted Hartley*)

This book is started by Ted Hartley, observer extraordinaire, who flew
in every Vulcan except one as a flight test observer. Much has been written
about the Vulcan and the way it flew but very little has been told by the
people in the flight development team who flew in it and helped to trans-
form a rather dangerous aircraft when flying at high speed into an effective
high and low altitude bomber. This chapter and the next relates some of the
stories told by the two most experienced flight test aircrew, Ted Hartley, observer and Bob Pogson, AEO. Like me they missed the very beginning of the
Vulcan flight testing but Ted joined Avros only a year later when the second
prototype flew. I have to say that I am envious of both of them as they flew
in one or two more than I did. Their recollections give an interesting and
challenging perspective to flying in the Vulcan.

The back of the Vulcan was a very different environment from the flight
deck; at least the pilots could look out even though the view has been compared to peering through pillar box slits, though of course pilots get used
to almost anything. The rear crew compartments of the Vulcan prototypes
were a mass of instruments with only two tiny windows in the roof and no
way of looking out at all. Add to this that the rear crew had absolutely no

control of the test manoeuvres, many at the corner of the flight envelope, and had no ejection seats if anything went wrong, and it is amazing that anyone volunteered to fly in the back of the aircraft at all. Certainly in the circumstances I find a lot of Ted's and Bob's descriptions very restrained.

Ted Hartley

I joined Avros in 1953 when I was twenty-four-years old and became a member of the flight research and development team when there was only one Vulcan flying, VX770. The second prototype Vulcan VX777 flew in September 1953 soon after I joined followed by the first production aircraft XA889 in 1955.

Luckily there was a shortage of pilots at Woodford so Jimmy Harrison, who was chief then, got Jack Haddock and myself approval from the powers that be in Whitehall to fly in the right-hand seat of the Vulcan during test flights even though we weren't qualified pilots, which proved to be very useful in progressing the actual tests.

Ted Hartley's authority to fly in the right-hand seat. (*Ted Hartley*)

Looking at Ted's letter of approval brought back many memories. It must be remembered that the aircraft we were flying were not the firm's aircraft but were all owned by the Royal Air Force. There was a department called flight operations in the Ministry of Defence headed by an air commodore that looked after all aspects of industry test flying. Ted's letter was signed by John Ratcliffe who was the worker in the department called 'Operations A'. He tried to ensure that all the flying that we did was done in accordance with RAF flying rules therefore we had an RAF authorisation book in which we entered all our flights before we went flying. Most of us were allowed to authorise our own flights but some had to be authorised by the chief test pilot or his deputy.

As they were RAF aircraft they had to be checked by an AID[1] inspector, on behalf of the MoD, who confirmed that the company had serviced the aircraft correctly and they had been inspected by their team. During all the twenty-two years I flew with Avros the ministry's inspector was Len Lee and he checked that each flight we were doing was in accordance with a par-

---

[1] Aeronautical Inspection Department.

ticular development contract. When he was satisfied that all was in order he would go out to the aircraft and, in our opinion, waste time functioning the flight controls since that was the first thing we always did. He would then go back to his office and sign the form 970 which then gave us authority to fly the aircraft. The whole flight development crew would have had a pre-flight briefing earlier in the day just in time to meet the flight time forecast by the foreman of flight sheds, Frank Sheehan or Jack Bolton while I was there, but they were always wildly optimistic; invariably we were hanging around for the preparatory maintenance work to be finished, for the firm's inspection to sign the aircraft off and then finally for Len Lee to waggle the controls, so poor Len always got blamed for holding us up and preventing us flying.

In 1954 (Ted continues) I joined the Territorial Army and did a parachute course which came in handy later on but I had to pretend I was only a clerk because in those days a flight test observer at Avros was a reserved occupation so I couldn't be called up to be sent to join the front line in an emergency.

In fact, having joined Avros I never looked back and I carried on flying with them until 1986 so that I flew in every Vulcan but one and every Nimrod. I also flew in the Victor K2 and even did some Avro 748 testing.

VX777 auto-observer panel. (*Ted Hartley*)

Our Vulcan tasks were either development or production testing. I started flying Vulcans in 1955 on the two prototypes, VX770 and VX777, and XA889 the first production aircraft. My first production flight test schedule (PFTS) was the second flight of XA890, the second production aircraft which at that time still had the original straight unmodified leading edge. There were forty-five Mk1 aircraft and the only one I missed was XH497. I flew on all the eighty-five Mk2s except for XM576 though not on all when they were first delivered. Fifty of the Mk2s were returned to Woodford to have their wings strengthened, these were called Skybolt modifications even though the Skybolt programme was later cancelled; as a result I was able to fly the Mk2 aircraft I had missed on initial delivery except XM576 which crashed at Scampton. One Mk2, XM596, never flew and went straight to the structural test rig. Initially all the Mk2s were painted white but when the deterrent role of the aircraft was changed to low level they started appearing in camouflage from XH497 onwards.

The first few production aircraft on both the Mk1s and the Mk2s were used as trials aircraft to test the aircraft handling and systems. Initially the instrumentation on the aircraft consisted of large banks of conventional pointer instruments mounted on a very large panel being photographed once a second with the rate being increased to ten a second during critical manoeuvres.

With the advent of the mach trimmer and the pitch damper, ultra violet paper instrumentation was used which meant that events could be tracked at a much higher speed and the results examined immediately after the flight. With the cameras, the films had to be developed and the gauges had to be read before the results could be examined; the problem was exacerbated for us in the air as we were continually having to change the film, which wasted a lot of time and was difficult to do, especially on 770 as it had two photo panels with two cameras and the film lasted for only a short time.

The first time I flew as an observer in the Vulcan was with the famous Roly Falk, then superintendent of flying, in the second prototype VX777 in June 1955. His call sign was Avro Vulcan unlike the other pilots who were Avro 2, Avro 3 etc. Tony Black-man tells a story that in 1956 Roly had to fly a Shackleton to get his hours up to five so that he could renew his private pilot's licence to fly at Farnborough and I often wondered what call sign he used.

> I remember the flight very well, though not his call sign. I was courting my fiancée to be at the time who was at Boscombe and so I wanted to get down there for the weekend. I had intended to fly the aircraft and was amazed and very puzzled when Roly appeared from nowhere and announced he was going to fly a Shackleton, something he never did. The weather at Boscombe was not all that good and Roly having got to Boscombe pretended it was too bad for him to land and we all returned to Woodford. Later we cross questioned his secretary and discovered that in the year since the previous SBAC show, 1955, he had flown less than the five hours needed to renew his private pilot's licence, which remarkably was all that we needed to fly as test pilots; hence Roly's need to fly the Shackleton. A day or so later he was flying at Farnborough giving an immaculate display.

Roly Falk joined Avros in the late '40s and did the initial flying on the 707s and the prototype Vulcans but left flight test in 1957 as the production aircraft emerged from flight sheds, but only after first recruiting Jimmy Harrison in 1950 and then Tony Blackman in 1956.

Roly used to give superb flying demonstrations but wasn't too keen on long test flights recording all the numbers. John McDaniel who was deputy chief of flight test to Cyril Bethwaite used to say that Roly's greatest contribution was recruiting Jimmy and Tony.

There have been many stories about Roly not telling the crew that he was going out to the aircraft and also that he flew in a grey pin-striped suit, and they were all true. The only time I saw him in white overalls was when he flew 770 with the canopy off, two flights in total. Stan Nicol, chief flight test observer at the time, remembered that for the sheer joy of flying nothing could touch the Vulcan with the canopy off; he said it was actually possible to see out instead of being enclosed in a metal box with no sensible view out at all. I continued to fly with Roly or Jimmy Harrison, mostly Jimmy, on development testing using 770 and 777 plus the first production aircraft 889. We didn't start doing formal PFTSs, until the second production aircraft 890 came along.

One of the early tests I remember was with Blue Danube, which was the name given to the UK's first atom bomb. It weighed 10,000lbs and only just fitted into the Vulcan's bomb bay. In one of Tony Blackman's test pilot books he says 'Roly dropped some small bombs' but maybe he was thinking of security since as far as I know the only bomb Roly ever dropped was the big one.

The Blue Danube flights were carried out taking off from Farnborough with very strict security and secrecy; the aircraft was put in a hangar which was inside a wired-off enclosure on the airfield. We had none of the inspection problems about being allowed to look at the bomb such as those encountered by Milt Cottee, a Boscombe test pilot but in the Royal Australian Air Force, described by Tony Blackman elsewhere, but maybe the UK didn't like Aussies looking at our bombs, even though we allowed them to fly the aircraft. We used XA892 and the drops were at Orford Ness off the Suffolk coast. There were five dropping flights between 30th April and 3rd May 1956.

The first four drops were from 1,000ft at speeds 310kt, 345kt, 380kt and 415kt, the Vulcan's maximum permitted indicated airspeed. On the final sortie the drop was from 30,000ft at .95 indicated Mach number. In all cases the bomb left the bomb bay cleanly. Our last flight was to measure the effects of 'g' on the beam supporting the Blue Danube; this comprised a number of pull-outs up to 3.0 g. Looking at the records later Roly actually applied between 3.2 and 3.3 g. On the return to Woodford some wing leading edge ribs were found to have buckled, as used to happen when we started doing rolls off the top.

The co-pilot on the Blue Danube flights was Squadron Leader 'Podge' Howard who later took the first RAF aircraft to New Zealand and back, finishing with that terrible accident at Heathrow with Sir Harry Broadhurst in the right-hand seat (mentioned in chapter 7 of *Vulcan Test Pilot*). In fact Sir Harry had been in the Vulcan before the New Zealand trip because on 26th March 1956 Jimmy took Broadhurst and his aide, AVM Sidney Bufton, on a demonstration flight. At one point in the flight Jimmy asked Broadhurst if he would like to see a roll; he chickened out giving 'chaps in the back' as an excuse. Sidney said that we in the back didn't mind but Broadhurst would not have it. However he would like to experience streaming the parachute which was hardly in the same league. After we had come to a stop I gave our passengers plenty of time to leave the aircraft but as I was last down I heard a squeal – I had trodden on the AVM's fingers. In fact when Sir Harry left the RAF he was recruited to run the Manchester factories, Chadderton and Woodford.

On the last flight, Podge Howard left the day before an RAF examiner arrived whose job it was to check out all the Avro pilots for fitness to be Vulcan test pilots, including Roly. That evening Roly wined and dined the designated examiner; however the next day the examiner was called away and replaced by another, much to Roly's chagrin. Throughout the flight Roly kept trying to 'give' the aircraft to the examiner but he would not have any of it, presumably because he wanted to watch Roly!

Much has been made over the years about Roly rolling the Vulcan at the SBAC show in 1955. On the 31st August I flew with him on an air test in XA899 a few days before Farnborough. Without telling anyone he rolled the aircraft four times. The only reason I knew this was because the sunlight through the top window went all the way round the cabin wall. At the time I couldn't work out what was happening which made a good story when we got back on the ground.

Really there was nothing to the actual manoeuvre; later on I actually did a few rolls myself when I was in the right-hand seat. I experienced over 100 between '55 and '58. Years later I flew with Al McDicken in a Chipmunk when he was chief test pilot and he said to me 'Go on, do a slow roll' which I did. He asked me what I thought and I think he was a bit taken aback when I said 'it was just like a Vulcan'. My last flight with Roly was on 13th April 1957 in XA902.

My early view of Jimmy Harrison was that he was somewhat of a martinet. I had been in the army on National Service from '47 to '49 and so I was used to officers. Jim once gave me a bollocking for dirty shoes. I seldom cleaned them because I travelled by motor-bike in boots and left the shoes in the office. He did soften a bit over the years and became more sociable but could now and again show a temper. I upset him once by saying my preferred pilot was Tony Blackman, which I suppose was not a very tactful thing to say. I considered Jim to be very able but he did make some mistakes. One I remember was in November 1955; we had gone to Waddington in 770 to do low level position error measurements calibrating the airspeed indicator and the altimeter. After the last run we pulled away and Jim went into a roll. This was not initially apparent until I saw the other observer Ken Yeomans curled up in the roof. Clearly Jim didn't get his barrel roll quite right and Ken wasn't strapped in. Another one was overstressing VX777 practising for the 1958 SBAC show...

Every time I think about Jimmy and the practising he did in 777 before the 1958 SBAC show I remember how lucky we all were. Jimmy had decided to practise in 777 because we were not sure if the first Vulcan Mk2 XH533 would be ready in time for the event; I was practising at the same time in XA891 since we were doing a synchronised display. I don't know what happened but somehow Jim made a mistake rolling the aircraft and pulled too much 'g' but nothing much was said at the time. In the event 533 was ready for the show and though 777 was positioned at Farnborough it was never used. In fact I flew it back in the middle of the week and it was my first flight in the aircraft since it had had the Mk2 wing fitted; I was a bit surprised to find that the lateral control on the approach left a lot to be desired and that the yaw damping needed attention, but that was another story. Coincidental with all this we had been demonstrating the Blue Steel on Mk1 XA903 and on the Wednesday of the show week the maintenance team decided that they needed to drop the Blue Steel off the aircraft for some reason and were horrified when bits of the aircraft structure came off at the same time. As a result it was decided to inspect 777 and the structural design experts were amazed that the structure was badly damaged. Had Jim had to use the aircraft at Farnborough the flight could have ended in disaster. The whole event had to be hushed up because 777 had been taken on our charge for the SBAC show and was no longer a ministry aircraft; strictly speaking we were liable for the repair bill of Jimmy's mistake.

Besides Jimmy Harrison and Tony Blackman more pilots were needed and Ossie Hawkins joined in 1958 when he left Glosters. Later Dickie Martin, having completed the extremely demanding Javelin spinning trials joined us, also from Glosters. Colin Allen came from the British Aircraft Corporation in 1960 but he was recruited to help in the Avro 748 development and didn't do much Vulcan flying.

Throughout the years that we flew the Vulcans we had RAF liaison officers attached to the pilots' office. The first was Squadron Leader Jock Calder who had been a member of 617 Squadron during the war and on 14th March 1945 in a Lancaster dropped the first Grand Slam bomb from 11,965ft (3,647m) on the Bielefeld Viaduct. More than 100 yards of the viaduct collapsed. I only flew with him a few times but my memories of him are positive.

Jock was appointed CO of the operational conversion unit (OCU) at Waddington just as the RAF were about to get their first Mk2. He hadn't done the course at this time or flown the aircraft so it was decided that I would deliver the first Mk2 to Waddington which was most unusual because the RAF normally always collected the new aircraft. Jock sat in the right-hand seat and on 1st July 1960 we flew to Waddington. Interestingly, the aircraft was XH558 which is the one still flying as I write this in 2013. It was the first and the last Mk2 and this came about because it had had a double-engine failure in the middle of its career and so was grounded for a long time being repaired. Back to Ted:

Jock Calder was replaced by Podge Howard; I flew with him as an observer. He was never allowed to fly the aircraft by himself but Jimmy let him fly in the left-hand seat occasionally on a few of the more mundane flights. He left in September 1957 preparing to take the first production aircraft XA897 to New Zealand and back. The story of the terrible accident at London airport has been told elsewhere but he clearly must have come below his permitted minimum altitude on the approach. Sometime later he reappeared at Woodford but he didn't stay very long.

Max Savage was next and proved to be very likeable and stayed until 1960. The final RAF attached officer was John 'Polly' Pollington. My first flight with him in the left-

hand seat was in XH534 on 5th December 1961. He was a super chap and a delight to
fly with and to know socially. By early 1963 an engine rapid air start was fitted to the
aircraft. Polly with Jack and me on board on XJ784 gave a demonstration to some RAF
visitors on how to get airborne in less than two minutes which from the Avro ramp
took some doing. Unfortunately Polly was called away to command a squadron as a
result of some fatal accident.

> Ted mentioning XJ784 reminds me of one of my great disappointments.
> I collected the aircraft from Moreton Vallance on 9th August 1961 after it
> had been fitted with the uprated Olympus 301 engines, 21,000lbs each, and
> compressed air starting for rapid scrambles. With one push of the button
> all four engines could be started and in no time at all the aircraft would
> be taking off. I was mad keen to demonstrate the aircraft at Farnborough
> visualising being towed out to the runway, air traffic firing a flare when the
> time came and the aircraft leaping, in no time flat, 'vertically' into the air.
> Alas it was not to be. Sir Harry Broadhurst had retired from the RAF and
> been appointed managing director of the Manchester Division of Hawker
> Siddeley. Jimmy Harrison asked if we could demonstrate the aircraft but for
> some reason he refused. I even asked him myself when he happened to be at
> Woodford but he said that we were behind in the programme and could not
> afford to waste the time at SBAC. I wasn't convinced that that was the real
> reason but maybe he wanted to convince the RAF how well he was doing.
> Somehow flying the Avro 748 that year at SBAC didn't seem so exciting but
> probably was more important from a sales viewpoint.

We always seemed to get on well with the attached RAF pilots perhaps because, unlike
the test pilots, they were pleased to be allowed to fly the aircraft and relied on us telling them what to do unlike the test pilots who frequently decided they wanted to do
something different from what had been planned.

Through the years there were various incidents I remember. In fact one of the first
which sticks in the mind was soon after I joined, although I was not on board. Jimmy Harrison was flying one of the prototypes with Podge Howard as co-pilot. Jimmy
wanted to use the urine tube and so he undid his parachute and seat straps. The tubes
were not of a robust design and Jimmy suddenly realised that the tube bottom bung
had fallen out. He tried to pick up the bung but in doing so he inadvertently operated
the emergency decompression switch. Podge – not realising what was happening –
pushed the stick forward to start a rapid descent and so Jim, not being strapped in, was
forced out of his seat on to the cockpit roof. Jim remarked afterwards: 'There I was. All
my straps undone, the aircraft falling to pieces around me and nothing useful in my
hand.' What Jim said to Podge was not recorded but he had only been attached to the
test pilots' office for a short time.

Tony has previously contested Charles Masefield's allegations that he started the
engines while climbing up the ladder but I have seen him do it. He tended to rush a bit
in the early days at Woodford but we other crew members soon caught up with him,

occasionally leaving him behind. When going flying we often went in the ambulance as transport from the changing room to the aircraft. Tony got to shouting 'scramble' as we reached the aircraft but we soon played him at his own game by all shouting scramble and leaving him in the ambulance. He seemed quite nonplussed.

All Vulcans were being rolled, it seemed an unwritten part of the PFTS. The other manoeuvre was a roll off the top, a half loop and a half roll back to level flight. The first one Tony did was in a Vulcan Mk1 low-powered aircraft XA894 with only Olympus 101 engines and 11,000lbs of thrust each. My job in the right-hand seat was to call out the acceleration to make sure that we never exceeded the limit of 3 g during the early part of the pull up. We started at 340 knots and his intention was gradually to lower this starting speed so that the pull-up could start before the end of the runway; he was preparing for the 1958 SBAC show.

Jimmy was also doing rolls off the top but in a Mk1A with 13,000lbs thrust engines. Then in June we went to Langar near Waddington where an Avro working party had installed the Olympus engines for the Vulcan Mk2 in Vulcan Mk1 XA891. Tony slowly reduced the starting speed for the manoeuvre and on 19th August we did the first roll off the top from take-off pulling up at 270kts before the end of the runway. Practices continued and on one flight we did twelve rolls off the top. By the time of the first demo at Farnborough we had done forty-five rolls off the top. After the SBAC show the rolls off the top were seldom done and were prohibited after the terrible accident to VX770 during a display flight at Syerston. A newspaper article of the period carried the headline 'Vulcan Loops the Loop in Secret'; certainly Jimmy and Tony never did a full loop as they said it might overstress the aircraft during the recovery if the wings were not level.

During the actual show Margaret, Tony's wife, came down to Farnborough and on one flight came with us in XA891 doing rolls off the top. I was in the right-hand seat. As we taxied back after the show I asked her if she enjoyed the flight and she said she did. Up to this point I'm sure Tony had completely forgotten Margaret was in the back because when Margaret said "did it make any difference, dear?", Tony looked stunned, but managed to recover and mutter "of course, dear".

> This next story still frightens me. It happened on the aircraft I was testing but we had gone away on holiday and so Jimmy had to fly it. We were having coffee at a café and I decided it was time to see what had been happening in the UK so I went to buy the *Daily Telegraph*. Suddenly I spotted a news item 'V Bomber Crashes in Lincolnshire' and then I read how Jimmy had had to bale out but that all the crew were safe. There must have been more detail in the clip than I can remember because somehow I knew it was 'my aircraft'. Reading the account I'm not sure I would have done as well as Jimmy. The thing that saved the day was his decision not to try and go back and land.

My most memorable trip was on 24th July 1959 in XA891. It was the Mk1 aircraft fitted with the Mk2 engines for development and in fact it was the one we had used at Farnborough doing rolls off the top. Tony had been doing all the engine handling but was sunning himself on a beach in Spain (for which I expect he was thankful) so it fell to Jimmy to fly the aircraft. We were to test the engine handling and take strain gauge measurements of the engines; it was expected to be another routine day. Because of the high altitude capability of the aircraft with the more powerful engines, in excess of 55,000ft, we were all wearing pressure suits.

The pressure suit comprised a ventilated suit, g-trousers, a bulky pressure jerkin (all on top of our flying overalls) and a Taylor helmet. We looked a bit like astronauts. Fortunately, we were able to put the helmets on in the aircraft. About a year earlier after protracted negotiations by Jimmy, we were awarded pay, not for flying, but for the discomfort of this gear.

The rear crew, observers and AEO had to fit their parachutes at the locker room before walking out to the aircraft. The pilots were spared this task as the parachute was part of the ejector seat. Bob Pogson was the AEO and while he was fitting on his parachute he remarked, "This harness is a bit tight". Having spent a short time in the 13th Battalion I seized his harness and in parachute jump instructor fashion gave it a good shake. I was able to pronounce it 'just right' – was this an omen? Thus encumbered we staggered up the sloping apron to the aircraft. Dickey Proudlove was in the right-hand seat and we had Phil Christie from Bristol Engines as an extra observer to control the engine tests.

Besides the fitment of the larger Mk2 engines to 891, the electrics on the aircraft were changed to test the AC electrics which were being fitted on the Mk2 instead of the DC generators. Consequently the port engines were to the Mk2 standard and fitted with Sundstrand constant speed drives (CSD) driving 200V alternators. The No 2 alternator was connected to loading mats in the bomb bay therefore supplying no power to the aircraft. No 1 alternator drove a motor generator set supplying DC power to the port main bus bar; this motor generator had to be run up to a synchronous speed to bring the generator onto the bus bar from ground power. The two starboard engines drove the DC generators, normal for the Mk1.

We were held by Manchester air traffic control at the Poynton end of Runway 260 for a couple of minutes, then the engines were opened up for take-off. Jimmy liked to do sporty noise abatement take-offs and with these new more powerful engines and a light all-up weight of 115,000lbs we were soon at 3,000ft. However trouble had started immediately long before we reached 3,000ft. Bob told Jimmy we had a big electrical problem. Jim asked what he should do. Land immediately should've been the answer but it was too late. We had flown 891 on engine tests for over sixty flights. They were not to last much longer.

The initial part of the take-off had been uneventful but soon, during the sporty climb for noise abatement, all the warning lights on the AEO's electrics panel had lit up, hence Bob's instruction. Instinctively Jimmy selected the airbrakes which required electrical power, which we didn't have and they probably didn't operate. Anyway we really had no electrics even though the No 4 generator was apparently still online; it was producing very little power, if anything. It seemed that a fault on No 4 generator had blown the bus bar interlink and also taken Nos 2 and 3 generators off so nothing could remedy the problem. There was no power to run up the motor generator on

No 1 engine. Because of the No 4 generator fault, No 3 generator could not be reset. The 112 volt battery which was advertised to last for about twenty minutes in the case of total generator failure had soon gone flat. It seemed just possible that the No 4 generator was supplying some power to the powered flying controls (PFCs) but to fly approximately straight and level Jimmy had to hold the stick fully forward and well right. He soon realised that landing was probably a non-starter.

It was about this time that Jim in his best commanding voice called: "Prepare to bale out." I realised this was positively not an immediate option. We were at 3,000ft inside an aircraft we could hardly control. I was of course expecting the order to bale out soon afterwards. Jim had transmitted a Mayday and was in touch with Woodford tower for any advice anyone could give. All the time we were steadily climbing to give us extra height for baling out. I had disconnected my personal equipment connector (PEC) so I had no intercom or oxygen. Luckily oxygen was not going to be needed, nor was pressurisation. This left the AEO to give us the signal to leave. I climbed down towards the door, now the escape hatch, and motioned the Bristol observer to do the same. I threw my now useless briefcase into the nose and tucked in my own and his loose parachute harness straps. We were now ready to go!

I had intended to open the hatch myself but some short time later Bob climbed down, opened the hatch, and gave me a thumbs up. I had a quick look up at the altimeter and saw we were at about 14,000ft, 170kts. I pulled my emergency oxygen knob out and threw it into the nose – I didn't want a tangle – moved to the door and slid out from a great roaring into a quiet calm. I found out afterwards that Jim had given another 'prepare to bale out' which caused Bob to open the door. Jim was apparently quite perplexed to learn later that two of us had already gone.

I have to say that the Taylor helmet, a real space man's affair, gave a feeling of being in one's own little world. I watched the aircraft pass over me, felt a little turbulence from the jet efflux, I suppose, then turned onto my front to observe the earth below. It was a lovely warm day, no clouds, really tremendous.

Freefalling is quite something. No falling sensation or height awareness. Having no altimeter, however, I eventually decided it must be time to 'dump' so I pulled the D-ring (rip cord), saw the drogue chute go over my shoulder, and moments later, with no jerk, I had a parachute canopy overhead. Now came the boring bit. I had still no idea what height I was at. There was a large river, the Ouse I later found out, in front which I did not expect to reach. After what seemed an age I realised that the ground was getting nearer and took my helmet off so that I could look down. Feet and knees together with the ground rushing up, hard landing (ground was very dry and rutted) and I realised how small a canopy the I-24 is. Still, it gets you home.

I had no idea what had gone on after I left the aircraft. So having landed I looked up expecting to see at least one parachute but there were none. What could have happened? I thought I had been abandoned in this field. I had little time to consider this because as I was rolling up my parachute two small boys arrived and they were able to direct me to a phone box. So with the three of us loaded with my 'baggage', off we tramped across fields and onto the road. There we passed a lady by a row of cottages, who remarked "oh, you are the cause of all the excitement". What could I say? In those days a red button in the box gave one the emergency call, a woman answered and asked if it was an emergency. A bit nonplussed I informed her that I had just baled out of a Vulcan! A sign in the box told me I was on Hook Road. She came back shortly to say that the only available car was busy at a school crossing but would come as soon as possible. So I went outside and sat on the grass to wait. The police car soon arrived and took me the short distance to Goole police station. At least now I knew where I was. Not long after the Bristol observer was also brought to Goole. He had landed on the other (east) side of the aforementioned river. We were given sandwiches and tea as well as a good stiff brandy which I thought was an excellent idea.

We found that the other members of the crew were safe and had been taken by helicopter to RAF Leconfield. We travelled there via the crash site and had a quick look round at the now smouldering wreckage of our aeroplane in a turnip field. Not a lot remained, the aircraft had landed quite flat, and the magnesium alloy skin and other parts had burned or melted. We were the first complete crew to escape from a Vulcan. We had taken off at 11.30 am and it was now after 6; all I wanted was to get to the mess at Leconfield for a few beers, and to swap stories, but this was denied us. As we climbed from the bus at the RAF base, the others, led by Jim, came out to meet us. We had to fly straight back to Woodford and no amount of protestation would alter things.

Our faithful Anson Aggy Paggy (G-AGPG) was waiting to take us there. A few snaps were taken for newspapers and thirty-five minutes later we were back from where we had taken off.

Our exciting day was over. We had earned £1 in 'discomfort' pay, of course. As a postscript, most of the newspapers carried the story the next day with lurid and mostly inaccurate reports. One

The imprint of XA891 on the ground with the delta shape clearly visible.

headline said 'Bat Plane Swoops on Women'. This was a reference to two elderly ladies who lived in a small cottage alongside the turnip field. Another reported that the matter was 'so secret' that Jim could not tell what had gone wrong even to the bosses at Woodford. Where do they get their stories?

As mentioned, XA891 had done a pair of rolls off the top each day at the Farnborough Air Show in 1958 and I have wondered, now and again, how things might have gone if we had had the problem during these manoeuvres.

A Royal Aeronautical Establishment (RAE) expert who examined the wreck remarked "The most likely cause was an earth fault on No 4 generator, which damaged No 3 generator. This put the motor generator offline and blew the starboard and battery bus bar fuses. The 28V battery then took over all the loads on the battery bus bar." It was also remarked that with only one generator supplying the port bus bar and with Mod 697 not incorporated the bus bar could not be reconnected. (This mod disconnected the bus bar on peak load and prevented reconnection unless manually connected.) Perhaps 908 in 1958 could have suffered a similar problem, crashing near Detroit during a demo when it lost all its electrics.

> On the Mk1 each engine had a 112V DC generator and 112V had to be available to drive the flying control motors. There was a bus bar on each side of the aircraft and the two bus bars could be joined together. In an emergency there was a bank of four 28V batteries which could keep the flying control motors going but even with four perfect fully charged batteries they could only last for twenty minutes. One aircraft was lost over Detroit as a result of which a modification was introduced which, had it been incorporated on 891, might have saved the day. With the introduction of the Mk2 the flying control motors were powered by 200V AC 400 cycle constant frequency alternators which was a much superior system, particularly as there was in-flight back-up of a ram air turbine and an auxiliary power unit so that there was no time limit for flying on emergency power.

Following this event and the terrible affair of 535 when Ossie Hawkins was flying the aircraft and it crashed after going into a spin and only the pilots escaped, a number of rear crew escape modifications were fitted to the test aircraft to help the rear crew stand up and get to the escape door under conditions of positive g.

We had done some trials of this 'electrical' door opening and we found that the door would not open with more than 1.5psi cabin pressure. On one of these door tests we ran out of pneumatic pressure for opening the door. It did not apparently cross anyone's mind that if we had then had a problem we wouldn't have been able to get out!

Interestingly, some aircraft always gave trouble and 555 was one of them. When we went over to Waddington to collect XM603 I was talking to the RAF guys and discovered they called XH555 'Trouble Five'. The end came for it when it did a heavy landing at Finningley and the remains were brought to Woodford for the structural test specimen.

Incidentally, when Dickie Martin wrote his flight test report on the firing of decoy flares just after coming to Woodford he wrote, 'the trials were successful in that the aircraft did not catch fire or explode', the remark possibly coloured by his recent experiences testing the Gloster Javelin. Jim was not impressed with this report and asked him to reissue it. Dickie wrote, 'all recipients of my previous report, please ignore all after successful'. I'm sure he was encouraged to write such a report by the test he was doing, firing the infra-red decoy cartridges and seeing the colour photographs of the underside of the aircraft as they were fired which looked rather startling with lots of sparks and flame from the underside of the aircraft.

Dickie was an excellent pilot and easy to get on with socially though occasionally went over the top. Just before take-off as he opened the throttles he would say "Hang on to your hats". One day we were taking off from Boscombe and he had just put a lot of papers and maps on the coaming which dropped onto his control column due to acceleration. Jack Haddock, who could fly an aeroplane in spite of a statement to the contrary by Tony, took control of the aircraft to continue the take-off. But Dickie with both hands dumped the papers on Jack much to his surprise so that no-one was in control.

I flew a great deal with Ossie Hawkins and after the 535 accident Tony seemed very keen to find the full story of his 'party piece' aircraft manoeuvre which was the cause of the aircraft going into a spin. Interestingly I am convinced that he never did the trick with anyone from Woodford on board the aircraft; certainly he never did it with me in spite of all the flying we did together. It was clearly illegal and inevitably the news of what he was doing would have got out. We only heard about it from Dickie Martin a short time before the accident when he mentioned it while we were on a test flight.

We were all appalled at Woodford when we heard that 535 had crashed on the approach to Boscombe and that the rear crew members had all been killed. It transpired that Ossie had developed a party trick which involved flying the aircraft very slowly using lots of power with the runway in sight in a seemingly impossible landing position below the nose of the aircraft; the aircraft descended at a very high rate and apparently he would then push the stick forward as the runway came into view from below so that the speed would build up and he was then able to land the aircraft normally. Harry Pollitt had had the manoeuvre demonstrated to him by Ossie and he told me that he was frightened all the way down looking at an airspeed between eighty and ninety knots (see Chapter Three).

On the fateful day while Ossie was demonstrating this trick the aircraft entered a spin, probably because he had allowed too much sideslip to build up, and he was unable to recover. What interested me after the event was who knew about this trick at Woodford. Clearly from Ted's account Dickie did and I often wondered whether Jimmy knew. Ted has made it plain that Ossie never carried out his manoeuvre with the flight test observers on board. Jimmy was very lucky not to lose his job as he was hauled up in front of the air commodore flying, Sidney Hughes, who had been at Farnborough when Jimmy was in Aeroflight. There is a letter from Hughes in the National Archives saying that he knew Jimmy from old but he didn't mention the story that Jimmy told me; apparently when Hughes had introduced some new regulation at Farnborough of which Jim disapproved, Squadron Leader Harrison said to Group Captain Hughes "you're trying to make flying as difficult as you find it". Ted again:

Earlier, another matter which got Ossie into a bit of trouble was damage to XA903 carrying Blue Steel whilst demonstrating at Farnborough when apparently he did a side trip to Moreton Vallance. In fact, the first flight I was on with Ossie was in a Mk1 production XH501 on 21st August 1958 only a couple of weeks before SBAC. We went to Moreton Vallance and he used his old call sign Pinkpill to call the Moreton Vallance tower. The airfield was situated in a dip as I remember, not very good for demos. I flew with him in 903 on the Saturday before SBAC as a practice and for photography and then on Monday we went to Farnborough and nothing out of the ordinary happened on my flights. I was not aware what went on the next two days as I don't know who was in the right-hand seat but apparently aircraft structure fell out when the dummy Blue Steel was unloaded.

Going back to 891 and engine testing, the engine slam accelerations were not satisfactory at low level as the engine would surge making the most tremendous bang which was rather alarming. The aircraft was returned to Rolls-Royce at Filton to try to fix the problem and on its return the handling was worse. Tony was getting very fed up with the lack of progress so he took the aircraft down to Filton and flew over the factory surging the engine leaving a trail of bangs behind. I think they got the message.

> I never did find out whether the bangs were heard at Filton. I think the engineers setting up the engines at that time did a really superb job as the fuel control system was all analogue with several large mechanical units metering the flow to the engine. Trying to adjust the fuel flows at all altitudes so that the engines did not surge on slam accelerations was extremely difficult. Luckily the engines never surged when handled normally.
>
> We delivered a 301-engined aircraft to Filton to set up the fuel system since by this time Rolls had set up a flight test department there. Tom Frost was the first chief test pilot there followed by the aforementioned Harry Pollitt. When they were satisfied that the engines were surge free we got the aircraft back but unfortunately they still surged at high altitude and more testing and adjusting was required.

One of the last tests we did was establishing the performance of the Vulcan Mk2 at maximum take-off weight of 204,000lbs. We flew from Bedford using XH539 and did twin-engine cut take-offs using lower and lower speeds at which to close the two starboard throttles. The last take-off in the series remains in my memory. Tony was doing the flying and when the engines were pulled back to idle at 135kts I really got concerned even though I was by now used to the fair amount of time and runway covered before becoming unstuck. This last one on 7th November 1969 seemed to take an inordinate length of time before getting airborne. In fact it was thirteen or fourteen seconds with the aircraft seeming to accelerate very slowly indeed with the wheels still on the concrete as the end of Bedford's very long runway came into view. It was with a huge sigh of relief that the stick was pulled back and we lumbered into the air.

My last flight on a Vulcan was in XH538 on 15th April 1969 doing a PFTS. In retrospect I was very fortunate to have taken part in such an interesting project and in particular to have been allowed to fly in the right-hand seat. Goodness knows what would have happened if the test pilot flying the aircraft had had a seizure and become incapacitated but I'm sure we would have sorted something out! My guess is that the people in MoD would have been trying to pass the buck back to Woodford.

Ted Hartley's account above is unique from a Vulcan flight test viewpoint. I'm still amazed that we were allowed to have unqualified pilots in the right-hand seat though as he has explained it certainly accelerated the flight testing.

Summing up Ted's splendid reminiscences it is clear that the Vulcan development work relied on a very large team. There were, of course, the crew that flew in the aircraft, the pilots, AEOs and the flight test observers of which Ted has mentioned just a few. I remember as well Derek Bentley with whom I did all the auto-landing trials. But the other people who deserve a mention were the large team of analysts who examined the flight records and worked out what had to be done to meet the handling and performance requirements. In the case of the auto stabilisers I remember Ken Wood and Svignev Olenski who made the Mach trimmers and pitch dampers work with the help of Newmarks who made the equipment; without them the Vulcan would never have been able to go into service.

Ted mentioned the instrumentation and this required a large team to install the gear headed, I remember, by Pete Elliott and then another team to read the results, though of course technology gradually made the thing simpler and less 'people intensive'.

Technology was changing all the time and I was very lucky to have been at Woodford as the digital revolution took place and computers had started to enter the aircraft, though the gear was heavy, unreliable, consumed large amounts of power but kept us all warm.

Many of the observers and AEOs are sadly no longer with us. However thanks to Ted and Bob, in the next chapter, I believe we get an appreciation of what was involved being in a crew flight testing the Vulcan and in my opinion they definitely qualified as Vulcan Boys.

Chapter Two

NAVIGATING THE TEST PILOTS

XM603's last flight, having been delivered to Woodford for static display. From left, Flight Lieutenant Jon Lazzari, Flight Lieutenant Terry Mitchell, Bob Pogson, Ted Hartley, Charles Masefield, Squadron Leader L'Estrange, Wg Cdr Baldwin.

Bob Pogson was the main Vulcan AEO at Avros during the aircraft's development and production. The minimum crew in a Vulcan was a pilot and an operator in the rear of the aircraft to control the electrics since the Vulcan was an all-electric aircraft; no power and the flying controls wouldn't work! This crew member in the back of the aircraft was called the air electronics officer (AEO) and he controlled the generators, the alternators, the batteries, transformer rectifier units, inverters, rotary converters etc depending on whether the aircraft was a Mk1 or a Mk2. In the RAF the AEO controlled other operational electronic gear such as the electronic counter measures; however on our test aircraft the AEO had no other duties except to look after the electrics and so had time to navigate the aircraft using a wartime hyperbolic navigation system call Gee. Even at the end of our Vulcan production we never fitted TACAN (tactical air navigation system) to our aircraft which would have given us bearing and distance from known beacons and we wouldn't have needed Gee.

The first AEO in the Vulcan was Eric Burgess who had been in the services operating with the Chindits in Burma. He was soon joined by Bob who had been a prisoner of war in Java and Japan for three-and-a-half years following the fall of Singapore. He had had to work 1,500ft down in a copper mine drilling the ore and then one day as their shift was finished they came up to hear about the Nagasaki bomb and the Japanese surrender. After a long journey home and then being demobbed he got a radio licence and joined the Merchant Marines. After a few years he joined Ferranti where he worked on developing a fighter radar. He saw an advert asking for radio operators at Woodford and eventually was told he had got the job. In the event he flew in nearly as many Vulcans as Ted Hartley and he was with Ted in XA891 when they had to bale out.

Bob was joined by two other AEOs, Jim Woodman and Peter Quinn in that order both from the RAF, but Bob, the test pilot's AEO, outstayed them all.

Bob Pogson

On 1st October 1956 I joined A.V. Roe at Woodford and was introduced to Eric Burgess who took me into the hangar, showed me round the Vulcan bomber and explained what I would be doing in the aircraft. Two days later I found myself in aircraft XA891 watching Eric demonstrate what I would have to do on the electrical panel. Jimmy Harrison was the pilot and in no time at all we were airborne to check the development of the Olympus 101 engine; suddenly there was a huge explosion. BANG! I asked Eric what it was. He chuckled and said the engines had blown out. I just wondered what I would be likely to hear next but I had no need to worry as the engines were relit followed by plenty more bangs! We were airborne for three hours twenty-five minutes. Four days later I was in aircraft XA892 on my own, looking after not only the electrical panel but also the Gee Mk3 navigation system. The following week I was introduced to the Shackleton Mk3 WR972 flown by Tony Blackman – a twenty-minute hop.

1957 proved to be a very busy year with Farnborough as always piling up the pressure. Saturday 31st August, the day before the SBAC press day, was extra busy. At 11.45am I flew with Tony in XA908 for forty-five minutes. Then I flew with Roly Falk in VX777, the second prototype, which had the new drooped leading edge for production Mk1s fitted, for just fifteen minutes from 6.30 to 6.45pm. On my way back to the hangar there was a group of people chatting away. As I walked past them Sir Roy Dobson, the managing director, reached out an arm and held my shoulders, "hurry up, Roly is waiting for you" was all he said. So I started the long walk up to the 08 runway where for some reason 889 was parked instead of at the flight sheds. On reaching the aircraft I checked all round, climbed aboard and called out to Roly, "all clear underneath. OK to close the door?" He replied in the affirmative. "We've got to be at Farnborough by 1925!" I used the aircraft battery to start the first engine and when it was running brought on the other three. Roly called for take-off to our tower and received the OK from Manchester. We were rushing down the runway while at the same time I was trying to find my maps. Having been released by Manchester we climbed very quickly. I had my first course south ready when we reached 40,000ft and in no time at all we were reaching Birmingham – thirteen miles west. I gave Roly our position and gave him the new course for Farnborough. Just after we had changed course Farnborough said they could see us on the radar. We were asked if we needed help by the radar operator. We responded with a no, to which they replied, "well Farnborough is closing at 1925". What speed we were doing I have no idea but I was convinced my course was good and as we approached Farnborough I waited until we were coming downwind and then I told Roly "abeam Farnborough, break left". He did, even though we were above the cloud and seconds later he called out, "now that's great navigation". Roly was pleased because a few seconds later we were on the ground at precisely 1925. During our time at Farnborough Roly managed to get important people into the aircraft and sometimes fly with us. Two passengers I remember were Prime Minister Anthony Eden and the Rt Hon George Ward, Secretary of State for Air.

Leysa Falk also flew with us and I remember she wasn't quite dressed for the event. I think she was the first lady to fly in the Vulcan. John, Roly's son, spoke to Leysa about it very recently. John takes up the story: "After Roly Falk first displayed the Avro Vulcan at Farnborough in 1952, he subsequently displayed the Vulcan for a number of years at Farnborough. In 1957 he asked Leysa, his wife, if she would like to go up during the display. As the daughter of another famous test pilot, Bill Thorn, Leysa was obviously open to having a go. She was also an ex-WREN and had worked on many aircraft herself before marrying.

"Leysa approached the Vulcan to be met by one of the Avro crew, Bob Pogson who asked Leysa to strap on a parachute. In those heady days of the '50s, the height of fashion at that time was skirts with multi-layered petticoats and Leysa was wearing one of these. With Bob Pogson trying to grab the crutch strap of the parachute through Leysa's legs and the layers of petticoat, his embarrassment was quite obvious and certainly it did not look decorous for Leysa! Leysa took the problem in hand, as only she could, by lifting the skirt and petticoats and telling Bob to grab the strap and get on with it!

"With Leysa duly joined to the parachute and strapped into her seat in the Vulcan, Roly did his display with Leysa unaware of exactly what manoeuvres were being done to display the Vulcan given the small portholes in the back. Anyone who has seen films of Roly displaying the Vulcan at Farnborough will be aware of how spectacular a display it could be – Roly even rolled the Vulcan at low level in 1955 – though not with Leysa on board.

The next day, Leysa was in the Avro chalet watching the display that Roly was giving and said: "If I had known or seen what Roly is now doing with the Vulcan in the display, I would never have gone up!"

The next year when I flew at Farnborough for the first time Leysa had obviously set a standard as there were a lot of secretary volunteers to fly in my aircraft during the show besides Margaret, my wife, and Jim's wife Maureen[2]. Looking back I shudder when I think of all the things that might have happened. Even though the aircraft were on Avro's charge we were still meant to operate to the book but somehow in those days what we were

[2] See *Tony Blackman Test Pilot* by the author.

doing didn't seem strange. Nowadays such impromptu behaviour would be unthinkable. Back to Bob:

One flight I remember some years later was with Dickie Martin. Taking off from Woodford in a southerly direction the navigation equipment seemed to be working, but as we travelled south I began to suspect that we weren't getting correct readings; one of the transmitters must have gone down. Dickie asked if we could have a long un-interrupted course as we were doing performance measurements so, as we were near the Bristol Channel, I of.ered him 245 degrees which would then take us down the Channel and out into the Atlantic. Still trying to find out why the equipment wasn't working I assumed we were on our way out over the Atlantic.

It was a long time later, flying at 40,000ft, that Dickie asked where we were. I as-sumed we were over the Atlantic to which Dickie replied that he had not turned off from due south. My reply to that was: "I think you must be three quarters of the way down into France. You'd better turn round now or the French fighters will be after you!"

Having turned and travelled for some time Dickie called Southern Radar for a po-sition but they couldn't see us and wanted to know where we were. Eventually Dickie informed them that everything was OK and that he could see the Bristol Channel. A very quiet voice replied, "I've got news for you, the coastline you can see is the south coast of England and the next one up is the Bristol Channel". It was a very quiet return home.

My other memory was when we had to bale out from XA891 (as relayed by Ted Hartley earlier). After receiving take-off clearance from Manchester air traffic we were on our way. It was only a short time after 'unstick' and with the wheels now up that I saw the generator warning red lights come on. We had lost all of the 115-volt gen-eration system. This was almost immediately followed by the three secondary supply fail lights on my electrics panel illuminating. Looking up to the top of my instrument panel I saw that the 100 amp inverter indicator lights were out. We had had a total electrical failure. Jimmy also told me that he had a red indicator light on. I had to tell him that we'd lost all the electrical supplies and must land immediately. He replied that this was not going to be possible, certainly not at Woodford as we were already at 3,000ft. It was at about this time that the No 4 generator warning light went out but it was clear that it was producing very little. Jimmy therefore commenced a climb to the less populated area to the east. We levelled out at some 15,000ft and were there able to have a thorough check with our chief engineer, Gilbert Whitehead, by radio back at Woodford. But it was soon clear that our problem could not be rectified and we should abandon the aircraft.

The moment Jimmy gave the second "prepare to leave" call I opened the door and gave him a thumbs up. I watched Ted as he slid out and expected to see a parachute but in a few seconds he was only a dot and then was gone. I held Phil back but immediately realised how unnecessary it was. I would be doing this soon. After Ted and Phil had gone Jimmy contacted RAF Waddington to explain our status and requested a course to steer for Waddington. This was given as 180 degrees but when the pilot tried to turn, the aircraft went almost out of control and the order was immediately given: "BALE OUT, BALE OUT." As I dropped down from my seat towards the door the co-pilot, Dickie Proudlove, ejected. I turned then to see that the escape hatch was slowly starting to close and realised that when we thought Waddington a possibility I had taken the door 'open' lever out of its catch .The airflow and the now open canopy were exerting their influence. I rapidly made my exit. Ted, who had done some parachute jumping, would have been disgusted – I went out all arms and legs. However, remembering a chat we had had about parachuting, I managed to get into a stable position and quite enjoyed the sensation of freefalling before pulling the D-ring. I had kept my Taylor helmet on just in case I might crack my head on landing. Having surveyed the ground, albeit from an angle, I prepared to land, though 'arrive' might be more appropriate. Feet and knees together, knees slightly bent, then WHAM. I had arrived.

I lay there for a while gazing at the sky before sitting up, pulling off my helmet and releasing my parachute harness. Having taken off my helmet I realised that I could hear a voice saying "thank God for that, I thought you were dead". It was a BP tanker driver who had seen me land and had come to see if he could help me. He told me that there was a helicopter just up the road looking for us. As we reached the road an ambulance stopped and invited me to hop in. Having done so I found myself in the company of a number of ladies all very pregnant. They were on their way home from a prenatal clinic. About a mile up the road I met the helicopter which took me to RAF Leconfield to be reunited with our two pilots. Apparently we had landed in the middle of a military exercise and our helicopter pilot was the station commander, he being the only pilot available. We three were taken to the officers' mess to be plied with lunch and many soothing brandies and ginger until some five hours later when Ted and Phil turned up; they had visited the crash site of our aircraft en route to Leconfield and arrived just in time to climb aboard the Anson for the flight home though we got the impression they would have preferred to go to the bar.

On Saturday morning the day after our escape a quite high-powered meeting was held at Woodford 'to investigate the cause of the accident to Vulcan XA891'. The Mk1 Vulcan's electrical power came from 4 DC generators; the Mk2 aircraft was to have 200 series engines of 17,000lbs thrust fitted with constant frequency AC generators (alternators). Vulcan XA891 was a development aircraft and electrically a Mk1 aircraft but fitted with Mk2 engines and so it was a 'lash up' with DC generators fitted to the starboard engines and a third DC generator to No 1 engine. No 2 engine had a Mk2 alternator driving a loading mat in the bomb bay, christened the 'toast rack'.

After the flight I was called on to report what had happened as I saw it, and of all the indications from the AEO's electrical instrument panel. Having heard all the evidence from both me and the pilot, the chief engineer put forward 'a case for consideration by the accident investigators'.

Ted Hartley has already explained on page 22 what the report's conclusions were. And that was about it. Nothing else to say and I was back to work on Monday.

Bob died on 31st May 2013 quite soon after I had spoken to him and he had given me the excerpts above. In this chapter he gives an appreciation of his contribution to flight testing the Vulcan. Bob went on to be an AEO on the Victor K2 and a flight engineer on the Nimrod, a lovely man and a sad loss. I'm so pleased to be able to include this chapter to retain his memory.

Chapter Three

ENGINE TEST BED

'Harry' James Pollitt joined Armstrong Siddeley at Bitteswell as a test pilot after leaving the RAF and so moved to Filton when Bristol Engines bought the company. He became chief test pilot in 1976 and flew not only heavy aircraft like the Vulcan and the Concorde but also hot ships like the Harrier. Like Harry I did a lot of engine testing myself of the Olympus engines in various marks of Vulcan and it wasn't particularly exciting, though there was a lot of engine relighting to be done as the engines flamed out. However, Harry's engine testing was much more demanding with forty different programmes including ten helicopters and all the engines were in the early stage of development. Perhaps one of his more interesting events was when an engine left the aircraft while firmly fixed to the ground as he graphically relates.

Flight test crew Concorde Engine Olympus 593: from left,
John Dickenson – flight test engineer (FTE), Jean Conche – SNECMA FTE
reheat, SNECMA FTE, Alan Baxter – FTE Olympus 593, Harry Pollitt –
chief test pilot, Mike Webber – test pilot. (*Harry Pollitt*)

The Rolls-Royce aero engine division took on a whole new lease of life when the firm bought Bristol Siddeley engines at Filton and moved their engine flight testing centre there. As far as the Vulcan was concerned we took over the engine testing of the Mks201 and 301 engines from Avros at Woodford in the early '60s and that was my

33

first involvement with the aircraft. It was routine flying, checking the handling and strain gauging the turbine blades and my log book says I did 340 hours on those flight tests.

The next thing that happened was the Concorde on which Rolls-Royce with SNEC-MA were responsible for providing the Olympus engine for the aircraft. A Vulcan was chosen for the test vehicle because it was the only UK aircraft that could carry it and the one allocated was a Mk1, XA903, which had been used to do the Blue Steel development trials in the UK. It first flew with the Olympus 593 engine slung underneath in 1966 just in time for the Farnborough Air Show.

Mind you it was a fairly tight fit underneath and we had to be very careful landing the aircraft not to scrape the back end – not for us the fancy nose-in-the air high drag landings which they used at Woodford, we had to come in above the recommended approach speeds and stream the parachute every time hoping that the brakes would work. There was a centre of gravity problem installing the engine so it had to be fitted as far forward as possible. The shorter Vulcan Mk2 nose leg was fitted to reduce the chance of our scraping the back of the engine on touchdown and a tail strut was fitted underneath the back of the engine nacelle which operated a light on the glare shield if the attitude of the aircraft was too high; I never regarded this warning as much use because it was far too late to do anything if the light came on. The engine installation weighed 30,000lbs so that our flight time was always limited as we were restricted to just over half the normal fuel capacity to avoid exceeding the maximum permitted take-off weight. Although we only flew the engine in the subsonic mode the inlet doors were modified so that we could close them completely during take-off and landing thus preventing any debris getting into the engine.

Despite the engine being called the Olympus it was significantly different from that being used on the Vulcan, having nearly 50% more thrust plus reheat as well. The actual testing of the Olympus 593 went very well, all subsonic of course but we did manage to get up to about .9 true Mach number. One interesting point about the installation was that the thrust line of the engine was six feet below the centre of gravity and we were expecting real problems as we adjusted the engine power. However, to our surprise, there was no trim change at all which the aerodynamicists explained by saying the pressure in the front of the engine disappeared as power was applied and so it all balanced out, which confirmed my view that aerodynamicists can always explain what we discover in the air, but usually only after the event.

We did a lot of handling on the engine checking things like acceleration times and surge behaviour plus we had to clear the reheat system. The thrust of the engine was about 30,000lbs plus another 17% for reheat, compared with 903's four engines of 11,000lbs each, so we had to plan our test conditions carefully and decide on which engine or engines were going to produce the power. The throttle of the test engine was controlled by the co-pilot while the pilot of the aircraft in the left-hand seat controlled the aircraft engines.

We also did the engine de-icing tests. We had a huge icing rig in front of the engine and a big water tank in the bomb bay. By pumping water into the rig we were able to simulate icing conditions and in fact we actually obtained the icing flight clearance for the Concorde on the Vulcan; no further tests were ever carried out.

We had a very worrying moment on one flight which nearly brought our test pro-gramme to a premature close. It was nothing to do with the test engine; the hydraulic pressure started to drop very rapidly to zero. I slowed down as fast as possible and managed to get the main legs down but we could see through the periscope that the nose leg only came down half way. We decided we needed a longer runway than Filton for landing but it was Friday and Boscombe Down was closed. I decided we had better call Mayday because we couldn't get the rear crew out with the nose leg being extend-ed. We elected to go to Fairford and by this time fuel was getting really low; I made an approach, touched down twice heavily trying to get the nose leg to lock down but it didn't move very far. I knew that we had some brake pressure because of there being hydraulic accumulators backing up the brakes even though the hydraulic pressure was zero; however, I also knew that if I braked hard the Maxaret anti-skid system would work and we would then lose the brake pressure so when we landed I would have to be very gentle with the brakes to avoid skidding.

We turned downwind and by then had the four low level fuel warning lights on which was rather unnerving but to our great relief when I banged the aircraft on the ground the nose leg locked down as the aircraft started to decelerate. However our troubles weren't over yet as when I streamed the 'chute it came out and burst; it clearly wasn't our day. Luckily, in spite of no parachute braking, I managed to stop the aircraft but we used every foot of the Fairford runway and the port brakes were on fire. When we got out the whole of the underside of the aircraft was covered with red hydraulic fuel. Looking back we had an incredibly lucky escape and so did the development pro-gramme as we were barely two thirds of the way through the planned tests. The flight test programme proved to be very successful comprising 219 flights and 417 flying hours of which I did 344.

Starboard RB199 engine installation underneath XA903, photographed from the front (*left*) and rear (*right*). (*Aviation Historian*)

After that we took the Concorde engine off and put the Tornado RB199 engine on. However, unlike the Olympus programme, the RB199 programme was bedevilled with test engine failures and shortages, the flying rate being seriously curtailed as a result. In the seven years that the programme continued, starting in 1972, we only managed 126 flights and a total of 286 hours flying time with the engine running for 203 hours in flight. I managed 117 hours on the trials and we flew Paul Millett who did the first flight of the Tornado. We did a lot of reheat filming using a formation aircraft to photograph the temperature gradients and in addition, towards the end of the trials, a 27mm Mauser cannon was fitted to the forebody, and we carried out several gun-firing trials under the control of Aberporth Radar over the Irish Sea. Even though the crew compartment was pressurised some of us swore we could smell the cordite. Perhaps we should have offered it to be fitted to the Vulcan for Operation Corporate and the Falklands!

TSR2 engine underneath the Vulcan. Note reheat (*left*)and bifurcated intake (*right*). (*Aviation Historian*)

The really fascinating programme was testing the TSR2. We used another Vulcan Mk1 XA894 but this time the installation was not really representative of the real aircraft as we had to move the engine right forward to keep the centre of gravity under control which meant that the intake had to be split around the nose leg. It was a completely new engine and we couldn't really guarantee that the work we did on the Vulcan was representative. We flew Roly Beamont in the aircraft on what proved to be the last flight to let him look at the engine behaviour but of course it was wildly unimpressive because the instrumentation was nothing like the aircraft with the actual instruments. I did twenty-one hours on the aircraft and twelve flights altogether before it blew up ground running which is a story in itself.

We were running the engine at full power on the ground when there was an almighty bang and all the fire warning lights came on. There were six of us in the aircraft and we all leapt out and started running. Luckily the fire at that stage was behind us. The main shaft on the engine gave way and the turbine came off which went out of the aircraft hit the ground, hit the wing then the ground again, went through the wing and then went nearly a mile before landing in the turning circle at the end of the runway at Filton, rolled round and round like an old penny and stopped about 50 yards from the A38. It was red hot. It only took a couple of seconds for the turbine to go and then the aircraft really caught fire as the fuel started to leak out; the flames went through several tanks but by then the fire was so intense that all the aluminium in the aircraft vaporised and all that was left at the end on the floor was the correct layout of a Vulcan with the four main engines and all fourteen booster pumps all beautifully in position. Presumably these were titanium or something. The fire engine was on the scene in seconds but then it got covered with burning fuel from the aircraft and was completely destroyed.

The reason for the failure was a resonance on the shaft which set up a natural vibration; as a demo the engineers hung a shaft in the assembly shop, and you could hit it when you went home and it was still ringing the next morning. It is called a bell mode vibration and luckily being resonance it was relatively easy to fix in the flight engines. In the end I flew a total of 820 hours on the Vulcan in many configurations and like other Vulcan pilots liked the responsive controls and soon got used to the rather restricted view out of the front.

When Harry retired he decided to do something entirely different and now runs a splendid horticultural business near Bristol.

Chapter Four

PILOTING THE VULCAN

Phil Leckenby graduated from RAF pilot training on Jet Provost and Vampire aircraft in 1964. He served two tours at RAF Waddington on Vulcans, the first as a B Mk1A co-pilot on 44 (Rhodesia) Squadron. Three months before his twenty-fourth birthday he became a captain on 101 Squadron flying the Mk2 Vulcan.

One of Phil Leckenby's (third from left) last flights collecting
aircraft from St Athan. (*Phil Leckenby*)

The Vulcan – A First Impression

It was the summer of 1964 and I had just finished RAF pilot training. We were all given our postings: a low-key ceremony conducted over a few beers in the bar of the officers' mess. Somewhat to my instructor's surprise, I had been judged runner-up in the aerobatics competition and I was therefore quietly confident that I would end up flying fighters, or at the very least, light bombers such as the Canberra. When the flight commander called my name and announced that I would be joining the huge majority of the course on V bombers, I was mortified. V bombers, *moi?* Surely not. There must have been some sort of mistake; a simple administrative error soon to be rectified by the personnel wonks. But alas, in those days the V Force was a large organisation hungry for recruits and all but three of our course started our flying careers as co-pilots on either Victors or Vulcans.

RAF Finningley, near Doncaster, was the operational conversion unit (OCU) for the Vulcan and on arriving there I discovered not only was I to become a Vulcan B Mk1A co-pilot but also the captain of our fledgling crew was none other than a certain Wg Cdr Mike D'Arcy. He turned out to be a thoroughly likeable man; tall, charismatic and imbued with a wicked sense of humour. He was to become the commanding officer of 44 (Rhodesia) Squadron and despite well-meant advice from senior squadron stalwarts that he should ditch the neophyte OCU crew he had arrived with in favour of a more experienced one, he insisted we would remain together throughout his squadron tour.

At the end of one of the early days of our course at Finningley, we were driven out to the dispersal to get our first look at the aircraft. The crew bus ground to a halt on a hardstanding between two hangars and there it was, a gigantic all-white Vulcan Mk1A, an aircraft like no other. Ted Marmont, our Australian nav plotter, a wise old bird with many hours of Canberra flying under his belt, muttered something dark and antipodean that I couldn't quite catch. James Walker, our young, debonair and über laid-back nav radar, smiled whimsically, probably wondering how many cases of duty-free liquor could be stacked into that cavernous bomb bay. Jock Lamont, our AEO from north of the border, broke off a lengthy dissertation on the merits of wiggly and straight amps and lapsed into silence. Even D'Arcy, normally never short of a *bon mot* or two, didn't say much as he gazed at the graceful delta.

It was unquestionably a weapon of war, but also a radical yet beautiful piece of engineering. Like other classic designs, such as the Hunter, Canberra, and the incomparable Spitfire, it simply looked so right. Its subtle curves would prove a challenge for countless aviation artists. There is no denying that the Victor, another of the trio of V bombers under simultaneous development, was also a handsome aircraft in its own right, but from any angle, the pure delta plan form of the Vulcan made it an unmistakable and jaw-dropping sight. In a word whose currency has been so devalued of late, she was truly awesome.

We all climbed in to be surprised by the modest dimensions of the crew cabin. We were assured it would be possible to squeeze seven people in, at a push, although the normal complement of five seemed crowded enough. The entrance ladder was attached to a hinged hatch hanging down below the forward fuselage. This hatch also served as an escape chute down which the rear crew would slide if disaster were to strike. The rear crew soon came to the sobering realisation that if the aircraft had to be abandoned with the undercarriage down, this escape chute was located immediately in front of the huge nose-wheel structure, making escape a tricky business for anybody who was not a talented gymnast. The dark interior contained a bewildering array of cables, pipes and lights beyond the three rearward-facing crew seats. Instrument dials and switches were scattered in what seemed to be a random fashion above a transverse desk where Jim, Ted and Jock would ply their trades. Other than the big H2S radar screen, their only glimpse of the world outside was afforded by a small circular window set high on each side of the cabin. Most of the time they would be travelling backwards in the dark at some 600mph.

The pilots' cockpit was reached by a further ladder between two Martin Baker ejection seats; the space was absurdly small and would be a real squeeze for two people

Vulcan Mk2 rear crew stations. (*Vulcan 655 MaPS*)

dressed in full flying kit. The layout of knobs, switches and dials reflected the aircraft's age, although most of the main instruments were placed logically enough. It looked as if some of the switches and controls on the side panels would be difficult to see when strapped in. A centre console housing fourteen fuel pump switches, fuel transfer switches and cross-feed cocks, hinged forward enabling it to be pulled down between the seats when the occupants were in place. Peering through the small circular side windows it was impossible to see the wing tips, which meant that when manoeuvring the aircraft in confined spaces there would have to be total reliance on guidance from a crew chief plugged in to the intercom on a long external lead.

The primary flight controls were unusual in that they consisted of two single-hand-ed fighter-type joysticks, one for each pilot, rather than the traditional control wheels more usually associated with aircraft of this size. A single set of engine throttles was located centrally so the pilot in the left-hand seat, usually the captain, was obliged to fly the aircraft using his left hand, adjusting the throttles with his right. Should the captain happen to be left-handed by nature, this arrangement would present no diffi-culty. However, right-handed pilots transitioning to the left seat had quickly to become ambidextrous. The pilots' forward view was a bit of a shock too, curtailed as it was by narrow windscreens above the curved top of the tall main instrument panel. It wasn't quite like peering out of a letterbox, but it wasn't that far off either. On each side was a small triangular window, optimistically called direct vision or DV windows, which although they did little to enhance the view, could at least be opened to allow some ventilation on the ground. The narrow windscreen combined with the rising curve of the cockpit combing meant that landing in a strong crosswind from the left could be challenging for the captain, as could a strong cross-wind component from the right prove highly demanding for a novice co-pilot. Like many aircraft, the cockpit interior had a distinctive smell: a curious cocktail of insulation, electrical wiring, hydraulic fluid and kerosene. This smell lingers on to this day in aircraft consigned to museums.

Whilst undeniably a thing of beauty, the aircraft did have a deadly purpose. The entire forward and side views from the cockpit could be blanked out by shutters and blinds zipped together to prevent the crew being blinded by high intensity flashes of nuclear detonations. For similar reasons the whole aircraft exterior was painted 'anti-flash' white. The colour scheme would later change to camouflage when the advent of more sophisticated enemy air defences would force V bombers to penetrate at low level.

Mike D'Arcy was quietly proud of the fact that before being posted to Finningley he had finally found the willpower to give up cigarettes. In the past he had flown a variety of aircraft, most of them small single-seat fighters, and his last operational tour had been on Hunters in Germany. As he resumed his seat in the crew bus after our introduction to the Vulcan, his resolve apparently evaporated. Looking over his shoulder at the behemoth he would soon be expected to fly, he suddenly said: "Ted, for pity's sake, give me a fag!"

Mk2 pilots' cockpit and instruments with Smiths Military
Flight System. (*Vulcan 655 MaPS*)

I was destined to do two tours of duty at Waddington – one as a Vulcan B Mk1A co-pilot, the second as a captain flying the more modern and powerful Vulcan B Mk2. It seemed that as far as the rest of the crew was concerned, the main responsibility of a co-pilot was to lug the in-flight ration box to and from the aircraft whenever we went flying. We rarely flew for less than five hours, sometimes more, and the availability of an endless supply of high-calorie, artery-clogging victuals was vitally important to my fellow crew members. My other duties, such as calculation of take-off performance, fuel and centre of gravity management, and indeed the trivial matter of being able to fly the aircraft safely from the right-hand seat, were of little or no interest. However, at the end of my co-pilot tour things were to change. I was sent back to Finningley for a second OCU course. This time there would be less emphasis on the provisioning of in-flight rations and rather more on the operation of the aircraft as an entity. I was to become a captain, not on the familiar old Mk1A, but on the new, improved Mk2 version of the Vulcan.

To the casual observer, there may have seemed little difference between the two versions, yet there were in fact quite a few fundamental changes. Externally, the Mk2, with its slightly shorter nose-wheel strut, sat a little flatter on the ground, and the wing was slightly bigger. The span had been increased by about twelve feet and there were subtle differences to the leading edge and the overall thickness/chord ratio. The jet pipes were larger to handle the increased power of the Olympus 201 engines and further ECM antennae were accommodated in a flat plate beneath the two starboard jet pipes.

But inside the differences were more pronounced. Systems-wise the electrics had been radically changed. The old 112 volt DC electrical system had been replaced by a 200 volt three-phase 400Hz AC system, supplied by four engine-driven alternators and backed up by a ram air turbine, RAT, which could be dropped into the airstream whenever required. Additionally there was a small Rover gas turbine, airborne auxiliary power plant (AAPP) buried in the wing just behind the starboard undercarriage leg, which supplied stand-by electrical power either in the air or on the ground. It seemed there would be no shortage of electrical power. RAT and AAPP were important acronyms now firmly established in the Mk2 lexicon.

Up front the cockpit looked more or less the same. Here too though, there were important differences. The old Mk1 engines were started by conventional electric motors powered by batteries; however, Mk2s could be started in a variety of ways. An external Palouste air starter (a sort of jet engine on wheels) could be connected by a large-bore flexible hose to supply low pressure air to the air starter motors of each engine. Air bled from a running engine could be used to start the others, either singly or simultaneously, depending on the configuration of the engine air switches. To start the other three simultaneously, the live engine would be opened up to 90% rpm, an extremely noisy way to get everything going in a hurry. In situations where Paloustes were unavailable, the engines could be started by 'rapid air', an autonomous system fed by on-board high pressure air bottles. In this case the engine's throttle would be set at the 50% rpm position and the rapid air bottle fired. The air bottles could only be recharged on the ground, so to conserve the rapid air supply, once one engine is started in this way cross-feed air would usually be bled from it to start the other three. Tucked away on the start panel on the captain's side panel was a deceptively ordinary button called the 'simultaneous' or 'mass rapid start button'. Just one finger pressing this modest little button would initiate an entertaining series of events: all four engines would start simultaneously, all powered flying control units ran up, as did the artificial feel units. Because of the high electrical loads, a 60 KVA ground power unit supplied electrical power during the rapid start cycle and flight instrument gyros received an initial voltage boost to spin them up quickly. The idea was to minimise the reaction time in the event of the aircraft being scrambled from a state of readiness. It was an impressive capability but unfortunately someone experienced a serious engine fire after initiating a mass rapid start and after that we were forbidden to use it.

Another system difference was the way in which the powered flying controls worked. The Mk1's control surfaces consisted of ailerons outboard and elevators inboard, each split into two for reasons of redundancy. The Mk2 had the same eight control surfaces on the wings but they were connected together through a sophisticated mixer box enabling them all to function in the aileron sense, or as elevators, or a mixture of both. This arrangement did have the effect of improving control authority in pitch and roll, but at a small cost of increased adverse yaw at low speeds.

The avionics suite of the Mk2 included the Smiths Military Flight System (MFS), a flight director system for primary flight instruments, sometimes rather unkindly referred to as the 'Smiths Mystery Flight System'. The MFS was cutting edge technology for its time and a significant upgrade over the conventional instrumentation on Mk1s. For the uninitiated however, it was necessary to devote many happy hours in the classroom and the flight simulator, getting to understand how it worked and master its capabilities.

When it came to actually getting airborne, the most noticeable difference was the huge amount of extra power when the throttles were opened. The Mk1A's Olympus 104s produced around 13,500lbs of thrust at full power, which was enough to give the aircraft a respectable enough performance. But the Olympus 201s, which powered the early versions of the Mk2, were rated at 17,000lbs each, an increase of almost 26%. On take-off the Mk2 was run up to 80% rpm against the brakes before releasing them and opening up to full power, accompanied by that characteristic 'Olympus howl'. It was as if the very air was being shredded in the engine intakes and the resulting noise was sweet music to the ears of Vulcan aircrew, if not to all of the nearby local residents. The aircraft would accelerate rapidly and it was necessary to rotate it and quickly establish a steepish climb attitude to avoid exceeding the undercarriage limiting speed.

At one point it was planned to equip Vulcans with two American Skybolt missiles carried on strengthened hard points beneath each wing. The programme was eventually cancelled, but not before a good number of the aircraft had undergone the necessary airframe modifications and re-engined with Olympus 301s, each of which had a whopping 21,000lbs of thrust. Now the Vulcan really did have some shove! So much so that full power was limited by a 'take-off/cruise' switch in the centre of the instrument panel. Normally this double-ganged switch would be left in the 'cruise' position, which limited maximum engine rpm to 97.5%, more than enough for all normal operations. Should full power ever become essential, in an emergency for example, 'take-off' could be selected and the final 2.5% would be instantly available.

The 1A was no slouch at high level but the additional thrust and increased wing area of the Mk2 enhanced turning performance even more. Fighter affiliation with contemporary fighters could be highly entertaining if all the electronic counter measures, passive warning, jamming and deception gear was functioning correctly. As with any simulated aerial combat, it is vital to know the whereabouts of the threat and, as already mentioned, unfortunately the cockpit afforded a poor field of view. However, if everything was going well and the interceptor had been detected, the usual ploy was to open up the throttles, turn towards the threat and climb rapidly. Climbing, even at high level, was something the Vulcan did rather well and it was only as a consideration to its oxygen equipment that the aircraft was limited to 56,000ft, an altitude at which it would still turn and climb quite happily. The most rewarding sight was to catch a glimpse of a steely-eyed Lightning pilot, several thousand feet below, hurtling along in afterburner at an outrageous supersonic speed, 180 degrees out and with ninety degrees of bank on, before having to limp back to base desperately short of fuel. Well yes, it's true that more often than not we did get shot down at high level, but the Mk2 Vulcan was certainly more than capable of causing a good deal of embarrassment to fighters.

There was no more dramatic reminder that the Warsaw Pact's air defences had become more capable than in May 1960, when Gary Powers, flying a U2 high-level reconnaissance aircraft, was

Vulcan Mk2 with Skybolts.

shot down by an SA-2 over Soviet Union airspace. This wake-up call made it clear that a high-level penetration into enemy airspace was becoming a risky business. The solution was to adopt a Hi-Lo-Hi mission profile, with the V bombers penetrating defences at low level. This evolution was enthusiastically embraced by Vulcan crews, who were flying an aircraft that would prove itself robust enough to cope with the additional fatigue of low-level flying. Terrain following radar (TFR) would be introduced in due course to enhance operations in poor weather or at night. In the meantime, switching crews from high level to low became a training priority. From a pilot's perspective this change was most welcome since, apart from anything else, there was much more to look at. However, the need to husband the aircraft's fatigue life was a constant preoccupation, leading to a number of severe operating restrictions. During training sorties, the cruising speed at low altitude was limited to a sedate 240 knots, with accelerations to more realistic attack speeds being permitted only during the final stages of a bombing run. Relatively little power was required in a low-level cruise at 240 knots and the engines had to be throttled well back; in fact, the throttles of the 301-engined variant spent most of their time not far beyond the flight idle gate.

Both versions of the Vulcan were pleasant to fly. Arguably the Mk1 with its limiting Mach No of .98 was very slightly faster at high level, although the Mk2's updated avionics, greater weight and increased engine power made it the more capable aircraft. If I had to cast my vote, I would have to go with the Mk2. After all, on that one I didn't have to cart that wretched ration box around.

> I feel I must make some comment after reading Phil's splendid description of the difference between the Mk1/1A and the Mk2. As he correctly points out, despite the cancellation of the Skybolt there proved to be a significant benefit from the programme since the wing strengthening enabled the aircraft to be used at low level and still have a reasonable fatigue life; however at the time of the cancellation I was a bit disappointed as I was the Skybolt project pilot dropping dummy weapons at random in Cardigan Bay!
>
> Electrically the aircraft was much safer because, besides having a lot more power, it no longer relied on its batteries in the event of a power failure to remain in the air.
>
> The speed difference between the Mk1/1A and the Mk2 was illusory as the Mk1/1A had a higher indicated Mach number error than the Mk2. Both aircraft built up drag and lost elevator control at about the same maximum true Mach number, nose diving uncontrollably towards the ground. However in my opinion, if not in Phil's, at cruise speeds and below the Mk2 was a far superior aircraft to handle and much nicer on the approach.
>
> He mentions the MFS which may have been at the 'cutting edge of technology' but it lost Smiths, my eventual employer, their place on the instrument panel as they chose for some inexplicable reason to have a moving pointer to show the heading instead of the accepted standard of a moving card. Back to Phil:

Waddington

By the time I first entered the gates of RAF Waddington in October 1964 quick reaction alert (QRA) had long since been an integral part of the lives of V Force air and ground crews regardless of aircraft type. The bombing of Hiroshima had changed everything fundamentally. Not only had it ushered in the nuclear age but no other single event emphasised so dramatically the crucial role of the manned strategic bomber. The quantum leap in Bomber Command's potency during the post-war years reached a pinnacle in the late '50s when each V Force squadron, and there were quite a few of them, had

Smiths MFS and the most important instrument for the display pilot is top right, the accelerometer. (*Charles Toop*)

an aircraft armed with a nuclear weapon continuously at fifteen minutes readiness for take-off. That alert state could be further elevated at any time to enable the force to get airborne within the four-minute threat posed by intercontinental ballistic missiles.

Crews were placed on QRA for twenty-four-hour periods, sometimes extended to forty-eight; whatever the duration, the seriousness of the undertaking was never underplayed. Brand new crews were excused QRA until they had fulfilled all the training requirements of the combat-ready qualification. This ensured that inexperienced crews were not saddled with such an onerous operational responsibility until they had acquired a firm foundation of tactical flying by day and night, competence in all modes of weapon delivery, become *au fait* with electronic warfare and were fully trained on the complexities of the mighty bomb. Finally there was the little matter of target study. Each month there was a requirement to complete a number of hours studying assigned targets so that, if push came to shove, every crew would be familiar with routes, enemy defences and every known detail of the targets they would hopefully never attack.

The QRA set up at Waddington was located at alpha dispersal on the northwestern side of the airfield. There were three Vulcan squadrons in residence, each of which continuously provided one combat-ready aircraft armed and ready to go at fifteen-minutes notice. A short distance away from the dispersal was a slightly shabby collection of Nissan huts providing accommodation for crews on QRA. They contained rudimentary dormitories with curtains affording basic privacy, an operations room equipped with an array of telephones and an intercom known appropriately as the 'bomber box'; in addition, there was a lounge area and a games room equipped with snooker and table tennis tables. The QRA huts may have been short on luxury but they did provide basic facilities adequate for the needs of the three resident Vulcan crews. As with sailors or prisoners, food took on a disproportionate importance for aircrew whiling away the tedious hours. Meals of generous proportions were taken in the aircrew dining room, predictably known as the 'greasy spoon', which was conveniently located nearby in ops wing HQ. The menu may not have been overly influenced by today's gospel of healthy eating but those of prodigious appetite could, if they wished, eat there as many times as they liked throughout the day. The QRA hut complex was not quite close enough to the aircraft for rapid access on foot, so each squadron had its own QRA vehicle in which they raced to their aircraft whenever the bomber controller raised the alert state from fifteen to five or even fewer minutes. Response times were critical and crews on QRA were never allowed to roam far from their aircraft. Essentially they were confined to alpha dispersal, ops wing HQ or the QRA hut itself. This restriction severely inhibited crew members' leisure activities and meant that the long hours could best be whiled away reading, watching TV, playing games or even working on the motley collection of old cars parked just outside the QRA hut.

Practice call-outs by day and night were a regular feature of life on QRA, providing brief moments of excitement during an otherwise dull period of duty. A service vehicle, often of humble origins, provided transport for a Vulcan crew sitting alert on QRA to its nuclear-armed aircraft on alpha dispersal. During my time at Waddington the QRA wagons were changed or upgraded a number of times. The requirements were modest: it had to start without difficulty, accommodate a Vulcan crew of five with all their flying kit, sport a flashing blue roof light to distinguish it from more mundane road traffic and be capable of covering the short distances to the waiting aircraft. A number of vehicles were assigned to QRA crews, the most memorable of which was an ancient minivan known as the Morris J2.

What the J2 lacked in elegance it more than made up for in temperament. The J2 could have been British Leyland's answer to the ubiquitous VW camper but for two small flaws; firstly, the woefully undersized engine was notoriously reluctant to start, even in a summer heat-wave it could be coaxed into life only with difficulty; in wet cold weather it was a toss-up as to whether the starter motor or the battery would give up the unequal struggle first, leaving the frustrated crew no option but to run to the aircraft as best they could. The second trifling imperfection lay with the J2's column-mounted gear change. These vehicles endured a hard life in the sometimes uncaring hands of RAF drivers and the older the vehicle became, the more imprecise was the selection of its three forward gears. As the linkage became worn, first and second gears would become increasingly difficult to engage, leaving the driver with the option of kangarooing uncertainly forward in third or accelerating away ignominiously in reverse. I have an enduring memory of a particular QRA exercise which required us to board the aircraft, start up and taxi to the runway threshold, as close as we ever got to a practice scramble. As we ran out of the QRA hut, I caught sight of 50 Squadron's van lurching towards the dispersal in a cloud of blue smoke and a series of hesitant leaps. As we drove off in pursuit, I noticed 101 Squadron's van motionless in its parking slot, its blue light flashing in anticipation and anxious faces peering out of the windows; eventually it must have coughed into life because soon afterwards we were treated to the bizarre spectacle of their J2 accelerating away rapidly in reverse, weaving an uncertain path backwards to the waiting aircraft.

A combat-ready Vulcan could be started and readied for flight very quickly. Four aircraft scrambled from the ORP at the end of the runway could all be airborne in less than two minutes, an impressive and ear-shattering feat often demonstrated to visiting dignitaries. Upping the QRA readiness state was a frequent exercise, initiated by the bomber controller and broadcast by tannoy throughout the QRA complex. Anything less than the normal fifteen minutes entailed manning the aircraft and 'readiness 02' meant the aircraft had to be started up and taxied to the runway threshold. Such rapid movement was not entirely without risk. The malevolent bomber controller, deep in his lair in the bowels of Bomber Command, was also fond of QRA call-outs during the night. On one occasion an unfortunate pilot, perhaps not yet fully awake and probably a little blinded by the sodium lights surrounding the pans, turned a little too tightly out of the dispersal and managed to drop a main wheel bogey off the concrete taxiway onto the grass. The fully loaded Vulcan quickly sank up to its axles and a spare aircraft had to be quickly brought on state.

The combat ready checks on a QRA aircraft tested all the systems and left the aircraft in a state ready for immediate engine start by means of an external ground power supply. The old Mk1 Vulcan's electrical system was DC and the engines were started using an external DC power supply. Engine start could be initiated by the crew chief

Demonstration scramble of Mk1As but Phil's vehicles appear to
have rejuvenated (*top right*).

pressing four buttons on the ground power unit. When all checks were complete, the
crew would lock the entrance door with a very small key, which looked suspiciously
like the sort of replacement car key supplied by Halfords. As ever with QRA, reaction

time was crucial and the approved engine starting procedure was to brief the crew chief that as soon as he saw the aircrew emerge from the wagon on the edge of the dispersal, he was to press all four start buttons. This could save a few precious seconds, allowing the engines to be winding up whilst the crew clambered into the crew compartment; as soon as the pilots reached the narrow confines of the cockpit they would open the throttles to the idle gate and the aircraft would be ready to taxi.

The custody of the aircraft key was usually entrusted to the co-pilot. During one exercise call-out, the inevitable happened. The kangarooing J2 lurched to a halt on the edge of the pan and the crew chief, who had already started the ground power unit, hit all four start buttons as briefed. The crew sprinted to beneath the entrance door and waited for the co-pilot to unlock it. The Rolls-Royce Olympus engines began their noisy wind up. The co-pilot repeatedly felt around his neck for the key lanyard but it wasn't there. He then went through a slap-stick comedy routine, furiously patting all the many pockets of his flying suit as he tried to locate the missing key. The penny finally dropped. The hapless co-pilot had committed the cardinal sin of leaving the key on his nightstand in the QRA dormitory where, until a few minutes ago, he had been enjoying a peaceful afternoon nap. Ashen-faced he was despatched back to the QRA hut to retrieve the key. Meanwhile the other two aircraft taxied out of the QRA dispersal towards the runway and the remainder of the stranded crew could only look on with mounting embarrassment from beneath their aircraft as the four mighty Olympus reached the peak of their start cycles.

Strange and sometimes humorous things did happen. Out on alpha dispersal, the small huts provided to shield the RAF Police guards from the elements were not immune from the effects of Olympus jet blast. I once saw one of them reduced to match wood as a Mk2 taxied out, the guard having had the good sense to retreat a safe distance away, but the threat from the Warsaw Pact has long since evaporated and QRA is now a fast-fading memory. The uneasy peace that prevailed throughout the cold war years can be interpreted as testament to the success of the policy of deterrence. QRA, in the strategic retaliatory sense, hopefully may never return. For the Vulcan crews of my era, the part we played in maintaining a credible nuclear deterrent evoked remarkably little emotion, even in the wake of the '62 Cuban missile crisis. If it now seems odd that the reality of our contribution to the nuclear stand-off was typified by almost passive acceptance, it is worth remembering that this was an era when a number of air ministry wonks held the equally strange tenet that it was somehow acceptable to provide Martin Baker ejection seats for the Vulcan's two pilots whereas the rest of the crew were left to escape through the entrance hatch as best they could.

Again I feel I must comment on Phil's remark relating to the fact that Vulcan rear crew did not have ejector seats. The specification for the V bombers came out in 1946 when the view was taken that the UK urgently needed an independent deterrent. There was no chance of getting a rearward-facing ejector seat in the same time frame as a forward one and it was judged that on a balance of risks the aircraft should be built with only pilot ejector seats, hoping that for most malfunctions it would be possible for the rear crew to escape before the pilots ejected. Nowadays it is easy to question whether the decision was a right one at the time; it is quite clear as the years go by that peoples' views on what is acceptable in a wartime environment are changing. It is my view that the politicians and defence chiefs got it right but I accept that such a decision today would be unthinkable. Phil continues:

Whilst QRA was the V Force's underlying active threat providing an immediate and continuous nuclear response around the clock, the policy of nuclear deterrence also needed to be sufficiently flexible to react to any developing strategic threat. In times of escalating tension, the QRA force could have been supplemented by the generation of additional combat-ready aircraft and weapons. However, to have all of the nuclear delivery vehicles concentrated at just a few permanent bases was to invite a pre-emptive strike that could well cripple our retaliatory capability. So in the event of things getting really serious, rather than leave all the eggs in one basket, V Force assets would be dispersed to a number of airfields around the UK. This dispersal was exercised on a regular basis, partly to get crews used to operating from a different and sometimes remote location and partly to make sure that all the logistical problems of doing so could be overcome.

Chief among these logistical problems was the weapon itself. Although armed QRA aircraft would routinely taxi to the runway threshold, we would never actually get airborne with a nuclear weapon on board unless there was an operational reason for doing so. For exercise purposes the engineers would generate the aircraft and once declared serviceable and fully-fuelled, a convoy of special vehicles would bring the weapons from the supplemental storage area ready to be loaded onto the combat-ready aircraft. Once a weapon had been married to an aircraft, the combination was known as a 'weapon system', which would then remain at a high state of readiness awaiting the order to disperse. The re-supply of nuclear weapons to dispersal airfields was not really an issue since any nuclear exchange was likely to be short and catastrophically decisive. Since as a matter of policy we would not fly with live nuclear weapons in peacetime, during exercises the weapons would be downloaded and returned to storage before the aircraft were flown off to their dispersed airfields.

So the impressive demonstration four-aircraft scrambles put on for every visiting dignitary and his dog, and so beloved by air show crowds around the country, were usually flown by aircraft with empty bomb bays, and often with reduced fuel loads to facilitate steep angles of climb after rotation. Of course, no such carriage restrictions applied to conventional weapons and aircraft could be scrambled with or without them.

Looking back now, it is interesting to reflect on how aircrew and ground crew all accepted so readily the onerous responsibility of being part of Britain's independent nuclear deterrent. To say that few of us seriously believed that the madness of a nuclear exchange would ever happen is simplistic but perhaps not too far from the truth. Everyone was aware of the calamitous consequences should the policy of tripwire response fail, yet most of us in the front line were secure in the belief that the retaliatory threat we posed was real enough to deter even the most fanatical of enemy regimes.

Certainly the stakes were high but we took comfort in the knowledge that our training, our aircraft and, of course the weapons we carried posed a credible threat.

It should be remembered that this was an era when the doctrine of communism was riding high and its overt policy of expansionism posed a very real threat to the western alliance. The Cuban missile crisis of October 1962 was a stark reminder that the game was indeed being played for real. Secretary of State Dean Rusk's memorable observation, "we're eyeball to eyeball and I think the other fellow just blinked," succinctly underlined the awful implications of brinkmanship. Much has since changed in the intervening forty-odd years but back in the 1960s there seemed no alternative to a defensive posture underwritten by the certainty of massive nuclear retaliation.

> After leaving 101 Squadron whilst serving as a flying instructor at the RAF College Cranwell, Phil lost his left eye in a car accident. There followed several lengthy battles with medical and personnel establishments, during which time he remained flying for a little over a year as Cranwell's unit test pilot. Ultimately though, he re-trained as a navigator in 1973. There followed two front-line tours on Buccaneer aircraft in the maritime strike/attack role, one of which was with the Royal Navy embarked on HMS *Ark Royal*.
>
> He left the RAF in 1982 and re-located to Florida, USA, working in property and hotel management until the parent company sold the business in 1986. Thereafter he worked as an aerial photographer, diversifying into freelance aviation journalism and documentary film production. He re-joined the RAF in 1990 and served in a number of operational appointments in the UK, Sardinia and Germany. On leaving the service for the second time he joined LGM, a French company, as a training consultant, working in Paris and Aachen. He finally retired in 2008 and now lives in Lincolnshire. Phil's absolutely splendid description of meeting the Vulcan for the first time took me back to my first climb into the aircraft at Boscombe Down. Everything was so very compact and, as Phil remarks, the view met none of the requirements for landing. But for me there was one splendid feature which I really loved. It was the stick, I started on fighters and I was left-handed.

Chapter Five

NAV RADAR AND H2S

Anthony Wright joined the RAF in 1960 and was trained as a navigator at Thorney Island, then Hullavington and Stradishall flying Vickers Varsities and Gloster Meteor 14 night fighters.

35 Squadron Sunspot Malta. Left to right: Jim Patterson – AEO, Anthony Wright – nav radar, Group Captain Roberts – station commander RAF Cottesmore, Nigel Baldwin – captain, Gordon Blackburn – nav plotter. (*Anthony Wright*)

Arrival on Vulcans and Straight Out to Indonesian Confrontation, 1965
My first taste of the V Force came in 1963 when after completing 97 Valiant Course at 232 OCU RAF Gaydon I was posted as a flying officer nav radar to 148 Squadron RAF Marham. However, in August 1964 metal fatigue was discovered in the Valiant fleet which caused them to undertake reduced flying. They were then grounded, except for a national emergency, on 9th December. The final crunch came on the evening of 26th January 1965 when I was on QRA. The wife of my nav plotter, Squadron Leader Ken Lewis, rang up to tell us that we were redundant. It had just been announced on the six o'clock news that the Valiants were to be withdrawn from service to take effect the next day. Shortly after the news the station commander, who had only been informed ten minutes before the announcement, arrived along with the three squadron commanders (OCs 49, 148 and 207 Squadrons) of the crews on QRA, with crates of beer. He told us that if there was a call-out we were not to react. The QRA aircraft would be unloaded the next day.

Although we knew that the demise of the Valiant had to come sometime it was still a bit of a shock. We all sat around talking of past times and wondering what the future held. As the days and weeks passed, some aircrew were posted while others awaiting their fate had to be kept occupied. After a compulsory Met briefing at 8am each day in the operations wing briefing room junior officers were ordered to give talks to all the other aircrew assembled, followed by daily coach trips to other service establishments. We also played the ground crew at various sports. Some extra Chipmunks were brought in to let the co-pilots and us younger nav radars take to the air. One co-pilot and I took full advantage of this by doing aerobatics and flying extremely low up and down the straight fenland dykes hopping over bridges and annoying farm workers and tractor drivers in the fields. Finally, it was decided that some of us, to keep our hand in flying V bombers, would also go and fly the Victor at 232 OCU. I was picked and subsequently spent one morning being briefed on the Victor electrics, followed by escape drills in the crew drill escape trainer in the afternoon. The next day I flew as the nav radar with four other 232 OCU Victor aircrew attacking high level radar bomb score unit (RBSU) targets on a four-hour sortie. As the radar kit was exactly the same as the Valiant there was no problem.

Shortly afterwards, back at Marham, my Valiant captain Norman Bevis was posted to Vulcans and wanted me to join him as part of his crew. However, I declined his invitation as I had decided that I wanted a change. I had now, by chance, already flown two of the three bombers and wasn't planning for there to be a third! Unfortunately, this was not to be and I ended up on 58 Vulcan Mk2 Course at 230 OCU RAF Finningley. There I teamed up with another navigator, Gordon Blackburn, who had flown B6 Canberras on 213 Squadron at RAF Brüggen in Germany. He was to be my future nav plotter. In September we joined IX(B) Squadron at RAF Cottesmore on the Atkinson crew who were without a nav team. Tony Atkinson was an ex Royal Navy Fleet Air Arm pilot who had served in Malta; the co-pilot Roger Neve was an engineering officer who, under a scheme running then, was one of a small number of engineers who were allowed to go through 'the training machine' a second time, to be trained as a pilot, and to complete one tour as aircrew. They then went back to their original engineering speciality. Finally, the AEO was Roger Hannaford.

Our crew was destined to join the second half of IX Squadron and go out to RAF Tengah, Singapore in November. This was part of the RAF's contribution to defending Malaysia in the conflict known as the Indonesian Confrontation, often called 'The Undeclared War'. Aircrew on the same squadron either flew a Vulcan out to the Far East or back. The other trip being in a Britannia courtesy of Transport Command. For us to meet the deadline it was imperative to get declared operational and thus combat ready. This combat status told everyone that a crew was capable of standing QRA and, therefore, capable of going to war. Thus the next two months were hectic. We carried out dinghy drills, navigation exercises, bombed on Holbeach Range with 100lb bombs, flew low level and high level attacks both with the H2S radar and the T4 bombsight, went on detachment to Luqa, Malta and dropped bombs on Tarhuna Range in North Africa. Squadron and weapons acceptance checks along with target study followed. Finally, we attended a three-day course at the Aviation Medicine Training Centre, RAF North Luffenham. There, in the decompression chamber, we experienced high altitude rapid decompression at 56,000ft wearing the Vulcan clothing we had just been issued, pressure jerkins, g-restrainers and air ventilated suits; we underwent lectures and practicals on anoxia, hypoxia, hyperventilation, oxygen deprivation and remedial actions. We also had to watch the gory details and effects of tropical diseases, prevalent in the Far East, on film. After completion of the inevitable RAF exam, and passing it, we departed for Cottesmore.

Finally, with our aircrew combat classification certificates signed by the station commander, we were declared operational and ready to go. Of course leave was a concession and not a right in those days. Indeed, I'd only had five days leave that year. We arrived back at our homes sometime on the Wednesday and travelled to RAF Lyneham on the Friday. On Saturday 6th November 1965 we were up early ready to depart en route for RAF Changi via RAF Akrotiri, Cyprus, RAF Muharraq, Bahrain and RAF Gan in the Maldive Islands. However, the Britannia went unserviceable and it took off late. It then went unserviceable at Muharraq and so we stayed the night, followed by a day and another night stopover for a propeller change at Gan. Thus, instead of it taking just over twenty-four hours to get to the Far East, the Britannia took three days. We weren't fussed at all, particularly as we reckoned we had four months to get there and back.

On arrival at RAF Changi, where the trooper aircraft of RAF Transport Command always landed, and having gone through the normal customs, we got our kit together and were then transported to RAF Tengah which was one of three RAF airfields in Singapore. The other two were RAF Changi and RAF Seletar. However, for aircraft strength alone Tengah was the largest. Our detachment of half a squadron of Vulcans supplemented the following: the permanent squadrons of 60 Squadron Javelins (FAW9), 64 Squadron Javelins (FAW9R), 45 Squadron Canberras (B15), 81 Squadron Canberras (PR7), 20 Squadron Hunters (FGA9) and 14 Squadron RNZAF Canberras (B15) on detachment. Periodically, one or two 13 Squadron Canberras (PR9) from Luqa, Malta, who only did a detachment of one month at a time, also took part. The latter's sole contribution was to overfly Borneo, take a few photographs, on two or three sorties during their stay and then return to Luqa! Finally, 63 Squadron RAF Regiment was also based at Tengah and armed with its Bofor guns, in the anti-aircraft role, guarded the airfield.

There is no doubt that Tengah possessed a large number of different types of aircraft with the commensurate number of aircrew. Added to that the ground crews, permanent and on detachment, plus the normal administrative back up that goes with every airfield, clearly made it an interesting and busy station.

Luckily our four-month detachment went without mishap. We underwent dinghy drills in the South China Sea and a short jungle survival course in the Mandai, an area in the north of Singapore Island. We were also issued with individual treescapes (a small capstan device with 200ft of nylon cord) from the flying clothing section at Tengah. This we were to carry in our flying suits in case we had to bale out and the parachute caught in a tree. A lot of flying both high and low level all over West Malaysia, up to the Thai border and out to Labuan and Kuching in Borneo was commonplace. We dropped 1,000lb bombs on Song Song Bombing Range, a sea range located off the coastline of the State of Kedah in the Malacca Straits and on China Rock Bombing Range, situated off the southeastern tip of the Malay Peninsula, in the South China Sea.

Apart from flying we checked our scores from the target runs on simulated targets in Malaysia and planned forthcoming sorties. We also had to study the targets allocated to each crew in the event that we had to bomb Indonesia. At the end of November we and three other crews, led by our flight commander Squadron Leader Butch Harris, flew across Indonesia at night, and at 60,000ft, down to RAAF Darwin in the Northern Territories of Australia. This was to take part in Exercise High Rigel, an air defence exercise (ADEX) with the RAAF. The aim was to check the capability of the RAAF in their air defence of Darwin. They used their ground controllers along with aircraft consisting of the Mirages III-O (F), from 75 Squadron RAAF and the CA-27 Sabres Mk32 of either 3 or 77 Squadron RAAF.

On 5th December we took off for RAAF Amberley situated just outside Brisbane. However, we couldn't head off directly as we first had to attack Darwin again, as part of the exercise, before we tackled the long leg to our destination. After a short stay of two days and a sightseeing trip to Surfers Paradise on the Gold Coast it was a return to attacking Darwin, through a horrendous tropical storm, followed by another two days of relaxation before returning to Tengah.

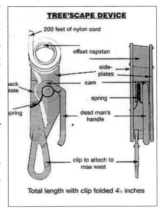

Treescapes as described by Tony Wright.

After a prolonged period of festive cheer during the Christmas stand down it was back to detachment life with all that that entailed. Obviously, the most important role during our detachment was to be on QRA. Therefore while we, as a squadron, were nominally detached to Tengah, one aircraft out of our four was always sitting by the end of the runway at RAAF Butterworth loaded with its 21 x 1,000lb bombs on QRA ready for take-off.

Butterworth town and the air base were situated on the west coast of West Malaysia opposite Georgetown on the island of Penang. The aircraft and crew stayed at Butterworth for one week then took off on a training sortie before returning to Tengah while another bombed-up aircraft and crew flew in to Butterworth to take over for their week's stay. As the crew on QRA was at twenty-four hours notice they could go across to Georgetown by ferry, swim, drink beer or just relax anywhere within reason. Gordon Blackburn and I particularly enjoyed this relaxed mode of life as our accommodation was situated on miles of sandy beach, which we walked regularly, and which looked as if it had come straight out of a travel brochure.

To be specific our QRA aircraft was loaded with 21 x 1,000lb MC (medium capacity) HE (high explosive) bombs each with varying types of nose and tail fuses, either for ground burst (instantaneous detonation when hitting the ground or delayed detonation on the ground at times set by our armourers), or airburst (detonating in the air at a certain height). The bombs were also varied in type to suit different situations. Therefore, some that were carried were used for hard targets while others were designed to fragment for soft targets. All of the targets were designated in Indonesia.

The 1,000lb bombs that we dropped on both Song Song and China Rock Bombing Range were from high level or medium level. However, some types of aircraft didn't use that form of attack. Another time it was decided that one of our IX Squadron Vulcans would drop a stick of 21 x 1,000lb bombs on China Rock while the rest of the squadron aircrew watched. I recall that the crew was chosen by lottery as we all wanted to do it. Unfortunately our crew missed out. However, we were able to watch the spectacle from the sea as we and some others went to Changi to board the marine craft from 1124 MCU or the MCRS RAF Seletar. We had a very pleasant trip out to the range, but not too near the Rock itself, then sunbathed and fished until the Vulcan came across and dropped the stick. We watched the bombs fall, watched the

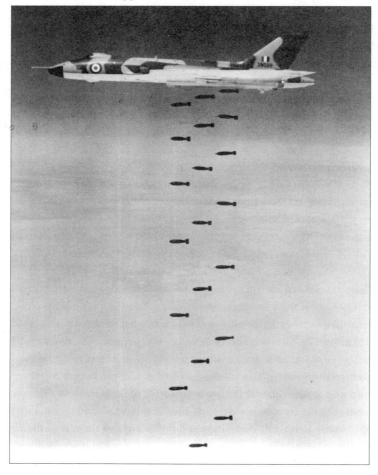

The photographer missed one! (*Jim Gardiner*)

splashes and counted the dull explosions. Not far away were some local fishermen waiting in boats. To make fishing easy they regularly nipped out after any range activity had finished to collect the dead or stunned fish which had risen to the surface! Years later I read that the fishermen regularly threw sticks of dynamite into the sea around the Rock to get their catch. We, unwittingly, had clearly started something.

February saw the end of the Atkinson crew four-month detachment. At that time many items were much cheaper in Singapore and could be bought for a fraction of the price in the UK. For example, one co-pilot purchased his wife a sewing machine, along with a 'gathering' attachment, and whiled away his evenings by 'gathering' copies of The Straits Times! We all had good buys too. Therefore, along with the aircraft spares, we loaded up the pannier in the bomb bay with our 'goodies' consisting of sets of Noritake china, my Kenwood Chef, Thai silk, Batik material and other souvenirs including Tony Atkinson's lamp shade and camphor wood chest plus countless other items bought by the crew chief and the rest of us. Tony's large lampshade and camphor wood chest were a real pain and we told him that if they took up too much space and we couldn't get all our things in then the chest and shade would be left behind. Tony quickly made sure that everything fitted, just!

On 26th February we took off to fly back to RAF Cottesmore, in Vulcan XM653. Our detachment commander, Squadron Leader Butch Harris, had nominated us to be the back-up aircraft for Victor XL513. It was being flown by a Victor training flight (VTF) crew from RAF Wittering. They in turn were carrying the Commander-in-Chief (C-in-C) Bomber Command, Air Chief Marshal Sir Wallace 'Wally' Kyle. He was an Australian, later to become governor of Western Australia, who had just visited Australia and was on his way back to the UK. Both aircraft took off from Tengah before noon, with an interval between, as we in the Vulcan were to follow the Victor some distance behind. It was planned that if the Victor suffered an unserviceability at any one of the various staging posts en route then it was our job to carry the C-in-C the rest of the way.

From our point of view everything was going smoothly, or so we thought, until on approaching RAF Gan we heard over the R/T from their air traffic control that the Victor was on fire. We then heard that it had landed. Clearly this was a very serious incident. Had the fire taken hold much earlier, the aircraft would undoubtedly have gone up in flames and they would have had to ditch or bale out somewhere into the Indian Ocean. Furthermore, they might not have survived in that vast area of sea. Luckily they had landed at Gan just in time. Therefore we, as a crew, decided that our first priority on landing was to go and see what a mess the Victor would be in.

Even from afar we were amazed to see the sorry state of the aircraft. We then walked over to inspect it at close quarters and saw the inside of the bomb bay which was covered in foam with the crew, crew chief and others standing around the aircraft. All that remained of Wally Kyle's golf clubs' bag, along with his, and the rest of the aircrew's, horseshoe-shaped issue-aircrew holdalls, were the skeletons of blackened wire hoops and bits of metal. Wally's golf clubs were reduced to long thin black rods with small black blobs on the end of each! His No 1 home dress (Best Blue) consisted of the remains of just one rank sleeve with only an air commodore stripe and the odd flying officer stripe on the cuff (whereas it should have been an air commodore stripe with three flying officer's stripes for an air chief marshal). Luckily for him, some of his civilian clothes for an overnight stopover at Gan, were packed in another small bag and carried in the aircraft cabin and thus went unscathed. Not so the rest of the crew who, we understood, had all their uniforms, civilian clothes, presents and other possessions destroyed by the fire in the bomb bay. That night, over a few beers on the patio of the officers' mess, we met up with a miserable Victor crew who were dressed in all manner of garb lent to them by other officers at Gan. Wally had no such problem. Obviously the main topic of conversation revolved around what might have caused the fire, at what point it was noticed and what actions were taken.

On 27th February, we left the Victor crew and their crew chief in Gan for them to await a subsequent inquiry. We took Wally onboard our Vulcan and flew him back to Cottesmore. Unfortunately for him our aircraft was not fitted out with the temporary 'VIP fit' of reading lamp, writing desk and comfortable cushioning like the Victor. Wally, as was required, had to sit in the sixth seat, effectively a ledge, behind my seat until airborne. However, at height he lay down on the co-pilot's li-lo, which we'd un-packed and put in the bomb aimer's position in the nose, and read Playboy!

Finally, to end the saga it did mean that the Victor incident brought a bit of luck to Gordon and myself. While we were out in Tengah we were told that we, as a nav team, were to be posted from IX Squadron to 35 Squadron, Cottesmore when we got back to the UK. We had not been on IX Squadron long and our objection was that it was 35 Squadron's turn next to take over the Confrontation rotation stint from IX at Tengah. Our moan was that we were to have two-weeks leave in UK and then have to return to Singapore. As both Gordon and I weren't green and were ready to stand up for ourselves we decided that as we were in the presence of the real 'Big Chief' on board we would bend his ear! Therefore, at one point during the flight when he looked over our shoulders to watch us working, we steered the conversation around to the subject of detachments and ours in particular. He conveniently asked us if we had enjoyed the four-month Singapore detachment. We politely told him that indeed we had. However, we added that we weren't very happy at being told by OC 35 Squadron, who was now at Tengah, that we were to get only two-weeks leave in the UK with our

White Vulcan Mk2s at RAF Cottesmore. (*Nigel Baldwin*)

families and then would have to go back out to Tengah for another four months with his squadron. We left it like that. Nothing more was said. We resigned ourselves to a swift return to the Far East as we didn't think that we had either got through to him or that he would do anything about our plight.

When we eventually arrived back at RAF Cottesmore, unknown to us, the station commanders had changed while we were away. Now a new station commander was awaiting our arrival, one that we didn't know. When the engines had stopped I opened the door and dropped down the ladder for the C-in-C to descend. There standing by our aircraft ready to greet the C-in-C was the new station commander, Group Captain 'Jack' Garden. After returning his salute and welcome, the first thing that the C-in-C said to him was "these two navigators are not going back out to Singapore". That was clearly that. We had both by this time come down the ladder and witnessed this exchange. The station commander, not expecting this statement out of the blue, was in no position to argue with the C-in-C. At the same time we knew that we weren't going to be very popular. Needless to say we navigators started off very low down in the popularity stakes with our new station commander; at the time we reckoned it was minus points, but so what! We'd got what we wanted and didn't have to go back out there for another four-month stint.

> The USAF Strategic Air Command bombing competition was an important event not only for the USAF but also for the RAF. It was first held in 1948 and in 1951 the RAF took part, flying B29s. In 1957 the V bombers became available and both Valiants and Vulcans took part in the competition though without any success against the USAF's B47s. The competition was renamed Giant Voice in 1967 and in 1974 the RAF flying Vulcans won both the bombing competition and the navigation trophy.
>
> Anthony was very much involved in one competition and almost in another!

SAC Combat Competition 1966 – Big Flight 28th October 1966
However, even before the end of the year we did get back into Jack Garden's good books. Although a new nav team on the Bill Downs crew on 35 Squadron, we were picked to take part in the United States Air Force (USAF) 1966 Strategic Air Command (SAC) Combat Bombing Competition named Big Flight. That year it was held at Fairchild Air Force Base (AFB) just outside Spokane in Washington State and consisted of flying bombing and navigation sorties competing against the best crews from the USAF SAC B52 and B58 Hustler Squadrons. Now we were on good terms with our station commander, he had decided to come out with us as the detachment commander, along with OC 35 Squadron; it was a very successful detachment.

After a number of fly-offs and scrutiny of past bomb scores of the RAF Cottesmore crews of IX(B), 12 and 35 Squadrons, four crews were chosen to fly to the Fairchild AFB to take part in Big Flight. Apart from 1965 the last competition was in 1961 as USAF operational requirements dictated the cancellation of the others. Our crew comprised Bill Downs as captain, Geoff Delmege co-pilot, myself Tony Wright nav radar, Gordon Blackburn nav plotter and Nigel Harding AEO. Prior to our arrival at Fairchild, for PR purposes, we all had to fill out forms saying who we were and where we lived in the

UK. It provided a bit of merriment on our part when the US PR machine got to work and erroneously reported one of our aircrew to be Flight Lieutenant Melton Mowbray!

I don't believe that any of our crews had quite grasped how important this competition was to SAC and the Americans until our arrival, when the local papers started to report on the event. For example on 2nd October *The Spokane Spokesman Review* announced, 'the region welcomes SAC competitors....SAC crews all over the world including Fairchild's own plus three top Royal Air Force crews from England are now on hand for participation in what has been described as the world series of precision bombing and navigation.' Then on 3rd October *The Spokane Daily Chronicle* proclaimed that:

> 'bomb tests due to start as Fairchild AFB today took on the look of a convention city. The majority of bomber aircraft converged on Fairchild yesterday to take part in the SAC combat competition. This is the fifteenth time that the competition has taken place. The bomber crews will fly 2,455 miles during the six hours of each of the two flights. Thirty-seven crews, one from each SAC bomber wing will take part in addition to three visiting bomber crews from the Royal Air Force. The forty crews taking part were selected as the best from their individual bomber bases. About 2,000 crewmen are at Fairchild for the meet, many for duties other than flying. Some are here to officiate at the meet or for servicing the competition aircraft.'

In addition *The Fairchild Times*, the on-base newspaper, published a blow-by-blow account of the competition on a daily basis.

For us, intensive training in the UK starting in August and lasting over two months, had been undertaken beforehand to master a type of attack, new to us, but which was operated by SAC. It was called 'The Large Charge'. This type of attack was to bomb two targets, one after another, approximately twenty to twenty-five miles apart. The competition itself required each participating crew to attack two targets at high level followed by four targets, using the Large Charge attack, at low level and then to complete a long high level navigation leg at night, the latter using limited aids including astro navigation. All bombing attacks were RBSU scored as was the accuracy of navigation at the end of the navigation leg. Two night sorties were required from each crew. The crew with the highest points in combined bombing and navigation for both missions would receive the Fairchild Trophy. Two other trophies were given, one for the crew with the highest points in bombing and the other for the crew with the highest points in navigation.

We all flew out from RAF Cottesmore on 15th September, each aircraft carrying crew chiefs in the sixth and seventh seats. Chief Technician Grantham and Chief Technician Perryman accompanied our crew. The early departure in September ensured that we could fly the USAF's 'oil burner' low level routes to practise our low level attacks along with high level bombing and navigation in the host's environment, prior to the event scheduled for 28th October.

The RAF crews were accommodated in a hotel downtown in Spokane. Each crew was provided with its own USAF Shooting Brake to get back and forth to the base. All the vehicles had seen better days and as all four doors on ours would only lock from the inside we had to open the rear window and crawl through the opening over the fixed tailgate which we could then lock from the outside. Getting in and out of the vehicle this way proved quite a sight for amazed passers-by in Spokane itself. At Fairchild Air Base the large competition hangar on the flight line was already prepared and divided up into many individual booth-type offices, just like an exhibition centre, to accommodate the different SAC bomb wings and RAF taking part. Each booth comprised a planning area within three temporary walls and open at the front. The open fronts facing the hangar walkway areas meant that anyone walking past could drop in to mingle and chat and 'spy' on a rival team's planning!

All the booths were decorated with various bomb wing and squadron memorabilia. We had posters and material from the English tourist board, beer posters, beer mats and other paraphernalia all designed to fly the flag for our squadrons, RAF Cottesmore, Rutland and England. As visitors, and Brits taking part, obviously we were a novelty and extremely popular. To add to our attraction we'd also taken over to the States, in one of our Vulcans, a large Stilton cheese from Melton Mowbray and a keg of Ruddles Rutland County ale to entertain our hosts when crews exchanged hospitality

at the party after the closing ceremony. Some of the SAC bomb wings went to great lengths to ensure that their crews stood out from the crowd. Rather than wear normal flying suits there was an assortment of coloured ones among the SAC crews. The home team, Major Thigpen's crew from the 92nd Strategic Aerospace Wing, who our crew got to know extremely well, clearly beat the rest as, much to their chagrin, they were forced to wear mauve-cum-lilac flying suits.
They were quickly dubbed the 'Lilac Ladies' by all at Fairchild, including their wives, a nickname that the crew hated. All the SAC crews wore the *de rigeur* coloured crew cravats around their necks above their T shirts. The RAF, understated as usual, just wore our normal light blue flying suits and blue RAF shirts, top button undone, apart from my plotter who, with no exceptions, always wore his black tie when flying. Apart from our squadron badges we, like all competitors, had to have the SAC bomb comp patch, which was the size of a small saucer and mandatory to wear, sewn onto the left breast of our flying suits.

As the RAF were working as a team it was decided to put up just one crew on the first night. My crew acted as the 'fall guys' to go first and to effectively be the reconnaissance aircraft to give the other two crews the best advantage. After we had flown our sortie the 35mm film taken of the radar screen by the R88 camera would then be removed from the aircraft, processed and scrutinised by our Joint Air Reconnaissance Intelligence Centre (JARIC) adviser Glyn Wady and HQ 1 Group representative Mo Hammond, both of whom were nav radars. They had already planned the bombing fix points and calculated the bombing offsets for us by touring the competition areas in a rental car taking photographs and marking maps. With my film available Glyn and Mo could alter any bombing offsets or fix points for better ones and the other two crews could study the target runs in detail and in slow time, ready for them to fly the same route and attack the same targets knowing exactly what to expect.

The opening ceremony was on 2nd October when the order of flight for the crews was drawn. At the same time umpires were allocated to each aircraft and there was much vying from the Americans to fly in the sixth seat of a Vulcan. That is despite them being amazed that a five-man crew, plus two crew chiefs, could be cooped up in such a small, dark cockpit. The first night of competition flying was on 3rd October. A KC 135 tanker and a B52 bomber were sent ahead to act as weather scouts for the competition route. They reported back that, unfortunately, the weather was deemed too poor on the Big Flight I route. Therefore, it was decided that all crews would fly the Big Flight II route. The first aircraft drawn to take off was a B58 Hustler followed by our crew's Vulcan then the B52s and other Hustlers. The six-hour sortie comprised much hard work and produced plenty of adrenalin, especially on my part.

We didn't know at the time until it was reported in the *Fairchild Times* that our crew got its own write up being the first Vulcan, and second aircraft, to take off in the competition. Under the heading 'Up, Up, and Away' the newspaper stated 'Along the runway, hundreds of people stood staring .....and waiting for the next bird to lift-off, the first of the Royal Air Force Vulcans... it was really the plane that everyone was there to see take off...'

On landing, the planning team and the other two flying crews and ops crew got to work to analyse my film, just as had been agreed. The following night the Arnott crew and Crowder crew flew their sorties, by now knowing their targets in depth, with the Arnott crew finishing in a very good position in the navigation part of the sortie and a strong contender for the Navigation Trophy.

I flew the second sortie on 5th October, experiencing another six hours of intensive work, and to my delight got a direct hit, or 'shack' as the Americans call it on my last target. I remember to this day that the final offset that I used was a small island in the middle of Tumtum Lake. A name not easily forgotten. On the huge score board against my name, in the large competition hangar, was a cartoon shack with a bomb through its roof, the symbol put up against anyone getting a shack.

The other two crews flew on 6th October, again using intelligence from my second sortie, but unfortunately didn't come away with a trophy. However, when the prizes were given out, in the huge auditorium on the base, the RAF went onto the stage to each receive an inscribed zippo lighter from General Ryan, SAC commander-in-chief. Both Bill and I still have those lighters today.

As to the social scene we had an RAF aircrew and ground crew team visit, organised by Fairchild, to the Grand Coulee Dam and were much sought after as guests at the houses of the Fairchild crew. So too to the home of the wing weapons officer major at Fairchild who we had got to know very well, and who had helped us during our training flights. Finally, on 11th October we flew back to the UK. As was often the case we routed ourselves via Bourne in Lincs just twenty miles from Cottesmore to fly over Bill and Geoff's houses. This was to warn their wives that we were back. It then gave them enough time to get in their cars to drive the twenty miles to Cottesmore ready to pick up their husbands once we had landed, unloaded, debriefed, changed and were ready for home.

SAC Combat Competition Giant Voice 1967
The next year Big Flight's name was, for the first time, changed to Giant Voice. The RAF were invited and our crew, now with a different AEO, Jim Patterson, was again selected to take part. However, this time the powers that be decided to use another station to train from to show the Americans that Vulcans were not just confined to RAF Cottesmore. RAF Waddington was chosen and crews from there as well as from Cottesmore would take part. OC 35 Squadron had relinquished command of the squadron by then but remained there to be the detachment commander of Giant Voice 1967. For our crew to train at RAF Waddington meant a round trip of at least ninety miles each day. Our sorties meant flying at all hours, we couldn't use RAF MT and to share transport wasn't feasible with crew members living in Bourne, Cottesmore, Melton Mowbray and Oakham. Therefore, we asked to claim payment for our mileage from the RAF as we were paying out money from our own pockets for something they wanted us to do. As our own station accounts wouldn't sanction payment our request escalated, via our detachment commander, to command accounts. The response, and meanness, was astounding when an air commodore at command HQ refused our submission with the statement that to represent the RAF and to get a good annual report (Form 1369) should be reward enough!

For five months from April until August we travelled daily to RAF Waddington to either plan or fly. After twenty-eight competition training sorties including two mini fly-offs to choose the final crews, our crew made it through as one of the crews finally selected. However, on 23rd August we got a shock. As we got out of the aircraft having flown our last training sortie we were greeted on the pan by Don Arnott who told us that because of their involvement in the Vietnam War, SAC had cancelled Giant Voice. Some of the RAF ground equipment had already arrived in the States and some was still on the high seas. It was a bitter disappointment to us after all our hard work, plus having paid out so much of our own petrol money, with no reward. There was not to be another Giant Voice until 1971.

Life returned to normal on the squadron with the usual duties and QRA. To speak of the latter our crew was on QRA on Christmas Day and the press came along to take some PR photographs ready for a national newspaper under the headline: 'Christmas is a Time For Work – For Some People.' Coloured photographs were also taken for another edition. In May 1968 our past hard work on Giant Voice was rewarded, so we believed, when our crew along with 'Buster' Skinner, one of the flight commanders, and his crew were both given the chance to fly out to Singapore west about and back the same way via RCAF Goose Bay, Offutt AFB (Omaha), McClellan AFB (Sacramento), Hickam AFB (Hawaii), Wake Island and Anderson AFB (Guam).

Both crews were due to depart on 20th May. However, on the day we all crewed in, after start up, our aircraft became unserviceable. The other aircraft, on the other hand, was serviceable and ready to take off. Buster told us they would wait in Offutt and with that he got airborne. After we had hung around for some time it was obvious that the snag couldn't be fixed that day and that it would take a few more hours. Therefore, with all our bags already packed in the bomb bay, and not wanting to unload anything, we all drove home, much to our wives' surprise, in our flying suits. The next morning, back at Cottesmore, with the aircraft now ready to go we crewed in again and took off for Goose Bay. On landing at Goose we heard that Buster's aircraft had now become unserviceable and so he couldn't take off. The crew had already gone back to their accommodation and so we didn't meet them at the flight line.

We hadn't forgotten Buster's comment about waiting for us in Offutt so without hesitation we immediately decided to double-stage which, dependent on crew duty time, was allowed. We asked the ground crew to refuel the aircraft as quickly as possible and told the RAF detachment operations staff at Goose not to inform the other crew. Then with a quick turnaround completed we handed the ground crew a note to be given to Buster once we had taken off. It said 'we'll wait for you in Hawaii', which we did for an enjoyable three days. Once again re-united with Buster's Vulcan in Hawaii we both took off for Wake then double-staged to Guam. On arrival at Guam quite a sight greeted us as there were a large number of B52s parked up and flying out of Guam to bomb Vietnam. What was interesting was that one end of the runway at Anderson AFB stopped at a cliff edge followed by a sheer drop into the sea. Watching the B52s lumbering down the runway struggling to get into the air in the hot climate and, with

full armament load, then having run out of runway sinking out of sight over the cliff edge until appearing again clawing their way back into the air was an amazing spectacle. Our MT soon arrived and we got into the rear of an open-backed lorry.

As we started off towards operations we could see a figure furiously pedalling his bike and waving an arm at us following our vehicle. We asked the driv-

A Douglas C-133B Cargomaster and three Avro Vulcan B2s at Offut. (*Andy Leitch*)

er to slow down and who should appear shouting and grinning but one of our American friends, a lieutenant colonel and participant, whom we had met in the 1966 Big Flight Bombing Competition. Apparently he and some others that we knew were on detachment to Guam for their Vietnam stint. He said that they'd be going off later on a bombing mission and, because they knew me from Fairchild and that I was a nav radar, asked me would I like to come and fly with them. Not only that, they'd let me drop the bombs! With great regret I declined their kind offer. They said that they'd meet up with us in the bar after they returned, which in due course they did. Later on I did fly in a B52 with a SAC crew so I did fulfil part of my wish.

A few days later we flew on to RAF Tengah, Singapore then retraced our route, eventually arriving back in the UK on 8th June. Before we had left on our trip MOD policy had determined that the two remaining Vulcan squadrons at Cottesmore, IX and 35 would move to RAF Akrotiri, Cyprus in January 1969 to form the Near East Air Force Bomber Wing. Therefore, most of my colleagues on the two squadrons knew their postings as they were still carrying on the same job on Vulcans but in Cyprus.

Post Giant Voice

I was, however, coming to the end of my tour as nav radar leader with 35 Squadron and was asked by my CO Wg Cdr Carver if I wanted a re-tour to Cyprus. Having done the job on Valiants then Vulcans, and flown the Victor I wanted a change from the V Force. I needed to move on, so I declined, and waited to see what my posting was to be. The 'move on' turned out to be a bit further than I bargained for. When I landed in the aircraft at Cottesmore I was greeted by one of my squadron colleagues with the statement that my overseas papers were in at SHQ. It was the rule then that whenever V Force crews wanted to holiday abroad you had to apply for permission. I had applied to go to Ibiza on holiday in the summer and thought that it was a bit over the top, although it was abroad, to call Ibiza overseas. In due course I went down to get the so-called papers and found to my amazement that it was a posting notice for me, on a ground tour, to be station intelligence officer at RAF Tengah, where I'd just been. I didn't know then but my absence from Vulcans was not to last for too long. Thus, after a tour in Singapore followed by another as station navigation officer and combat survival rescue officer instructor at the RAF College Cranwell I returned to Vulcans. By this time the Bomber Command Bombing School which used to train nav radars on bombing had been integrated into 230 OCU so that the Hastings training aircraft, which contained the H2S radar used in the Vulcans, were part of the aircraft fleet. I became an instructor on 230 OCU at RAF Scampton flying both Vulcans and Hastings instructing on radar navigation and bombing for Vulcan, Victor, Buccaneer and Phantom aircrew (1975-1978).

Tasks that the Hastings and nav radars undertook were Operation Tapestry patrolling the oil rigs round the UK and taking part in the 'Cod War', Operation Heliotrope. Iceland was continually trying to extend its fishing boundaries

Not exactly a Vulcan but at the OCU the Hastings radar equipment was the same. (*Anthony Wright*)

and in doing so its gun boats were cutting the warps or lines of our trawlers and ramming both them and the Royal Navy ships sent out to protect our fishing fleet. This was the Third Cod War where Iceland was trying to extend its territorial waters and hence increase its fishing area to a 200-mile limit from its coast.

My tour on 230 OCU ended with promotion and I was posted to RAF Waddington as squadron leader bombing and navigation systems in operations wing. This proved to be highly enjoyable as I was able to fly with crews from IX, 44, 50 and 101 Squadrons, on a regular basis, and join them on the odd over-seas detachment. One in particular was a NATO exercise called Teamwork, with 50 Squadron, at Royal Norwegian Air Force (RNoAF) Bodø, Norway (right). The fly-ing was excellent and the scenery remark-able. However, it was the constant aroma

of fish in the air and around the port, and the Scandinavian meatballs, which appeared regularly on the menu, and termed 'reindeer balls' by some of our more discerning aircrew, that I can't seem to forget.

Finally, I joined 50 Squadron at Waddington as nav radar leader flying Vulcans and was selected for the Red Flag night flying and bombing exercises in Nevada, USA in early 1982 (described later on). This was followed by Operation Corporate when I was posted to Northwood to help in planning the later Black Buck Raids.

Surprisingly the end of Corporate didn't mean that it was the death knell of the Vulcan. Although all the other Vulcan squadrons had disbanded by the end of 1982, mine was given a reprieve and was still going strong. The reason, put quite simply, was that we were now going to become tankers. So back from Northwood I became the only Vulcan tanker leader until 31st March 1984 when the squadron was disbanded.

So Anthony, having taken part in Red Flag found himself involved in the Falklands campaign, Operation Corporate, and was detached to RAF Northwood as a Vulcan advisor which he describes in Chapter Twelve. Then his squadron was reprieved from being disbanded as the Vulcans were turned into tankers and he tells the story in Chapter Fifteen. Finally after Anthony's flying days were over he was posted to the Nuclear Directorate in the Ministry of Defence in Whitehall.

On leaving the RAF in 1998 he took a post at Headquarters Air Cadets, RAF Cranwell which was responsible for both the Air Training Corps (ATC) and the Combined Cadet Force (CCF) RAF as a squadron leader in the Roy-al Air Force Reserve (RAFR) in a post entitled squadron leader corporate business. He decided to retire finally on 1st January 2003 – his sixty-first birthday.

Chapter Six

'DOWN UNDER' NAVIGATOR

Ted Marmont joined the Royal Australian Air Force on 1st October 1951 as an aircrew trainee hoping to be a pilot. He passed the initial flight grading on the Tiger Moth aircraft and moved to pilot's school but he obviously had problems. He found it difficult to maintain height and though he could make approaches he wasn't able to do three pointers on landing. His instructor reported his progress to his CO and he was duly programmed for the inevitable scrub test. So the fifteen hours he did training to be a pilot were the only true piloting that he ever achieved.

His story reminded me of my scrub check at thirteen hours but somehow I got through and managed to get my wings. I blame the Percival Prentice for my lack of progress as I raced through the Harvard; pity Ted couldn't have done the same.

Ted's CO suggested that because of his good education and fairly high marks in ground subjects he was a suitable candidate for navigation and reluctantly he agreed; he reckons it was the best decision he ever made. He was duly posted to the School of Air Navigation (SAN) RAAF Base, East Sale, Victoria, and graduated as a sergeant navigator in early 1953.

Ted Marmont, Phil Leckenby and Jim Walker not on QRA.
(*Ted Marmont*)

I flew in Dakotas, Lincolns and converted onto Canberras at RAAF Base Amberley, Queensland, in 1958. Flying in a Canberra was most enjoyable. My Lincoln flying at

1,000 feet above the water using maritime techniques consolidated my earlier navigational experiences. Our aids were the Mk9 sextant, drift recorder and a set of eye balls. Hence, to become the navigator of high-flying fast-jet Canberra bombers, equipped with Green Satin and GPI Mk4, was a wonderful promotion and I enjoyed every minute. That experience was later to become vital to my future flying career.

However, the RAAF did not want to give me a permanent commission in the general duties branch so I became an equipment officer and handed in my plotting gear and flying clothing. By mid-1963 I had suffered a gutful of this role and talked to an ex-RAF navigator who had joined the RAAF as, would you believe, an equipment officer. He suggested it might be a good idea to enquire if the RAF could use my experience. My wife Jackie, who was born in the UK at Wythenshawe, Greater Manchester, agreed that it would be wonderful for me to go flying again. I made an enquiry of the RAF and was advised that provided I was medically fit and passed an interview, they would have me and advise details of the offer that would be made. My medical and interview were successful and the RAF stuck by their word and made a positive offer which I accepted. It included a permanent commission in the supplementary branch with the rank of flight lieutenant, with free transport to England for me, Jackie and our daughter Susie. I was to arrive in the UK by 9th March 1964. I had been selected, by a process known as 'Predetermined – Locked and Welded Destiny', to fly in Vulcans.

I departed Melbourne for Singapore in early March by BOAC Comet 4. Three days later I was off to the UK, this time in an RAF Comet 4 via Gan, Aden and El Adem, arriving at Lyneham on a cold grey winter's day. I looked around and thought, 'what the hell am I doing here?' It was too late to get to London to sign up, so I had to wait until the next day – and lost a day's pay!

Having done the due signing at Adastral House, I was directed to RAF Hendon, where I spent a most enjoyable two weeks. The next move was to RAF Stradishall, Suffolk, where I did a nav refresher course: the most enjoyable course I have ever done. Then to RAF Lindholme for my third visual bomb aimer's course and down the road to RAF Finningley, where I waited for the rest of the crew to arrive. They were Wing Commander Mike D'Arcy, OC of 44(Rhodesia) Squadron elect, co-pilot Phil Leckenby, nav radar Jim Walker and AEO John Lamont. After ground school was completed we began flying; Flight Lieutenant Derek Bryce being the flying instructor.

Our first training sortie was in Vulcan Mk1 XA901 on 2nd September 1964. I imagined that on that trip I would be supervised by an OCU staff nav plotter, but instead, they placed great faith in me and off I went on my own. At least I had a nav radar operator and Gee Mk3 to help me find our way and my years on the Canberra had fine-tuned my ability; consequently I had the type of experience suitable for the RAF V Force and I was soon to learn about the absolute orgasmic delight of having one's body being dragged backwards in the dark at 480kts. In answer to the question "what is it like to navigate a Vulcan at 40,000ft?" I answer: "it's much easier than at 53,000ft while wearing a g-suit and pressure jerkin in a confined space."

Jackie arrived at the conclusion of the OCU and joined in the 'end of course party'. Next day we drove to RAF Waddington and occupied our married quarter at 15 Edinburgh Square. We handed in the dining room furniture and I built a bar. We had many visits from single living-in aircrew who preferred to enter via the bar window instead of the front door. The cheapest strong drink available locally was 'Grotty Port' at five shillings a bottle from the corner shop in Waddington village. They did a roaring trade.

Upon our arrival at Waddington in October 1964, Mike took over command of the squadron and was asked if he would like to take over the existing OC's crew but he declined, declaring that he had flown with his crew during conversion, was happy with them and wanted to continue with them. He was extremely loyal to us and I will always honour and respect my memory not only of him but of Phil , Jim and John: Mike and John have since departed this earth, Phil, Jim and I being the survivors.

Waddington was equipped with Mk1A Vulcans hence it was necessary that a squadron flight commander, firstly Squadron Leader Albert Wallace, be co-pilot on the first two flights which were day and night checks. For a pilot, there was little difference between Mk1 and Mk1A aircraft except for engine power. The next check was an introduction into low-level flying, under the supervision of Squadron Leader Richard Goldring. We then began our training for war.

> I did the initial flying of the Mk1A and Ted seems to have forgotten that the Mk1A introduced the now very familiar bulged tail shape of the aircraft to house the new electronic counter-measure equipment of the time; but then the new gear was operated by the AEO! There was a change for the pilot because the Mk1 had a strong nose-down trim change when the bomb doors were opened and this very conveniently disappeared with the introduction of the Mk1A back end. Ted again:

We spent many hours planning and flying a type of sortie called a 'hi-lo-hi' profile. Peace-time low-level training involved flying at 500ft above ground by day and at 1,000ft above the highest ground within ten nautical miles of track at night and at an indicated air speed of 240kts. We were allowed to increase to 250kts for timing purposes. That was not so good if you were unlucky enough to meet a head wind and still have to be on time at one's destination. No forgiveness for bad luck just: TCT which translates to 'Tough Cheddar Ted'.

My favourite low-level route was close to Fort William at the northeast end of Loch Linnhe from where we would follow the route for a simulated attack on a target near Gateshead and Newcastle-on-Tyne. Such targets could be anything from a display sign at a corner of a pub or the centre of a road bridge. Letting down to an entry point could sometimes be tricky depending upon its geographic position; however, letting down over the middle of Loch Linnhe was easy. Be at the correct position at the start of the let down and fly the correct heading. The nav radar then gave advice to the captain to make necessary heading changes to ensure that the aircraft remained over the centre of the Loch. When the aircraft was below cloud and the steely-eyed pilots could see the water and had a clear view ahead, I could breathe a sigh of relief and think 'so far so good, there's more to do yet especially our attack on the Newcastle target'.

Immediately at the end of the attack came the announcement: "Bomb gone, bomb doors closed." That was the time when the nav plotter needed four sets of eyes and three right hands because, at bomb release, he had to read all the dials on the navigation and bombing computer panel and record the data for the nav radar who was probably still staring at the radar tube at least once wondering if he had got it right. The plotter had also to continue with his own job while the captain turned the aircraft through 90 degrees to point its rear to the target and begin to climb. All retired nav radars who read this will remember the embarrassment of their failing to switch in their aiming point offsets[3]. I know one such person who once got a direct hit on his offset. He is a good friend and great fellow and, sorry, I can't give his name.

Trying to plan and complete a hi-lo-hi sortie in England in winter was very frustrating. We were required to complete several such flights in order to maintain our crew category, the highest of which was 'Select Star', and the whole exercise depended on the weather factor but bad weather was not the only obstacle. I remember being told, on many occasions after I had just completed the flight plan, then booked our entry/exit points, worked out target attack time and was completely ready to go that some other crew, for some reason having a higher priority than ours, had been allocated those time and place slots. "So Ted, do another plan and make it snappy for the aircrew bus will arrive any minute to take us to our aircraft."

Flying on solo flights became somewhat mundane – next trip more of the same. However, there was one exercise which I really enjoyed called a Groupex. That entailed all No 1 Group aircraft flying the same route with ten to fifteen-minute spacing, a very pleasant game of follow the leader, but don't make any silly errors. There were a few and they caused much laughter when they were announced over the radio. Each crew tried to obtain the best bombing results, something like a mini navigation and bombing competition. Why so much high-level flying and why so much emphasis on bombing runs? The answers are fairly self-evident. None of the production V type aircraft were designed for low-level flying and we still had to retain our bombing skills.

On one day in early April 1965 Mike D'Arcy told us that we might possibly be flying to Southern Rhodesia for a goodwill visit to meet and enjoy some time with men who had been members of 44 Squadron during World War 2. In fact, the name of the squadron had been changed during the war to No 44 (Rhodesia) because most of the crewmen were Rhodesians. Anyway, upon Mike's instruction I set to work and busily planned the trip with the odd request from him as to how I was progressing. Mike kept us informed of pertinent news and then one day said that the visit had been approved and that we would go. My next task was to make out a detailed flight plan and to nominate reporting point times in order that diplomatic clearances could be obtained. I was very happy that we were to go and realised that there were some real advantages in being a member of the CO's crew. Here was another chance for adventure and I put all the enthusiasm I could muster into the whole task.

The route outbound was: Waddington-El Adem (Tobruk)-Bahrain-Aden and thence to Salisbury. The return was a back track except that we were given a day off in Akrotiri, Cyprus. I later found out that the person who organised the day off was

---

[3]Offsets were easily recognisable radar responses which were used to identify targets.

none other than Wg Cdr Vic McNabney who took over command of 44 upon Mike's departure in June 1966. One of Wing Commander D'Arcy's friends was based in Akrotiri and when he heard that Mike and crew were present, he took us all into Limassol to the Romantic Bar for a kebab even though we had just finished dinner in the No 2 officers' mess. Some enterprising local RAF members told us about a wine called Kokkinelli and advised us to drink as much as possible because it was so good. We took their advice but did not feel so well the next day. Sunbathing with a rotten hangover is bad news.

The leg from Bahrain to Aden, Khormaksar, took us over the island of Masirah where the RAF had a base and where I was to spend some time on detachment from RAF Akrotiri in June 1969 flying in Vulcan Mk2 aircraft. Wg Cdr D'Arcy was keen to have a look at Masirah so with clearance to let down he did two overshoots, said goodbye and climbed to height and thence to Aden. The tower controller said they seldom saw a V bomber out their way and it was XA910.

A TV team filmed our arrival at Salisbury airfield and we put on a small display of what a Vulcan can do; if the g meter read 2.0g instead of the permitted 1.5g then someone must have interfered with the instrument! The time was about 11.10am on 8th July 1965 and it was a magnificent sunny day. In fact, the weather remained the same for the whole of the next week. First up we were taken to a good hotel and were entertained to lunch by Salisbury Rotarians, a very pleasant way to welcome us. We met several dignitaries including the chief of staff of the then Royal Rhodesian Air Force: Air Vice-Marshal Harold Hawkins CBE, AFC an Australian who came from Toowoomba, Queensland. We met also our host Group Captain Johns, the RAF air attaché in Salisbury.

On that first evening we were invited to Group Captain Johns' residence for cocktails and to meet his other guests including AVM Hawkins. I told the AVM of my air force background including my great desire to become a pilot. I said that I had some experience in manually flying a Dakota which I discovered he remembered the next day.

Salisbury was a lovely city and I found to my surprise that there were many beautiful large tall gum trees growing along the streets. I had the feeling that I was back home in Australia. We were shown around the city and went to see and listen to tobacco auctions, very interesting if one spoke the auctioneer's language. In the evenings we were entertained by ex-44 Squadron members.

AVM Hawkins arranged for a small group of people, including us, to travel to Victoria Falls in his VIP Dakota and we all wore civilian clothes. I was sat minding my own business peering out the window when he came from the crew compartment and told me to go sit in the captain's seat and fly the machine. I said: "Sir, I am not a pilot." He said: "I have kicked the captain out of his seat, go and fly the aircraft." Now how could I disobey such and order from an AVM? I was absolutely delighted but thought 'bloody hell, I hope I can do a fair job'. In fact I did pretty well, plus or minus three degrees of heading and some variation in height. There were no complaints from the passengers nor did any of them become airsick. I got the thrill of my life plus a little more adventure thrown in. It was a beautiful, fine day and the mist from the falls was

Canada low-level routes checking navigation.
(*Nigel Baldwin*)

visible for about thirty miles. After lunch and then a flight to Kariba Dam it was back
to Salisbury. We then departed from Salisbury at 7.54am on 12th July for our return
to UK via Cyprus.

Our turn to go to 'the Goose', RCAF Goose Bay, arrived on 15th November 1965
and off we went. The route took us within radar range of the southern tip of Green-
land so that we could fix the aircraft's position before entering Canadian air space.
Magnetic Variation changes in large amounts and fairly quickly across the Atlantic so I
had to keep altering the setting on the G4B compass main indicator. We flew low-level
routes numbers two, four and three in that order on 16th, 17th and 19th November
and returned on the 20th. It was a very interesting experience and the snowfalls had
already begun. One had to watch the G4B compass main indicator very carefully because there were some strange magnetic anomalies in a few places along the routes
which could upset the compass and where this occurred we just kept flying straight
ahead until the instrument settled down.

In early June 1966 Vic McNabney arrived to take over command of 44 Squadron
and we flew with Mike for his last trip on the 23rd. Our new captain called us together
to discuss the sort of flying that we had been doing and possibly to get a feel for what
sort of a bunch he had inherited. After we had flown a few sorties including Libyan low
level without any hiccups, he discovered that we were a reasonable lot who knew what
we were doing. I think that he may have just felt fairly impressed with us. We achieved
'harmony on the flight deck' easily and thereafter enjoyed a happy association, except
for one embarrassing action on my part. It could possibly be called a minor social
hiccup which I will never forget. It was 21st November 1966; it was the foggy season in
Lincolnshire with visibilities sometimes dropping to 100 yards or zero with horizontal
icicles on small bushes. I forget the officer's name but he held the position of wing

commander ops at Waddington and was a qualified nav plotter, also a great friend of Vic McNabney. He wanted to navigate our aircraft to RAF Luqa, Malta for the exercise and I was asked to be at operations by 6.00am to complete the flight plan for him.

One of my best friends is a man called Roly Taylor who now lives in Wall, Northumberland. I was his best man when he and Jill were married in St Clement Danes Church, London in 1967. On the evening prior to our departure for Malta, Roly and I plus a few more mates enjoyed a few pints of Whitbread Tankard in the mess. I enquired of Roly if he had packed his clothes ready for the next day. He said he hadn't. I

Ted's first RAF crew. Left to right: Phil Leckenby – co-pilot, Mike D'Arcy – captain, Jim Walker – nav radar, Jock Lamont – AEO, Ted Marmont – nav plotter. (*Ted Marmont*)

replied that he ought to do so because he would be short of time in the morning. Off we went to his room to complete the task but were interrupted by the appearance of a comrade wielding a bottle of Tequila which of course we emptied in the proper way. Neat Tequila is an excellent sleeping draft, so much so that I was woken at 7.00am next morning by Jim Walker, our nav radar, who told me that I was in it right up to my ears and that Vic McNabney was furious.

I arrived at ops ASAP and did the flight plan. The only thing that saved me was the fog which had caused the airfield to be temporarily closed. I will admit that I felt a right 'git', Ted Marmont the Aussie navigator who had not to this point put up even a minor black was now possibly facing a charge. I apologised and accepted the warning; we then went on to complete some very successful high and low-level sorties. I put every bit of effort I could into them.

Mk1A machines were being gradually replaced with Mk2s and it was time to go to 230 OCU at RAF Finningley for conversion and to receive a new co-pilot, Pilot Officer Graham McKay. Phil Leckenby had completed his intermediate co-pilot's course on

14th November 1966 and was soon to begin his captain's conversion. I had my first flight in Mk2 XH559 on 7th March 1967 and we finished our conversion on 6th April by which time I had flown for a grand total of 3,970 hours and thirty minutes. With our conversion to Mk2 aircraft completed we returned to Waddington and got on with the usual tasks.

Mk2 Vulcans had a better navigation aids fitment than Mk1As. The Doppler navigator called Green Satin, which provided very accurate drift and groundspeed together with the faithful old radio compass were retained. Gee Mk3 was replaced by TACAN, ground position indicator (GPI) Mk6 replaced the Mk4. Smiths Military Flight System (MFS) replaced the G4B compass and zero reader. A highly stable orthogonal gyro flight director designed for Lightning aircraft was modified for fitment in Vulcans called the heading reference system (HRS) and it had an output of azimuth which could be adjusted to provide true heading.

Many Vulcan crews have flown around the world westwards on what was then called a 'westabout'. During those days the Far East Air Force was still very active, especially at RAF Tengah in Singapore. Our masters desired a westerly route to Singapore should the easterly route become blocked. In March 1968 and, if my memory is correct, Air Commodore G C (Larry) Lamb had been appointed air commodore bomber operations and he wanted to visit Strategic Air Command Headquarters at Offutt Air Base, Nebraska USA, and the Headquarters Far East Air Force, Singapore. 44 Squadron was tasked to provide two aircraft to fly him to those bases and return. Vic was selected to fly the spare/support aircraft.

I was delighted to hear about the forthcoming trip and began to plan it immediately. The route had already been set and it was just a matter of drawing tracks on plotting charts and compiling basic flight plans. That sounds easy but it involved a great deal of effort, more so perhaps because right from the very outset I was determined to make it the best trip I had ever done and today I am very happy to say that it was.

The route took in McClellan AFB Sacramento and Honolulu, Hawaii and it is time for a very short slice of theory. As the earth rotates towards the east, the sun appears to move to the west. Hawaii is approximately south-west of McClellan AFB and, since we made an early departure, the sun was travelling almost in the same direction and it remained on our port wingtip most of the way to Hawaii. I asked the nav radar to take sextant shots of the sun every forty minutes in order to check if we had departed from our required track and found we had by small amounts; the sun shots allowed me to adjust the GPI Mk6 latitude and longitude readings and so alter heading to regain track and continue.

We had to report to air traffic control and request permission to enter Hawaiian air space upon our arrival at the ADIZ (air defence interception zone) entry point. When we reached our ETA I plotted the GPI position and a TACAN fix. The distance between the GPI position and the entry point was two miles, not too bad after some four hours and forty minutes over water. I was gradually winning back some lost brownie points from my previously mentioned Malta flight plan saga. From Hawaii we continued around the world without any drama and arrived home at Waddington on 30th April in foul weather for a GCA approach and landing.

I was interested that Ted forgot to mention an idiosyncrasy of the GPI6, that it wasn't designed for global navigation; on crossing the 180° meridian the longitude would carry on counting upwards 190°,…200° until reaching destination; in the case of Wake Island Ted would have been looking at 19° 18'N 213° 24'W. Apparently they used to carry a spare GPI they would change after they had crossed the date line and live with numbers above 180°, doing the necessary subtraction and conversion to get easterly longitude. It was a time-consuming process making the analogue GPI fly backwards and round the Greenwich Meridian to get back to the same place with the correct read-out.

By that time Vic was nearing the end of his posting as OC 44 Squadron; I last flew with him on 15th May 1968. On May 29th I flew in the famous Vulcan XM607 with Flight Lieutenant Nick Dennis doing formation. My last trip as a member of 44 Squadron was on 18th July '68 having accrued 4,280 hours twenty-five minutes flying time.

By June 1968 plans were well under way to bring Canberras back from RAF Akrotiri and to replace them with two squadrons of Vulcan Mk2s – Nos IX and 35 which were then based at RAF Cottesmore in Rutland. We were hoping that we might be lucky enough

Ted found USN FDR Roosevelt on one of his maritime sorties. (*Andy Leitch*)

to be posted to Cyprus. Our good commander said that he had declared us to be available for posting but not to hold our breath. Sure enough our posting advice arrived, John Lamont and I went to IX Squadron, Jim Walker and Graham McKay to 35. Initially I flew with a very capable captain – a pleasant Scot – Flight Lieutenant Andy Jones. We were together from 24th July to the end of August.

About one week later I was told that I would join the Bencke crew. Flight Lieutenant Rodney Bencke was an Australian, who had just completed his captain's course and returned to IX. Unlike most other up and coming captains, Rod had completed his course without having a regular crew. I never asked why I had been selected to fly with a fellow Aussie but I thought it something of a novelty. I was a member of the RAF accustomed to flying with – I hope you will forgive me – Poms, and I had to re-programme my hard drive.

We began flying together on 4th September 1968 doing all of the typical continuation training exercises including the inevitable low-level trips. October saw us in Luqa, Malta for another sunspot including lots of low level. November was a fairly busy month, December was quiet. At exactly midnight on 31st December we ceased doing QRA standby and headed for the officers' mess bar to celebrate the arrival of 1969. The Royal Navy took over the QRA role with Polaris submarines. However, perhaps one should not forget that with the RAF V Force crews beside fully armed, fuelled aircraft ready to go and with USAF B52 bombers already airborne and loaded with powerful atomic weapons, the rest of the world was able to get on with their daily tasks and sleep soundly. Those were the days of the Cold War and if we had been called forth to action I would have willingly done my duty.

On 26th February 1969 we flew to RAF Akrotiri in the first wave of four aircraft. On 4th March we commenced flying in Cyprus and for me, another 529 hours twenty-five minutes of interesting and varying types of exercises including low level in Cyprus, Iran, Libya, Sicily, Calabria, maritime reconnaissance in the Mediterranean and of course England during our regular visits back home for refresher training.

In fact I was involved in two bombing and navigation competitions, first in April 1970 when we slept at Cranwell and flew from Waddington, the second in March/April 1971, all activities from Waddington. In the 1970 job we were the standby crew; however, we did a fair amount of flying and as I look back I think we were being trained for the 1971 season. By 1971 the name had changed from Bomber Command to Strike Command. IX and 35 Squadrons were then based at RAF Akrotiri, Cyprus and were under the operational control of Near East Air Force (NEAF). It was natural for NEAF crews to be invited to join in the competition with UK-based squadrons and USAF B52s.

I was a member of IX Squadron, our crew members being Flight Lieutenant Rod Bencke captain, Flight Lieutenant Mike Horton co-pilot, Flight Lieutenant Ray Hollett nav radar, Flight Lieutenant Julian Grenfell AEO, Flight Lieutenant Ted Marmont nav plotter (yours truly). We commenced competition training in Cyprus on 1st March 1971 then moved to Waddington on the 19th to begin an intensive period of flight planning and flying. Group Captain Mike D'Arcy was then the commanding officer of RAF Waddington. He took a great interest in our activities and it was a pleasure to talk to him.

The bombing phase consisted of one high-level attack where the aircraft was tracked by a radar bomb scoring unit (an RBSU site) then descending to low level and flying a specially-prescribed route to carry out three RBS-scored attacks. A typical low-level target would be the intersection of four hedges near a road which speared way off to the right.

Mike spent hours drawing up his own topographical maps which indicated the objects he would be able to identify out of the starboard window on the bombing run. He map read all the way to bomb release point which occurred when a mark on the refuelling probe was over the target and the radio tone was switched off. Meanwhile both navigators were flat out with their own jobs and at the end of low level we ascended to height under radar control and recovered to base.

The high-level run was the smoothest bombing run I ever witnessed; after a 90°

starboard turn onto west, Ray switched in his offset aiming points and the target was dead ahead. It remained so until bomb release point but our score was about 580 yards direct undershoot. Rubbish! We challenged the umpire and compared the photo of the radar tube at bomb release point with a map of the target to the same scale; the error was about 230 yards undershoot but our challenge was not accepted. Our low-level runs were commendable and we scored 245 points out of a 400.

We achieved excellent results from the navigation stage and having started off with 400 points we returned with 358; our NTP error was 5,000 yards. It was one of those wonderful nights when there was no upper air turbulence and the actual winds were almost the same as the forecast. We were a capable coordinated crew and we paid proper respect to each other for our individual skills and disciplines.

A rare photo of the triumphant crew on return to Akrotiri. Left to right: Ray Hollett, Mike Horton, Rod Bencke, Ted and Julian Grenfell. (*Ted Marmont*)

A few days after we returned to Akrotiri our squadron commander, Wing Commander Ron Dick, called me aside and said: "Ted, I am sorry but I cannot offer you any more flying. You guys have already used up much of the squadron's allocation of flying hours and we are a bit short." I replied: "Sir, don't worry, I have had enough." And so I ended my flying career of 5,073 hours and thirty minutes. The breakdown on Vulcans being: 517 hours and five minutes on Mk1 and 1,167 hours and ten minutes on Mk2 aircraft. Those hours that I flew on limited aids sorties both in training for and during the competition were of great help when I applied for a flight navigator's licence which I received before I departed from England.

When I joined the RAF, air ministry offered me the choice of a straight sixteen-year pensionable service or, should I wish to count my RAAF service of twelve years and 144 days as reckonable service toward a pension and pay to the UK authorities the value of that time, I could serve eight years only and retire with a pension. I chose offer number two hence, at the end of the competition I had six months to go until repatriation to Australia.

We spent most of our disembarkation leave in Cyprus going water skiing at Akrotiri each day. My final and very enjoyable posting was to the Joint Air Reconnaissance

Intelligence Centre at RAF Brampton. I worked in the section where low-level route maps were made in book form, just the job for a worn-out nav plotter.

There is one very important person whom I must mention and it is my very positive wife Jacquelyn, Jackie for short, who pushed and encouraged me to apply to the RAF. Phil and Janet Leckenby arranged a farewell party in Waddington officers' mess for us. Thereafter we found our way to RAF Lyneham where we spent the night prior to departure from Brize Norton the following day. Soon after becoming airborne the VC10 developed a problem and the captain had to dump fuel over the Bristol Channel then return to Brize.

We spent the rest of the day in the departure lounge. Later in the evening we contacted Mike D'Arcy, CO Queen's Flight, and told of our predicament whereupon he and his wife Clover came to sit with us for an hour or so. We had a very pleasant talk over thirty bobs' worth of brandy. We had to return to Lyneham for the night and try again the following day, which we did and successfully made it home.

> Ted was born on 27th August 1929 and is one of a select few Australians officially retired from the Royal Air Force and the Royal Australian Air Force. He was repatriated to Australia in 1972 and included among his pensions (English and Australian), he receives an old age job of 52p per week from the UK.
>
> I showed **Phil Leckenby** this splendid account of an Aussie in the RAF and he remembered a particular flight with Ted on Vulcan Mk1As when Ted's watch stopped at the critical moment. Here Phil relates the flight:

The night was very dark and up front Mike D'Arcy and I had little to do except marvel at the stars, keep an eye on fuel, eat too many in-flight rations and listen to the navigators beavering away in the murky depths below.

D'Arcy ventured to ask Ted how much longer it would be before astro. Clearly all was still going well down the back because Ted confidently replied, "navigator to captain – ten minutes to astro". Mike pondered this last announcement for a while and, looking a trifle concerned, leaned over and quietly asked me, "you know, I've got a feeling that's exactly what Ted said the last time. What do you think, Phil?" "Er, yes… I rather think it was," I whispered back. Mike switched on his microphone to clear up the matter, "Ted, unless I'm mistaken, I could have sworn you said it was ten minutes to go the last time you gave us a heads-up."

There was an extended pause, then over the intercom there came a terrible howl of anguish as Ted realised the dreadful misfortune that had overtaken him. He stared incredulously at his aircrew watch, a faithful instrument upon which he relied so heavily. It had stopped. We had sailed right through every planned time for the pre-computed sextant shots, rendering his hours of work in the planning room utterly useless. 'Livid' doesn't even begin to adequately describe the change in Ted's mood. He had gone nuclear. An irretrievable meltdown. A towering antipodean inferno. A cruel world had conspired against him and he was incandescent with rage. From the cockpit we could plainly hear him ranting and thrashing around the crew compartment, arms flailing like a windmill disintegrating before a gale. Peeking cautiously back through the black-out curtain we could see that Ted, now helmetless, was in the grip of an almighty strop, the like of which we'd never seen before. Jim had the good sense to suppress any hint of mirth as he cowered to the cabin wall trying to avoid whatever missiles Ted had begun to hurl around the cabin. Running out of things to throw, Ted then picked up his charts and started shredding them. He tore them into small pieces, scattered them like giant confetti and then, as if entranced in some sort of wild voodoo dance, he stamped on the fragments as they fell to the cabin floor.

While all this mayhem was going on, Jock, the AEO, who had seriously underestimated the true extent of Ted's wrath, made some flippant comment or other. Whirling round to face his tormentor, Ted looked for a suitable weapon. He grabbed a pencil, raised his arm and tried to nail Jock's hand to the desk. Fortunately his aim was slightly off and Jock escaped with little more than a severe fright.

Meanwhile, as the drama unfolded, we steamed on across the Atlantic in an uncomfortable silence. On the way back Ted's reactor core eventually cooled sufficiently for profuse apologies all round and even he was able to see the funny side of what had happened.

The human memory has a comforting ability to obscure or erase particularly unpleasant experiences; some sort of natural defence mechanism. So it is not altogether surprising that Ted now professes he remembers little of the incident described above. However, the story has been corroborated by Jim and it is one I am unlikely ever to forget.

Chapter Seven

AN AEO'S STORY

Wing Commander Peter West started his aviation career as a member of the ATC and as a result of gaining a proficiency certificate in navigation and engineering he was able to join the RAF. A year or two later he remustered as an air signaller and after a tour on Shackletons retrained to become an early AEO on Valiants. From there to Vulcans and 1 Group in 1962 was a short step. Peter shows just what you can achieve with a bad back!

On reaching 1 Group I learnt to fly in the Vulcan Mk2. The OCU was at RAF Finningley where I was lucky to pick up the best crew I have ever experienced, (and I've had some excellent crews over the years). Our skipper was Wg Cdr Phil Lagesen, a South African veteran of WW2, the co-pilot was Cyril Parker who was from New Zealand, the nav plotter was Gerry Taylor who had come to us from the RCAF, the nav radar was Paul Berkeley who was born in Australia and me as the only Pommie Bastard, Limey, and bloody Reunek! All were in the RAF in spite of their origins. We hit it off immediately and bonded quickly into an efficient and very happy crew. Phil was destined to take over as CO of 12 (Bomber) Squadron at RAF Coningsby, Lincolnshire. We were allocated married quarters there straight away which made a nice change. However, Paul already owned a house in nearby Horncastle so didn't need accommodation. It wasn't long before we were declared to be 'combat' which meant that as a crew and as individual crew members we were ready to be employed in a war role if necessary. Following that, and over the next couple of years, our rating improved steadily until we reached the pinnacle for a bomber crew of 'Select Star'. We spent many hours in the vault studying our target in the USSR until we became as familiar with it as with our own home towns.

The high spot of the tour came in late October 1962 when we were involved in the Cuban missile crisis. Our involvement lasted only a few days but it was the closest this country ever came to an all-out nuclear war. Our status meant frequent changes of readiness introduced with, "this is the bomber controller, readiness state 05". This required us to enter the aircraft and prepare to start engines. Later we heard, "this is the bomber controller, resume readiness state 15". The bomber controller's radio transmitted a background note every minute which indicated that we were still connected and could hear any change in readiness. It was assumed that the bomber controller was located deep underground in the war bunker at Strike Command HQ, High Wycombe, although we did not really care where he was. The instructions were relayed over a tannoy system from air traffic and, once in the aircraft, over our intercom system. There was no attempt to conceal these broadcasts and it occurred to us that NATO wanted the Warsaw Pact to know what we were doing in order that they would take our threat seriously; normal practice in the world of intelligence as I learned later when I joined that organisation.

We were confident that a scramble wouldn't happen as the prevention of such a conflict was our whole purpose. If we had taken off then we would have failed in our mission. However, the deterrent worked, Campaign for Nuclear Disarmament had got it all wrong, but they will never admit it. As an illustration of this, during the stand-by when we were confined to a caravan a few yards from the aircraft, Paul got up from his seat, walked across to the aircraft which had its bomb doors open and the sinister nuclear weapon loaded, took out of his pocket a china-graph pencil and scrawled a CND symbol on the side of the bomb. "Why on earth did you do that?" I asked. "Because if we have to drop that bugger those bastards were right!" We did not have to drop 'that bugger', 'those bastards' were wrong. My dear old pal Paul, one of the best friends I had in my RAF career, kindly, well informed and thoroughly decent died recently. Goodbye old friend, I treasure your memory and will never forget you.

Mess functions were great fun as were squadron social events. I had a lot to do with the latter as Phil made me entertainments officer, a task which I enjoyed. One day he came into the squadron briefing room, looked at the long blank wall and shouted: "Peter that wall needs a mural. Get on with it!" I had, for long, enjoyed drawing cartoons and the RAF encouraged my hobby as humour is a very important feature of the British armed forces in maintaining morale. 12 Squadron's motto was 'Leads the Field' and our emblem a fox mask. This was to be the basis of my mural which, when finished, portrayed the whole squadron chasing a fox...in the wrong direction!

The fox was doubled up with mirth at the far end of the picture. I had lots of help from the guys on the squadron who would pop in from time to time to see how I was doing and get stuck in themselves painting large areas of sky, grass etc. The finished product seemed to go down well and formed a pleasing background to our parties. Sadly it was eventually bulldozed with the rest of the building when we were moved on.

Peter West's 12 Squadron fresco in Coningsby's officers' mess bar.
(*12 Squadron History*)

We had a trip to RCAF Goose low flying over Canada and then came our first 'Western Ranger', a trip to Offutt AFB in Nebraska. This was the first of many visits to the USA all of which were thoroughly enjoyable. By this time we had lost Cyril as he was given a captaincy and left us to form up with his own crew. His replacement was one of the few real characters in the RAF, Jules Brett, a highly amusing and thoroughly delightful fellow of whom we all became fond. He was eventually posted to become the staff pilot with the Sir Vivian Fuchs Antarctic expedition. We sadly lost touch with him but I learned recently that he eventually became a captain with Cathay Pacific airline. For him flying as co-pilot to Phil Lagesen was a trial as Phil regularly punched his left shoulder and rarely let him do a landing without a constant stream of teases and taunts aimed at putting poor old Jules off. Some rough landings resulted but we in the back seats never blamed Jules. We knew that Phil would never have behaved so had he not had a high opinion of Jules's abilities as a pilot.

All good things have to come to an end and as Phil was the CO we knew his tour would be only two and a half years. He went on to become Air Marshal Sir Philip Lagesen but sadly died aged seventy back in his home, South Africa. Our new CO was an equally good chap but very different from Phil. He was Bob Tanner, an excellent pilot who had flown ground-attack Spitfires during WW2 and handled a Vulcan like a Spitfire. He kept the same crew but after a short while it became clear that there was a serious clash of personalities between him and our nav plotter, Gerry Taylor. Gerry was posted off bombers and his place on the crew was filled by Dave Lowe. This all happened at a busy time for the squadron as we and the other two Vulcan squadrons, IX and 35, were moved to RAF Cottesmore near Oakham as Coningsby was needed to house the new TSR2 aircraft....which never actually materialised – surprise! surprise!

On arrival at Cottesmore it became clear that even though I was by now a Flight Lieutenant married with three children I would have no chance of getting a married quarter. We bought a house and my wife Mary had to bear the brunt of over-seeing its building as at this time our squadron was ordered out to Malaysia to bolster up their air capability against Indonesia which had threatened the country with destruction. We staged out via El Adem, Khormaksar (Aden) and Gan. We had to hold there for a couple of weeks with no flying as we were loaded up with 21 x 1,000 pounders. We were delayed because Malaya was full up with aircraft and troops! When we eventually arrived in Malaya we were put on an RAAF base in the north of the country near Penang. This was Butterworth where the Aussies had a squadron of F86 Sabres and one of helicopters. We flew regularly, giving the Aussie fighter pilots practice in dogfighting. For the F86s to get any real benefit from these sorties we had to reduce height and speed as well as avoiding any violent evasive action. The Vulcan, as I've said before, was an excellent aircraft in a dogfight.

The chopper pilots offered us flights from time to time and these were great fun, especially a trip up into the Cameron Highlands where we visited a fascinating tribe of negritoes, a primitive people who carried spears and wore war paint. Later we were sent down to Singapore for about a week which included a jungle survival course. This was very interesting and involved, after a series of lectures, a trek through the jungle carrying nothing but a snake stick. This is a pole about six-feet long at the end of which is a running noose. The theory is that after spotting a snake you slip the noose over its head, pull tight, but not too tight, and return to base with a live snake ready to kill, skin and cook for a meal. We didn't even see a snake, for which we were all grateful. When we eventually reached the rendezvous a team of marine commandos which had reached the rendezvous much earlier, were making a 'brew' and had, on the end of their stick, a lively Russell's viper. We had to wait some time for the third and last team to arrive. They were all light bomber (Canberra) aircrew who eventually turned up an hour or two late all smiles and covered in mud. On the end of their snake stick was an indignant looking tortoise!

Our detachments to Singapore were all part of a deception plan arranged by our intelligence services who wanted the Indonesians to think that the Vulcans were carrying nuclear weapons. Such deception activities were a normal part of the overall intelligence war against the Soviets who were, themselves, past masters at the game.

Bob Tanner was an excellent display pilot and it was through this that we had a most interesting detachment to Iran as guests of the Shah. We were required to fly for him and his entourage as part of an air display. This also included a parachute demonstration by the RAF parachute display team who, at the main briefing, were given a hero's welcome. This turned a bit sour for them, however, as after giving them a big build up the Iranian host officer told the assembled throng that the RAF team would be preceded by a mass parachute jump by the Boy Scouts and Girl Guides of Iran! Bob, as usual, flew a brilliant display and afterwards was presented to the Shah and his air force officers who were excellent hosts.

During my time on 12 Squadron I was recommended for a General List Permanent Commission. This would mean that my future would, hopefully, see promotion and, from time to time, staff appointments. It also ensured a full career to the age of fifty-five. The problem for me was my age. I had spent nearly eight years in the ranks before being commissioned so was considered by some to be too old for a PC. However, I eventually achieved this goal which changed the pattern of my career. When

my second tour with 12 Squadron ended in 1966 I was posted as an instructor to the Vulcan OCU at Finningley where I taught electronic warfare in the ground school.

Vulcan Mk2 AEO's panels with alternator control panel central on side wall.

(*Charles Toop*)

After five years of training officer cadets, which included a promotion to squadron leader, I was at last posted back to flying duties, this time as AEO leader on 44 (Rhodesia) Squadron at Waddington. Whilst I was delighted to be returning to flying I was disappointed not to be a flight commander. At this time there were too many squadron leaders and not enough executive flying appointments hence the decision to make all 'leaders' squadron leaders. Going through the OCU again was fun, especially as I had been an instructor there five years earlier. Prior to this I had to undergo a refresher course at the AEO School at RAF Topcliffe. The OCU was interesting and useful, helping me to remember my role in the Vulcan. Unfortunately I noticed that I was developing lower back pain which was becoming progressively worse. In the end I had to see the medical officer just after I had joined the squadron and had begun to settle in. The 'Doc' diagnosed a slipped disc and I spent four weeks in hospital on traction. All seemed well again but I was forbidden to fly for a while so was transferred, temporarily, to the operations wing for administrative duties. This brought me into closer contact with the CO and OC Ops Wg both of whom were kind enough to commend my work, useful for future advancement!

Having returned to flying duties with 44 Squadron at Waddington I was flying one day with our co-pilot and the OCU instructor pilot, Squadron Leader Ken Gowers, an old friend of mine. We were carrying out 'handling' off Spurn Head and Ken was having trouble with the radio link to Scampton Tower. I was pretty sure that I could fix the problem and asked him to fly straight and level whilst I left my seat and crawled under the nav crate to get at the radio. I did not remove my parachute as I would have to lie on the door, a risk I was not prepared to take without a 'chute. I managed to sort the problem and a quick radio check proved all was well. As I was extricating myself from under the nav crate I heard Ken say to the co-pilot, "OK Co, I'm putting the aircraft into an unusual attitude so be prepared to sort it out". I tried to intervene to get Ken to wait until I was safely back in my seat but to no avail. As the g forces swung in I felt a sudden sharp pain in my lower spine then, as I got back into my seat, all feeling left my legs. I reported my situation to Ken who made an immediate return to base calling the tower for an ambulance to meet us on landing. When we got into the dispersal the doctor clambered aboard and started to explore my back, causing me more than a little discomfort. The two navs lifted me out of my seat and, having removed the door ladder, slid me down into the waiting arms of the medics below. Then it was straight to hospital again. As I was wheeled into the officers' orthopaedic ward in full flying kit I was asked by the other patients if I had baled out; I felt like a proper 'Charlie' telling them that I had slipped a disc!

A month on traction again, not good, then the awful prospect of a flightless future as the senior orthopaedic surgeon, Group Captain Povey, (known by us as 'His Holiness the Pove') suggested that I should consider an alternative career. I was not at all happy at this suggestion and asked him to be specific. He told me that low-level flying, the normal routine for bomber operations, would almost certainly result in more back trouble. "What about high-level flying?" I asked. He said that he knew of no high-level Vulcan squadrons so I told him that 27 Squadron at Scampton had recently reformed in the reconnaissance role which was all high-altitude flying. He then demonstrated to me the power of the medics in the RAF by saying that he would arrange for me to be posted there, which he did!

27's role was, primarily, maritime radar reconnaissance (MRR) which involved flying over the North Atlantic at high level searching on radar for ships which were likely to be of the Soviet navy. They usually sailed in a small group with a cruiser, oiler and occasionally a destroyer all in close formation. Initially when such a ship was sighted we would home in a flight of Buccaneers to overfly and photograph the surface action group (SAG). We suggested, after a short while, that it would save the Buccaneer squadrons the trouble if we, the Vulcans, did the job ourselves. This manoeuvre we called 'self-probe' and it worked very well making our sorties much more interesting and enjoyable. On one occasion we detected a SAG about fifty miles east of Norway and descended to about 250ft with all of our radar equipment switched to 'stand-by'. This meant that the SAG was unaware of our presence and we were able to identify a Kresta 2 cruiser with an accompanying oiler. Then, when we were about ten miles from them we switched on our radars. This prompted the reaction we hoped for; all of the Kresta's radars suddenly sprang into life and I was able to record the cacophony of sound emanating from the cruiser; all very useful for our intelligence team. I didn't let Group Captain Povey know that I was flying low level again! Another of our roles was code-named Tapestry and involved our 'showing the flag' by flying at very low level around our North Sea oil and gas rigs to ensure their safety from terrorists or other potential troublemakers.

Operation Tapestry watching oil rigs.
(*Aviation Historian*)

Our third, and for many most enjoyable, role was to monitor Chinese nuclear tests. Unlike the other nuclear powers the Chinese carried out their tests singly, not as a series. This meant that in order for us to get in position we needed good intelligence so that we might deploy in time. Our deployment was to the US Navy base on the island of Midway in the central Pacific. The deployment for the two Vulcans was from Scampton to Goose Bay in Labrador, then on to Offutt AFB Nebraska where the crew night stopped. The next morning it was Offutt to McClellan AFB California then to Midway. If we had sufficient time we would night stop at each base enabling us to arrive in a reasonably fresh state. Meantime the third crew and twenty-five ground crew flew across Canada and down to Midway in a transport aircraft, either a Britannia or VC10, with no night stops. Midway is the northern-most island of the Hawaiian Islands and is about 1,500 miles northwest of Honolulu. It is uninhabited and was a US Navy base employed as an occasional transit field for aircraft deploying to the Far East, but rarely used. The one runway was usually covered in nesting or roosting Laysan Albatrosses, huge seabirds with wing spans of about twelve feet. Up to 20,000 of these birds call at this island home and breed there before flying to their feeding grounds in the Sea of Japan. There are many other birds which use the islands and it is impossible for anyone to visit there without becoming enchanted by these delightful creatures which have no fear of man. Our sorties were guided by two civilian experts who were detached with us, one from the Met Office the other from Atomic Warfare Research Establishment, Aldermaston. Flights were over the Northern

Pacific where we searched for any fallout from the Chinese nuclear tests, real 'needle in a haystack' stuff. Radioactive detection devices were fitted to our aircraft and a pod un-

der the wing housed a paper filter which was to collect any samples we might find. The fact that we were sometimes successful was nothing short of miraculous.

Not many months before leaving 27 Squadron I was, with my crew, scheduled for a flight with two trappers[4]. We were

Vulcan with large and small sampling pods. (*Nigel Baldwin*)

assigned to fly in Vulcan XH558, nowadays the most famous Vulcan of all. As usual with a trapper ride we were expecting our take-off to be interrupted by a simulated double-engine failure after take-off. As we thundered down the runway we came to the 'unstick' point which is the moment the aircraft leaves the ground; there was a sudden loud bang which caused me, initially, to think: 'that was clever, how did they do that?' Then, in a nanosecond I realised that this was real. Like the two pilots I immediately began the procedures for an emergency on take-off, the most dangerous part of any flight. I raised the periscope which enabled me to look aft. I could see straight away that the two starboard engines were on fire and reported this to the captain who had already pushed the fire extinguisher buttons.

Initially I thought that the fire had not gone out and told the captain; I then realised that what I had thought was fire was in fact the rotating navigation lights reflecting on the jagged metal following the explosion of the two starboard engines. I reported this to the captain and immediately started the checks to settle the aircraft electrical system, essential to enable us to stay airborne. I then, for the first and only time in my flying career, pressed the transmit key and sent a Mayday message to the control tower. Our two pilots, Squadron Leaders Courtney Guest (trapper) and John Porter (crew captain) carried out a perfect circuit and immediate landing, first rate. The two navigators carried out their duties calmly but the poor old trapper navigator, Squadron Leader Mike Doyle-Davidson, could only sit on the sixth seat and listen to the intercom. It must have been deeply disturbing for him poor chap. We landed safely being escorted down the runway by several emergency vehicles, and when we stopped we were met by the senior engineering officer who, bless him, had brought with him a most welcome crate of beer! This incident, as were so many, was caused by a bird entering the engine which blew up scattering bits of metal into the neighbouring engine which followed suit, hence the fire and loss of power. XH558 was very sick and spent

---

[4] Examiners from Group to ensure proficiency and standardisation.

about a year in the hangar being made well again, which is probably why it is now the only flying Vulcan. The incident proved not only that we had very good pilots, but also a remarkably strong, forgiving aircraft. John Porter later told me that had I not reported to him my error identifying the strobing nav lights reflecting on the jagged metal he would have ordered us to abandon aircraft. Thank God I told him in time!

A few months later my tour ended and, although I didn't realise it at the time, I was never to have another flying tour. However, my ground appointments were all interesting and enjoyable and led to promotion to wing commander and the award of the MBE. I still regret that there was no more flying for me, though.

I have, on more than one occasion, been asked by pilots why I was content to fly as non-pilot aircrew. It had become clear to me early in my life when I first became fascinated by flying that I was not cut out to be a pilot. I had, whilst an Air Training Corps cadet, been given lessons in gliders and had found that I was unable to judge height. This had resulted in my doing some pretty heavy (and hairy) landings. Notwithstanding this disappointment I was determined still to pursue a flying career and attendance at an officer aircrew selection centre revealed an aptitude for the role of air signaller. This too came as no surprise as my education had been somewhat erratic due to it taking place during the years 1939-47. In this time I had attended eight different schools and although I was selected for a grammar school I had to leave at fourteen as my parents divorced and both moved overseas. I then lived in Egypt with my father who was a soldier, and there was no schooling for children over fourteen. Hence my having no educational qualifications and I considered myself lucky to be selected for NCO aircrew. This role I enjoyed as I did later as a commissioned AEO. It was a fascinating and important job keeping the country safe from enemy attack.

When Peter stopped flying he got briefly involved with the Falklands campaign and Operation Corporate like quite a few contributors to this book, this time on intelligence. From there he went to NATO intelligence, then left the RAF but still worked in the same area. When he finished that he nominally retired but still kept on working...

Chapter Eight

BLUE STEEL

Chris Reid did two tours as a nav radar from 1965-70 on 83 and 617 Squadrons at Scampton, gaining 1,500 hours on type in the Blue Steel role. He chose the Vulcan because he was courting and didn't want to be posted overseas; the aircraft proved to be a good choice as he has now been married for fifty years. On leaving 617 he had a tour at the Strike Command Bombing School at Lindholme as an instructor on the Vulcan NBS.

Chris's second crew on 617 Squadron, all flight lieutenants. Left to right: Simon Baldwin – nav plotter, Chris Reid – nav radar, Val Ventham – captain, Bob Bolton – AEO, Chris Abram – co-pilot. (*Chris Reid*)

A Good Jolly

When I first went to the Vulcan operational conversion unit in early 1965, the RAF was still using an old traditional method of forming the five-man crews. In my case twenty aircrew met in the mess bar on the evening before classes were to start next day and, with the help of beer, mixed and mingled until formed up crews appeared. Three crews formed quickly. A good friend and I, as brand new nav radars, were certain of one thing, neither of us wanted to fly with one of the two remaining captains, a squadron leader destined to be a flight commander on 83 Squadron. Who wanted to fly with a

senior officer breathing down your neck? We played darts, the winner to get the captain of his choice. I lost and as it happened, I had a lucky choice forced on me as the
squadron leader became a lifelong friend.

Once on the squadron it became clear that rank had its privileges as our captain
collected several of the more interesting trips away from base. These were known as
'jollies'. In September 1966 a good jolly turned up. We were to take an aircraft to Australia, show the flag at an air show at Adelaide, overfly the Cenotaph in Sydney on a
memorial day, and then continue on across the Pacific through Guam, Wake, Honolulu and San Francisco and complete a round the world trip home. Clearly this was going
to be an arduous duty, but someone had to do it.

The downside was that, rank having its privileges, we were to be captained for part
of the circumnavigation by the air commodore senior air staff officer (SASO) from
HQ 1 Group, a man known for a degree of irascibility. In fairness, being a V Force
SASO in 1966 was probably demanding enough to try the patience of a saint.

He arrived at the pre-flight briefings and seemed pretty normal. We junior aircrew
kept out of his way while our captain danced attendance. The first couple of sorties
went well until we arrived at RAF Muharraq, now Bahrain International Airport, but
then a hot dusty staging airfield en route to the Far East. SASO was miffed early on
when he found that only Transport Command crews were entitled to air conditioned
rooms. Another annoyance was the need for a dawn take-off as the Mk1 Victor that
was accompanying us, having only two thirds of the power of our Vulcan, needed the
coolest air possible if it was to get airborne from the runway available with a full fuel
load needed to reach Gan in the Maldive Islands. Departure did not go well. The Victor was delayed by a snag, the sun rose, and the temperature climbed. The Victor then
needed to be defuelled to achieve a safe take-off weight. Time passed, a lot of time. It
was eventually ready to go. We had climbed out of our baking aircraft and watched it
take off. After an impossibly long run it staggered into the air and flew off at nought
feet across the desert leaving a huge plume of dust behind it!

Our departure was uneventful and we overtook the Victor en route, arriving at Gan
first. SASO who had fumed throughout the whole sorry departure process was mono-
syllabic throughout the flight, and the rest of the crew kept conversation to operating
essentials. The landing on Gan's single runway was straightforward until we reached
its end. There was/is no taxiway at Gan airfield so that at the end of the runway aircraft
had to make a 360° turn on a circular dumb-bell patch of tarmac and backtrack up
the runway until a turn off at its middle point. This would not normally be an issue
but our Vulcan's nose-wheel steering chose this moment to fail. Attempts to turn using
differential throttle proved fruitless as the nose wheels just scrubbed sideways and we
risked them going off the tarmac on to the sand. SASO called the tower reporting that
he was shutting down and calling for a tug with the Vulcan nose-wheel tow bar which
was held on the unit. There was a long delay and SASO started to get cross, turning
to rage when the tower revealed that the tow bar could not be found. Meantime an
increasingly unhappy Victor was circling overhead making plaintive cries about fuel
shortage. It no longer had enough fuel to fly 500 miles north to Ceylon.

Since we could do nothing to help, the rear crew quietly left the aircraft and sat on the seashore admiring the sunlit palm trees and the azure sea, while trying to ignore the muffled shouts from the Vulcan cockpit as SASO decided whether the Victor could risk landing on the runway with a Vulcan parked at the far end. All ended well. The tow bar was found, and our Vulcan towed off the runway before things got really fraught for the Victor. Later that day, SASO mellowed when we discovered that the spirits in the bar were free – the drawer of the last tot from the covered bottles bought the next bottle. Somehow that evening broke the ice, and SASO became more human from then on.

Blue Steel and High Test Peroxide

I joined 83 Squadron at RAF Scampton in 1965 as a new nav radar. The squadron was equipped with Mk2 Vulcans and the Blue Steel missile. Blue Steel was a giant, thirty-five feet long and weighing 16,000lbs, a two megaton bomb in its own right with rocket motors fuelled with high test peroxide (HTP) of an 85-95% concentration and kerosene. It had the capability of being launched from low level, fifty miles from a target – Moscow!

Blue Steel on 617 Squadron before camouflaging. (*Aviation Historian*)

HTP is fearsome stuff. It is a violent oxidiser and if it comes into contact with any inflammable material, spontaneous combustion results. We were given demonstrations where a few drops of the water-like liquid dripped on to a rag burst into flame seconds later. The jolly missile bay crew chief giving the brief warned that standing in a puddle of the stuff would promptly set your shoes on fire!

We never flew with armed real missiles, but we did fly with practice missiles which were fully fuelled but had an inert mass instead of the bomb. These were known as 'wet rounds'. In the air the HTP in the missile needed constant temperature monitoring by the nav plotter. The bomb bay heating was designed to keep the HTP at just the right temperature for if it got too hot it could start to decompose releasing lots of oxygen into the bomb-bay area with potentially disastrous results. Rising HTP temperatures were an emergency situation requiring immediate diversion to the nearest airfield, preferably a V bomber base which was set up to handle an emergency HTP offload. Normally, at the end of a wet-round sortie we could expect to have to go through the emergency HTP offload procedure.

This is where the nav radar came into his own, as he was the lucky guy who got to do the business. After landing, the aircraft would taxi to the offload area where fire tenders would already be in place spraying the pan surfaces with water. Inside the aircraft, I would open a large chest of kit and don wellies, an all-enveloping plastic suit, heavy industrial protective gloves and a helmet with a clear face piece. Once the aircraft had come to a stop, I would climb down carrying a long length of hose and suitable tools for attaching the hose to the HTP tank. The far end of the hose was first led to a concrete offload pit containing lots of water. Next to it was a bath of water the size of a horse trough. This was for me should I get splashed with HTP and start to smoulder.

To defuel the HTP, a panel on the missile had to be opened, and a large screw cap on the fuel tank removed with a special tool and the hose inserted in a self-attaching valve opening fitting, just like a hozelock connector on a garden hose. It all sounds pretty straight forward, but by this time I would be sweating buckets inside the plastic suit, the face piece would have completely steamed up and handling precision tools in heavy rubber gloves was tricky to say the least. I used to clear the face piece by rubbing my nose on the inside to clear a small window and utter small prayers as I inserted the hose that HTP wouldn't spurt out and go up my sleeve – the gloves were too short for complete coverage. Once I had got the HTP to flow, the exercise was mercifully terminated and the missile ground crew took over to do a complete defuelling into a tanker. I then joined a wholly unsympathetic crew for a sortie debrief and a V Force post-flight meal in the 'feeder'.

Brake Fire

On Blue Steel squadrons the process of preparing for war was the subject of continuous exercises. Exercise 'Mickey Finn' involved the loading of simulated live missiles and then flying the loaded aircraft to a bomber dispersal, a remote airfield far away from the main base. After landing, the aircraft was refuelled and the crew declared it ready for action and assumed QRA status. The dispersed aircraft could not all be destroyed at once by any enemy attack and so those remaining after a first nuclear strike would retaliate. The concept of mutually assured destruction (MAD) would ensure deterrence, and thus no enemy attack. At the height of the Cold War, we took such stuff very seriously, and station commanders' careers depended on success in generating armed aircraft on dispersed QRA as quickly as possible.

It came to pass one dark and windy night on 617 Squadron that my crew were tasked to fly our generated aircraft from RAF Scampton to the V Force dispersal at Lossiemouth in Scotland. Speed was of the essence. My newish aircraft captain was comprehensively briefed. "Don't stream the brake parachute", instructed the authorising officer, "it will delay the aircraft getting on state if we have to reload it. Mind you, with the missile and a lot of fuel you will be heavy, so be prepared to brake hard, just get up there and on state ASAP."

After a short flight to Lossiemouth, inevitably the wind dictated the use of their shortest runway. The captain landed and braked hard and the aircraft came to a successful halt at the end of the runway. At that point, the control tower informed us that we had a brake fire, and that fire tenders were being scrambled. The AEO looked through his periscope and confirmed there was indeed a fire. As the nav radar, it was my job to seize a, very small, fire extinguisher and leave the aircraft to take first action on the fire to inhibit its spreading. We had been briefed on this at the operational conversion unit. The big danger with a brake fire was that a wheel and tyre might explode with the heat with a high risk of injury from flying fragments. It was recommended that the fire be approached either on a line parallel to the tyre, or at ninety degrees to that, pointing at the axle. For the life of me, I could not remember which it was. So, I carefully advanced at forty-five degrees to the undercarriage leg in the hope that I was minimising the risk.

Fortunately the fire turned out to be the light from the brilliantly orange glowing brake units being reflected off the billowing smoke. The fire crew foamed it just in case a fire appeared, and all was well. We didn't get to put the aircraft on readiness and received a very cool reaction from Scampton.

The next day it was found on wheel removal that the axles had gone blue with the heat, and the engineering view was that the metal had lost its strengthening heat treatment and thus the undercarriage would have to be changed – a long job at a remote base. Exercise imperatives being what they were, HQ 1 Group authorised one flight back to Scampton – in the hands of an experienced crew! We made the lengthy journey back by train.

Double Trouble

It was September 1968 at RAF Scampton and we were rolling for take-off in Vulcan Mk2 XL425 armed with a fuelled Blue Steel training missile. No live nuclear weapon of course, but the 16,000lb missile, full of high test peroxide and kerosene, was a large bomb in its own right. Shortly after the call to rotate at about 140Kts, there was a double bang and the aircraft shuddered. We had flown into a flock of seagulls wrecking an engine, which had then spat compressor blades into its neighbour, doubling our trouble. Trouble it was, on two engines, low and slow, at maximum all-up weight.

Birds were always a problem, particularly sea gulls.
(*Tim O'Brien GAvA*)

Abandoning the aircraft was a real possibility.

My task, as the nav radar, was to leave my seat and prepare to open the crew access door in the floor four feet below me. The rear crew would use their manual parachutes for escape, the pilots their ejection seats: still a controversial issue in the V Force at the time. Our getaway was going to be hindered by the presence of the nose-wheel leg immediately behind the door. In the crew trainer we had practised escape in these conditions, which involved using the door jacks and advanced gymnastics to swing around the leg. Easy enough on the training rig, but harder in a 150kt slipstream. The nav plotter and AEO reckoned that this wasn't a problem as the undercarriage leg would be padded with the body of the nav radar who was scheduled to leave first.

Jet engines love eating birds but their digestion isn't very good. (*Chris Reid*)

I sat by the door waiting for the abandon aircraft call. Looking up at the navigation instruments I saw that both airspeed and altitude were reading 150 and in slow decline. Remembering that my static line parachute needed 300ft for deployment, I returned to my seat to sit it out with my buddies. Observers on the ground, who had heard the destruction of our engines, watched the aircraft descend slowly out of sight over the Lincolnshire Edge, and waited for the much bigger bang that was to follow.

I'm still here because the drop into the Trent valley enabled the captain to find the few knots of airspeed necessary to fly the big delta through to the other side of the drag curve and accelerate to a safe flying speed. We thought about jettisoning the missile, and found that we couldn't: but that's another story. Fifteen minutes later after a very overweight landing, my shortest, hairiest, Vulcan sortie was over.

In 1973 after escaping from the clutches of the V Force Chris flew Phantoms and then had a variety of staff jobs including maritime operations at Northwood and being on the directing staff at Staff College. He now lives in Cheltenham.

Chapter Nine

Taceval – On Being Combat Ready

Taceval was a vital part of Bomber Command's system to make sure that the V Force, the UK's ultimate deterrent, was really effective. It is initially described by **Squadron Leader Ray Leach** followed by Group Captain John Laycock, then a Vulcan crew member, and Flight Lieutenant Mel James, squadron engineer, who describes what it was like to be at the receiving end.

Left to right: Back row: Fg Off Chris Williams – co-pilot, Squadron Leader Ray Leach, Flight Lieutenant Paul Millikin – pilot, Flight Lieutenant David Bradford – nav radar, Flight Lieutenant Barry Masefield – AEO. Front row: Cpl Kevin Ball, C/T Dave Thorp, SAC Mark Jordan, Cpl Mick Howarth. (*Ray Leach*)

As a navigator I served on the UK Taceval team for three years and remember the impact of these exercises. Tactical evaluation was a NATO initiative to test the operational capability of air force units assigned to Saceur (Strategic Air Command Europe). However, the UK decided that it did not wish to share its nuclear secrets with any other nation, so elected to form its own team based at HQ Strike Command. The team was led by a wing commander who reported directly to the senior air staff officer to ensure that no diplomatic manipulation of results occurred in the chain of command. At first the NATO Taceval department was suspicious of the UK's 'go it alone' policy but, on having members of its team co-opted to the UK as observers, came to realise that far from being a rubber stamp, the UK team was demanding higher standards than those of its continental counterparts.

The UK Taceval team consisted of aircrew officers of the rank of squadron leader, plus specialist ground branch personnel. The aircrew were drawn from strike (nuclear) units, attack (conventional) units, air defence (air and ground) units, as well as transport and maritime units. The particular specialist acted as team controller and coordinator when undertaking an evaluation of a unit in whose role he was the specialist. It was his responsibility to devise the evaluation scenario and to deliver to the Strike Command control room a complete set of signals, each to be relayed to the station in question, at the date and time specified. At the completion of an evaluation, the team members produced a field report which was presented either to the station commander in the case of a Part I, or to the station executives plus others at the conclusion of a Part II.

A Part I evaluation was a 'no notice' evaluation lasting approximately twelve hours. The team would arrive unannounced, usually in the early hours of the morning. The guardroom personnel would be constrained from taking any action until all the team members were in place; at that stage the senior person on duty was directed to sound the station alert siren. From this point on the station would often resemble an upset ants' nest. With team members spread across the unit, all manner of 'interesting' activities were, on occasion, observed. (The amount of traffic between the WRAF and RAF accommodation had to be seen to be believed!) A Part I evaluation required the station to generate its aircraft and weapon systems within a specified period of time. At the same time all necessary active and passive defence operations were initiated. Once the team chief was satisfied he would call a halt to the evaluation, gather his team together and commence writing the field report. This was usually delivered to the station commander by the team chief in a matter of hours, at the conclusion of which he would advise the station commander when the Part II evaluation would take place.

A Part II evaluation commenced at a given start time. In essence, it started where the Part I left off. Stations and units were tested on their ability to cope with a wide range of problems such as intruders, accidents, demonstrations, battle damage repair, deployments, aid to the civil power and many more. Unlike many of the continental units, it was not acceptable for a station to say "well, what we would do in this case is…", they *had* to do it. A Part II could last for three to four days, at the conclusion of which the Taceval team would retire to write their reports, which would cover all aspects of the evaluation, including administration, catering, medical etc., as well as the operational aspects. The final copy of the report was delivered by the team chief to SASO STC in person. Units that failed to come up to the standards required could be subjected to a repeat evaluation in a relatively short period of time. I did three of these in my three years with the team.

Though by no means popular Taceval made air forces assigned to NATO get their act together and strive to achieve the required standards. Although some nations never did make it, the UK units invariably did well despite the disadvantages some had with little or no works improvements since the end of WWII.

John Laycock now tells the story of Waddington's first Taceval when he was based there.

Waddington's first Taceval, a Part I evaluation, began, as most no notice exercises do, with the station siren being sounded at four o'clock in the morning. The well promul-

Top: Vulcan XM645 enjoying low flypast. (*Copyright, 2001. Stuart H Bourne © 1971*)

Above: Vulcan Mk1 XA903 test bed for Concorde engine Olympus 593, with deicing rig. (*Aviation Historian*)

Opposite top: Vulcan carrying Blue Steel. (*Mel James*)
Opposite bottom: Vulcan scramble carrying Blue Steels. (*Aviation Historian*)
Top: Vulcan B2 XL386 being prepared at Waddington.
Above: Vulcan B2s at RAF Akrotiri. (*Nigel Baldwin*)

Above: Vulcan Mk2s at Offut in winter. (*Adrian Sumner*)
Below: Vulcan Mk2 flying one of Canada's approved low level routes. (*Nigel Baldwin*)

Opposite top: Pilot's view of flying an approved low level route in Canada.
Opposite bottom: Vulcan B2s at Richmond, Australia, 27th November 1962. XH556 on left, XL392 on right. (*RAAF Point Cook Museum*)

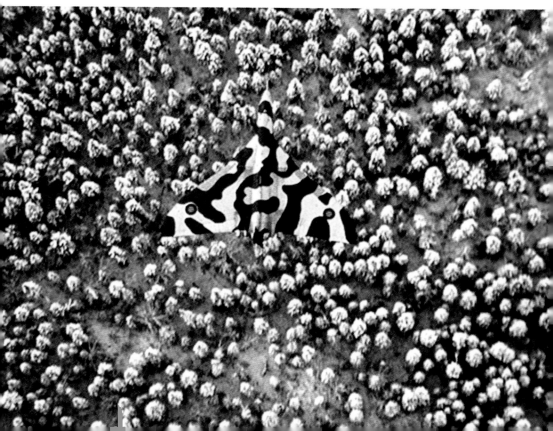

Opposite top: Vulcan XH480 demonstrating in Australia.
Opposite bottom: Vulcans and RAAF Mirages over Sydney Harbour Bridge while the Opera House was under construction, c 1970. (*RAAF Point Cook Museum*)
Above: Getting ready for a night sortie before crew in.
Left: Giant Voice 74. The stage of the massive auditorium (interior of a temporarily converted hangar) is being prepared for the prize-giving ceremony.

Top: RAF Benson 19th November 1974 (on return the USA) — GV 74 Nav and Mathis Trophy winne Centre: Captains — Left, Flt Lt Paddy Langdown 1 Sqn with Navigation Trophy; Right, Flt Lt Peter Pe 230 OCU with Mathis Trophy (Bombing and Navig combined). Semi circle from left: Ch Tech John Bea cham, Flt Lt Ed Candlish, Flt Lt Jim Vinales, Flt Lt Dee, Flt Lt Colin Hinge, Ch Tech Prickett, Flt Lt Ki Hunter, Flt Lt Pip Wort, Flt Lt Stevie Stevenson, Fl Peter Elliot, Ch Tech Weller.

Above: Vulcan B2 at Nellis Field during Red Flag 1 (*Bill Perrins*)

Left: Waddington Wing Vulcans positioned on the Operational Readiness Platform (ORP) ready for a scramble take-off. (*Jim Gardiner*)

gated and familiar recall plus aircraft generation procedures swung into action; station personnel, suitably dressed, attended their well-practised drills and aircrew assembled to be paired with an aircraft.

One significant difference between Waddington and the other V bomber main bases was that the nuclear weapons storage area, the supplemental storage area (SSA) lay on the eastern side of the A15 Lincoln to Sleaford road, separated from the rest of the base by this busy main road. Thus, at the point in an exercise or operation when nuclear weapons were loaded on the aircraft, the weapons convoys had to cross the A15 under traffic light control exercised from the air traffic control tower. As ATC and the lights were over half a mile apart there was always the possibility of control difficulty in reduced visibility and the unthinkable prospect of a road traffic accident involving a nuclear weapon.

Some three hours into the exercise, aircraft generation was well advanced and aircrews were either at fifteen minutes readiness in operations, combat checking aircraft or in the squadron offices awaiting allocation. My crew was in the 44 Squadron offices, which had a view across the perimeter track from the hangar to ATC and we noticed that visibility was beginning to deteriorate. I decided to walk across to operations for a few moments and left the squadron. When I entered the front hall of the operations block, which was empty, I noticed an official publication lying on a table and checked to see if it was a classified document. The document was entitled, 'Waddington Taceval – Incident List' and classified 'Taceval Team Eyes Only'. I retrieved the book, entered operations and asked to see the station commander who was in the control centre, known as 'the bridge'. I was admitted and, when asked what I wanted, I offered the book to the station commander for safe keeping which he accepted. I then returned to the squadron but on the way I noticed that visibility was now down to about half a mile. Shortly thereafter the order came to cease further weapon loading.

At this point it should be explained that a weapons convoy consisted of a police Land Rover with a driver and armed escort, a weapons trailer drawn by a tractor and a further police Land Rover with driver and armed escort. Also, that the station commander's wife owned a horse and a donkey, which were stabled on the south side of the airfield. The route from the station commander's house to the stables was across the road between married quarters and the guardroom entrance to the station, straight between the hangars to the perimeter track then clockwise on the peritrack past the hangars, operations and the eastern end of the airfield crossing the end of the runway at the point where the weapons convoys crossed the A15. The station commander's wife drove a grey VW Beetle.

Within a few minutes visibility had dropped to less than 100 metres. Looking out of the squadron offices we could just see the perimeter track but nothing more. To our surprise we then saw a weapons convoy pass the offices consisting of a lead Land Rover, a weapons tractor and trailer, a grey VW Beetle and a second Land Rover with the escort climbing out and advancing on the Beetle with weapons drawn. The station commander's wife was arrested and taken to the guardroom. She was a feisty lady with something of a fierce reputation.

The NCO in charge of the guardroom reported the incident up the chain of command and OC ops wing informed the station commander who consulted the incident list. He sent the word back to continue treating the incident as part of the exercise. Not long elapsed before the NCO in charge raised the issue with higher authority as his prisoner was demanding to speak to the station commander, in person, and would not take 'no' for an answer. Eventually, OC security squadron, having secured the nuclear weapon problem, attained access to the station commander and pleaded for his wife's release as it was causing more problems for his squadron than the rest of the Taceval. The station commander approved her release after some two hours custody. He was a brave man!

> **Mel James** was an engineer on 44 Squadron, also based at Waddington, and describes another Taceval.

Squadron Leader Ron Helen, OC eng ops, had a star role in a Taceval. It started in pretty much the usual way. At around 3am, the Taceval team arrive unannounced at the station guardroom. Within minutes, if not seconds, the station duty officer and night duty staff are alerted and the station siren or hooter is activated – the same undulating drone that signalled an air raid during World War 2. Each squadron or unit on the station has its own contact chains to alert personnel – whether living on the station or surrounding married quarters – or off base in the Lincolnshire countryside. Man 1 rings Man 2, Man 3 and Man 4. Man 2, 3 and 4 then phone the people on their contact list, etc. No time to wash or shave, working uniform on, and out of the door. I arrive at 'D' dispersal – and the kettle is already on. The shift flight sergeant has despatched his flight line mechanics to the aircraft on the dispersal, checking oil levels, fuel states, nitrogen and oxygen gas bottles. If it is a cold winter, the de-icing truck has been plugged into the electricity mains all night – heating the de-icing fluid in its 1,000 gallon tank. The aircraft serviceability states are confirmed with eng ops and technicians are allocated to aircraft which need maintenance in order to bring them up to 'S'. Eng ops need to know how long it will take to 'fix' all the u/s jets so they can start to prioritise aircraft for operations. The Vulcan crews will make their way to the squadron HQ and confirm the crew allocations to targets. Over on the engineering dispersal, we don't care what the targets are at this stage; we just fill the fuel tanks to the top. Some aircraft may already have been prepared on standby for special missions. The navigation bombing systems (NBS) will have been tweaked for optimum performance and to make sure nothing is touched, the captain or nav radar may have taken the aircraft key with him. But that's not a problem; I can still get in the aircraft if I need to. I can open any Vulcan crew door with a Wilmot Breeden Ford Cortina Mk1 ignition key. My key was handed down to me by my predecessor, and I have still got it.

The Taceval may go on for a couple of days, so the shift boss sends some of his team to the exercise messing location to grab a meal. Minutes after the hooter went, the station messing staff would have started cooking. If you're busy and late getting your first meal, you could be looking at bacon and eggs which were cooked hours ago. When the main meals are cooked, a favourite exercise choice is a four or five-inch round minced-meat ball – colloquially known in the RAF as 'babies heads' – which staves off hunger for hours. Progressively, we work on the u/s jets, call in to eng ops with updates and prepare for the final fly off. Over in eng ops, things are heating up. Some aircraft are not reaching serviceability as fast as expected, and the station commander is demanding action. Ron Helen's voice – never that tempered – can now be heard throughout eng ops. As yet another delay is reported, he stops speaking, looks vacantly at the eng ops team of young aircraftwomen preparing the status boards and grabs his upper left arm. His face turns redder, he mumbles incoherently and crashes to the floor. The Taceval team, standing by with their clipboards, wait to see what the eng ops team will do next. Call an ambulance maybe? Decide who will take over from Ron? But all that can be seen and heard is the screaming of the girls as they stare at Ron's motionless body on the ground. Then Ron turns his head slowly, looks up at the girls, and winks. The Taceval team, recognising Ron's pivotal role in running eng ops, had already briefed him as the exercise started. They wanted him to feign a heart attack so they could see how the team would cope! The Taceval team tie a label with the word 'casualty' on Ron's arm. And that is the end of Ron's part in the exercise.

Waddington did a Taceval for real in the Falklands conflict described in a later chapter.

Chapter Ten

VULCAN CREW TRAINING IN NORTH AMERICA

In this chapter John Laycock explains how the RAF worked closely with the USAF taking part in their training competitions Giant Voice and latterly Red Flag. This chapter has personal accounts of Giant Voice competitions by David Bourne and Jim Vinales, then finally Anthony Wright describes Red Flag, but first **John Laycock** sets the scene.

V bomber operations began in North America as early as the mid-1950s with the testing of atomic weapons at Christmas Island. To support these operations, Bomber Command detachments were established at Goose Bay, Labrador and Offutt AFB, Nebraska. Transport Command detachments were set up at Gander, Newfoundland, a joint detachment at Offutt, McClellan AFB at Sacramento, California and Hickam AFB, Honolulu. Bomber Command aircraft transiting further west than Offutt AFB used the Transport detachments.

Regular training flights to the area began in the late-1950s when crews of all three V bombers were required to fly across the Atlantic and operate in North American airspace. A flight to RCAF Goose Bay and back was called a Goose Ranger and to Offutt and back, via Goose Bay, a Western Ranger. On the Western Ranger, facilities were provided by Strategic Air Command (SAC) to use their RBSUs to practise high-level radar bombing and receive accurate scoring en route.

By the early 1960s, regular V bomber detachments to the Far East were established under the commitment to reinforce the South East Asia Treaty Organisation (SEATO), except for the Blue Steel squadrons. The normal transit route to the Far East was via Cyprus, Aden, Gan and Singapore. However, in the event of this route being unavailable, a western deployment route was established via the North American detachments, as far as Honolulu, then via US bases at Wake Island and Guam. Squadrons practised these deployment routes, with up to four aircraft, until the early 1970s when Far East deployments ceased.

Operational Training
When the Soviet Air Defence capability forced the V bomber crews to retrain for defence penetration at low level, the Canadian and US governments were asked to provide low-level training airspace for crews operating out of Goose Bay and Offutt. Starting in 1964, the Goose Ranger was extended to allow low-level navigation on four routes out of Goose Bay, two local routes in Labrador and two long-range routes with the low-level stages in Ontario. By this time, SAC had established a variety of low-level routes for their bomber crews, known as 'oil burners', which terminated in scored low-level attacks against RBSUs. Western Ranger crews were given the facility to fly some of the oil burner routes when operating in US airspace. To support this additional training task the detachments at Goose Bay and Offutt were given an increased

establishment which eventually rose to about thirty-five personnel at each base. By the end of the 1960s the Vulcan was the last remaining V bomber in the low-level role. Extensive use was made of the North American training with Goose Bay and Offutt established to support up to two crews at a time at each location.

SAC Bombing and Navigation Competition (Giant Voice)
Bomber Command introduced an inter-squadron bombing competition for the emerging V Force in the late 1950s. SAC had done the same for their B52 bomber wings. It wasn't long before SAC invited Bomber Command to compete in the competition, at wing strength, i.e. four aircraft with crews and Bomber Command reciprocated. The Bomber, later Strike, Command competition was called Double Top. By the early 1960s, 1 Group was tasked to select their top Vulcan crews to train for the SAC competition. To achieve this, a temporary training flight was established with four aircraft and crews and matching support personnel. In 1966 the project was known as Big Flight but the following year it was re-named Giant Voice (GV) although due to Vietnam it was cancelled. Initially, the detachment deployed to selected SAC bomber wing bases, but in 1974 a permanent arrangement was made for the GV detachment to deploy to Barksdale AFB, Louisiana, the HQ of SAC's 8th Air Force. This arrangement lasted until the final year of the competition (1980).

Red Flag
By the mid-1970s and in the aftermath of experience in Korea and Vietnam, the US Air Force was planning to provide realistic operational training, within Tactical Air Command (TAC), to reduce the vulnerability and high loss rate of pilots in their first five combat missions. The concept was to establish a training complex of air defence fighters, radars, electronic counter

Vulcan at Nellis Air Force Base. (*Alastair Montgomery*)

measures, guns and missiles which simulated Soviet air defences and used their operating procedures. The concept became known as Exercise Red Flag and was based at Nellis AFB, Nevada, with operations in the desert training ranges to the north of the base.

Initial experience with the exercise led to its rapid expansion and, by 1977, invitations to participate went to other US Air Commands, the US Navy and the Marine Corps. At an early stage the RAF was invited to participate with both tactical aircraft and the Vulcan. Selected crews deployed to Nellis with a GV-sized support staff and flew both day and night exercises at low level on the ranges. This training was considered the most valuable that crews could experience and two of the crews which flew the Red Flag of February 1982, captained by Monty Montgomery and Martin Withers, were selected for Black Buck a month after returning.

Flight Safety and Displays

Remarkably, bearing in mind the quantity of flying and the demanding nature of the training, no aircraft were lost during training in North America[5]. The Vulcan was extremely popular and much in demand for displays in North America. Selected crews performed at up to ten locations each year and special locations were allocated displays every year for over twenty years. At the end of its service life, four aircraft were allocated to museums in North America: XM573 to the SAC Aerospace Museum at Offutt AFB, XM606 to 8th Air Force at Barksdale, XM605 to Castle AFB, California, the main B52 OCU, and XL361 to Goose Bay.

> **David Bourne** was involved with the first RAF involvement in Giant Voice and also in winning the competition in 1974. He was later posted to Offutt as he describes in Chapter Eleven.

Giant Voice 1970

Blue Steel had been taken out of service and 27 Squadron had reverted to a conventional bombing role when Strike Command received its invitation to compete in the 1970 SAC Bombing competition. Because of our Blue Steel role the Scampton squadrons were not included in previous years. Now in the conventional role 27 and 617 Squadrons were required to produce a crew each to join the Giant Voice Training Flight (GVTF) at Waddington. In previous years of the competition Waddington had the monopoly and they were not keen on Scampton crews becoming involved. The invitation was for four crews to fly with a fifth reserve crew. However when we were given our initial briefing we were told that only three Vulcans would compete with one crew to go as reserve; with five squadrons, each providing a crew, one crew would be eliminated during the Waddington training period from the privilege of flying in the competition. This had been the form of training on previous SAC competitions but with no success. This meant that from the start the GVTF was a house divided against itself. If one crew had a particular, and successful, way of doing any part of the competition they were hardly likely to share it with the others.

The Vulcans had been specially selected for the task. They had been tuned up by the ground crew and there had been additions to the bombing and navigation equipment. For example the radars had extra offset controls (potentiometers) to improve the bombing accuracy. The whole navigation and radar equipment was kept tuned by the use of the 'Tardis', named by the ground crew after the police box in the Doctor Who series.

Not knowing the best of the Vulcans our crew accepted whatever we were given to fly and it was not until we were given a much more superior Vulcan for the job that

---

[5] Although two were lost earlier, see *Vulcan Test Pilot*.

we realised the distinct difference between them; with that aircraft we turned in the best score for one of the practice sorties. However it was a very strange experience when there was no mutual discussion between the crews. In the end we were the crew eliminated and as booby prize we were given 'Command Crew' status and returned to Scampton where we were immediately included in the squadron detachment to Tengah and then on to Darwin. As I suspected, not having changed their training system, the GVTF returned empty handed from the SAC competition.

Giant Voice 1974

In May 1971 I had been posted to Wildenrath as OC GD Flt. I had transferred, by then, to the specialist aircrew list and this posting was definitely not what I should have been given. I was only in Germany for seventeen months and in October 1972 I was back at Scampton and in January 1973 I was promoted and transferred back to the single list and was the new flight commander on 617 Squadron. The SAC bombing competition was scheduled for 1974 and I was made the pilot leader. In the interim we had our own competition in which the Vulcan squadrons in Cyprus had been involved.

I was determined that if I was to get involved then the flight would not be a house divided against itself but would observe the principles of war in that we would make a maximum effort using all the sorties offered us in the competition and we would pool all the experience in a concentration of effort. When I met the other staff members I was glad to hear that Simon Baldwin, nav plotter, and Mac McLachlan, nav radar, had reached the same conclusion as they had used that system to good effect in our bombing competition by winning it for a Cyprus squadron, if I remember rightly. However, we still had to persuade the boss Wg Cdr Colin King. By the time we went over to Bawtry to see the AOC, 1 Group, we had Colin's support. The AOC was not happy but agreed our plans saying we had better come back with a trophy. With conspicuous failures in the past, under the crew competition system, we could hardly do worse than had already been achieved.

The training started at Waddington in late July. One of the crews was from the OCU, which had not been a source in previous competitions, but was undoubtedly where the most experienced crew members could be found. Friday was set aside each week for a ground day when all five crews came together to discuss what had been achieved, and how. It was agreed that we would fly all four slots offered us in the competition which would be based at Barksdale AFB in Louisiana.

Once at Barksdale we were accommodated very well and the training continued. All of the SAC bomber bases sent competitors and each base had a booth in a huge hangar. As the bases were from all over the States each booth was decorated to show something of that geographic area. The recruiting PR part of the RAF had come up with a booth decorated like an old timber-framed pub for us. Unfortunately C-in-C SAC had decreed that the whole hangar was to be dry as previous competitions had seen some heavy drinking which he was not impressed by. This meant that our booth rapidly became an Olde English Tea Room. There was a trophy for the best booth which was judged before the competition got under way and we won. One pain in the posterior was that we had a civilian PR man allotted to us who had been with us since Waddington; he was given the honorary rank of squadron leader and was forever attempting to involve the crews when we wanted to get on with the training. At Barksdale he was lent a Stetson by an American colonel which was of a colour that earned the PR man the title of 'The Lavender Cowboy'. He also forgot to return it at the end of the detachment which caused a slight furore.

The training went well and on the nights of the competition the crews performed superbly. Fortunately the 111s which were flying, who might have been a problem, all had computer problems. We won two of the three trophies which were available; Colin King was possibly the most relieved man.

Jim Vinales was the nav plotter in the winning crew. He gives a splendid account of how it was done.

David Bourne receiving Boeing rings for the winning crew. (*David Bourne*)

13th November 1974 – Vulcan XM606

The aircraft rolled wings level and steadied on heading. I looked at the Doppler and noted our ground-speed – 510 knots. Excellent! Just as expected on flight plan. We'd just completed a timed high-level simulated bombing attack and now it was time to set up for the celestial navigation leg of the mission. We needed a stable platform and the relatively gentle thirty-five knot wind from the northwest at 37,000ft was unlikely to give us problems of wind shear and therefore turbulence. We had an enormous number of these celestial sextant shots to get through and we should have no trouble completing them all satisfactorily. Here we were, smack in the middle of the United States in the small hours of the morning on the second night of a prestigious bombing and navigation competition, Giant Voice 74, against the might of Strategic Air Command. Our opposition were twenty-four B52 bombers, twenty-seven KC135 tankers and, of course, our three other Vulcans representing RAF Strike Command. On the first night of the competition, we'd flown a sortie of six and a half hours. The states had rolled by fast underneath the aircraft: Louisiana, Arkansas, Missouri, Kansas, Nebraska, Colorado, Texas, Oklahoma, Louisiana again, Mississippi and recovery to our base, USAF Barksdale, in Louisiana. The names were redolent of the legendary cowboy films of my boyhood and it had thrilled me to think I was flying over all these mid-Western states heavily committed to our own showdown with the great Strategic Air Command. Tonight the sortie was an hour shorter and fully contained within the states of Louisiana, Texas, Arkansas and Mississippi and a stretch over the Gulf of Mexico. But at this stage the navigation termination point (NTP) was still a couple of hours away and there was a lot of work left to do.

Our crew had been nominated by our boss, Wing Commander Hopkins, to represent 101 Squadron, within Strike Command's 1 Group. We'd done reasonably well in the first leg of the competition several days earlier, earning ourselves 176 points out of 200. Not brilliant, but it put us in the top ten aircraft out of fifty-one competitors. I sensed that we stood a very good chance of winning the nav trophy. If only we could shave a mile off our 2.4-mile first attempt, we'd be in with a very good chance. Our four Vulcans were in for three trophies: the bombing trophy, the navigation trophy and the bombing and navigation combined (Mathis Trophy). Sadly, in the weeks running up to the competition, our aircraft navigation and bombing system had developed an annoying fault. At the critical moment in a bombing run, the nav radar's screen would appear to 'jump' and spoil his finely-judged aiming. Not for nothing was our aircraft, XM606, nicknamed 'Sick O Sick'. It had a history of spurious faults.

On the other hand, I was very happy with the way the navigation system, which we'd been monitoring and tweaking towards perfection over four months of training, was behaving and I had no desire for us to change over to the reserve aircraft. I insisted we were in with a very good chance for the navigation trophy and we should concentrate on correcting the bombing fault. Although Ed Candish, our nav radar, specialised in primarily radar bombing, he was also excellent with the periscopic sextant and we'd had some very positive results in the weeks since he'd replaced our regular nav radar, Flying Officer Tony Thornthwaite, who had picked up a virus which was proving slow to clear.

Ed was a tall, dark Scot; some might have accused him of a slight touch of dourness except for the fact that he was a very nice guy. But he was a dedicated professional and he would flagellate himself unmercifully if he felt his performance was not up to scratch. Although he was relatively new to the crew we'd all developed a great deal of confidence in him and constantly reassured him that he was certainly pulling his weight. We all knew he'd do his best when the chips were down.

Giant Voice mattered to the Vulcan Force. Competition between RAF Strike Command and Strategic Air Command was always intense but, over the previous twenty years, the Americans were certainly ahead with the trophies. Indeed, no RAF crew had won any trophy in the States but the Americans had certainly put in some very good results in the RAF's own competition, Double Top. The format of the competition varied marginally from year to year but it had not been held over the previous two years as the Americans had been far too involved in Vietnam. The competition was revived in 1974 and the RAF had received both the invitation and the document detailing the format and rules of the competition. Our directing staff were hopeful of a good result this year. Although there was little change in the format of the bombing, the rules for the navigation stages slightly favoured our aircraft. These were the days before GPS, and celestial navigation was still considered important.

The rules were simple: the method of fixing was to be purely by manual sextants. The only other systems allowed would be the aircraft's compass systems and the Doppler radar which gave us accurate displays of groundspeed and drift. All other indications of position were to be either switched off or covered over with black tape just before the start of the navigation stage. An aircrew officer, appointed by the competition's governing staff, would fly in one of the spare seats as umpire to ensure that all rules were observed fairly. The competition would be flown over two nights. The first half of each sortie would be the high-level phase: a timed simulated bombing run plus a long celestial navigation stage ending at a navigation termination point. The second half was the low-level part of the sortie consisting of four simulated bombing attacks on two sets of targets, each set with two targets in close proximity.

Within our Doppler system was a set of distance-gone counters, slightly superior to the Americans' own system, and we would exploit this tiny advantage to the utmost. A crew would be allocated 200 points each night for a perfect navigation score and this would be reduced by one point for each tenth of a mile distance from the termination point. On approaching the NTP, crews were to transmit a continuous RT tone for about twenty seconds and the aircraft's position at cessation of the tone would be taken as the crew's declaration of arrival at the NTP. On the ground, radar scoring units would note the position of the aircraft at tone cessation and work out the error in nautical miles. A similar system would be employed to assess the accuracy of all simulated bombs. No hardware would ever be dropped from any aircraft. Scores would be passed directly and exclusively to directing staff at USAF Barksdale in Louisiana where the competition HQ was based.

Our periscopic sextants bore little resemblance to marine sextants but they did exactly the same job: the measuring of the angular altitude of a heavenly body above the horizon. But how to observe the horizon at night from an aircraft at altitudes around 40,000ft? This problem was resolved by incorporating a spirit level within the body of the sextant. Later sextants, such as the ones we now had, had a pendulous reference, in effect, a plumb line. Both systems were prone to the same errors. If the aircraft moved from stable flight, the bubble or pendulous reference would be disturbed and an error in the recorded angular altitude would result. For that reason, it was important to avoid turbulence and to record, as accurately as possible, changes in airspeed and heading between the start and finish of the shot; a composite correction for disturbance to the levelling datum could then be calculated and applied. Each shot lasted a minute and was the aggregate of 60 x 1-second shots. A clockwork mechanism within the sextant averaged out the sixty shots.

The sextant operator had to be both slick and able to concentrate. Especially as he was expected to do as many as eleven shots on the one star with only thirty seconds between each shot. In that brief interlude, he had to rewind the clockwork mechanism and realign the sextant to the star. The whole process took ten or sixteen minutes, depending on whether it was a seven or eleven-shot sequence. Every member of the crew cooperated to ensure the shot's success. The co-pilot timed down to the start of every shot, to the second; the captain observed and recorded the exact change in airspeed between start and finish of the shot; as nav plotter I coordinated all activity and carefully observed changes in the heading of the aircraft; Ed, the nav radar would concentrate on the actual 'shooting'. At the end of each shot the other crew members passed their data to me and I then processed it as carefully as I could. Then, using a very sharp pencil, I carefully plotted the position line and compared it against the Doppler in formation, checking and rechecking my calculations as accurately as I could. Figures abounded and great concentration was required to avoid simple arithmetical mistakes. The AEO took no part in the exercise, as such. His job was to monitor the radios and talk to air traffic as required.

Periscopic sextant (*Norman Bonner*) and (right) placed in position in roof of rear cabin. (*Jeff Jefford*)

Flight Lieutenant Tony Dee was the co-pilot. A graduate of Cranwell, he was keen and very competent and I knew I could rely on him to be spot-on with the timing. As all celestial navigators knew, seconds were essential in the quest for accurate determination of position. A very pleasant and self-effacing man, it amused him to describe himself as 'thoroughly average'. He'd been told that at Cranwell, so it must have been true! However average at Cranwell was an accolade in itself. With few exceptions, tending to prove the rule, the RAF did not recruit mediocre candidates into the 'College of Knowledge'. Like Peter Hoskins before him, Tony would do very well in his RAF career.

Flight Lieutenant Paddy Langdown, the captain, was in many ways very different from his contemporaries. Possessing a quick mind, he loved his job and took his position as aircraft captain very seriously. But he was honest to a fault and would never hesitate to 'tell it as it was'. In other words, tact and diplomacy were encumbrances that got in the way of business. This invariably led to senior officers harrumphing at him, particularly when, as squadron instrument rating examiner, he was tasked to check them out. He would go on to become an excellent pub landlord and, thereafter, a great insurance salesman.

Several minutes into the long navigation leg, the aircraft had settled down and there was little sign of any appreciable turbulence. I sighed with relief; the way was open for Ed to turn in some excellent star sights. We would be starting our sextant work in a few minutes and, sensing a brief lull in activity, Colin Hinge (the AEO) offered to get coffees all round. Colin was always ready to get at the coffee whenever things quietened down in flight. One now, he reckoned, would set us all up for the several hours of high-level flight towards the NTP, and the high-energy low-level work which would follow. Ed had, fortunately, experienced no trouble with his radar and he was happy with the way he had performed on the high-level simulated attack.

Flight Lieutenant Colin Hinge was a highly-experienced AEO. Indeed, this was the third time he'd been selected for the prestigious task of representing the RAF in the Giant Voice competition. Colin, in his mid-thirties like Paddy, hailed from the Valleys, a broad Welshman, utterly true to his origins and a faithful labour supporter, "Michael Foot, man! He's brilliant!" A short stocky man with a highly-active metabolism, he was always laughing, joking and generally taking the mickey. Easy going and utterly devoid of all pretence, it was quite impossible to keep up with him on a night out. There he'd be, sweat beads on his forehead, the night always too short for him, always ready for loads more fun. And God help any man who tried to be pompous with him.

Right now, he reached across the chart table to offer me my coffee and, somehow or other, spilled it all over my chart. Disaster! I'd spent hours getting that chart prepared in minute detail. It was absolutely essential to the execution of the task in hand. I looked back at him in horror and he looked back at me and burst out laughing. Insult to injury! I was livid. Spawn of the devil, wretched son of the valleys, the swine – how could he? But the insensitive so-and-so just carried on laughing – absolutely no sense of decency or occasion. The rest of the crew were more sympathetic, and concerned. Like me they knew how much was at stake and quickly, out of nowhere, cloths appeared. I carefully dabbed the chart, desperately trying to retain and not distort essential detail. I was sweating now; it was time to get on with business and Tony was already counting down to the start of the first star shot. I took one look at the chart and saw it was just about usable. Perhaps, as it dried up properly, more detail would reappear. Heaven alone knows what the USAF major in the 'rumble' seat was making of all this. He'd been told by his colleague, who'd flown with us on the first sortie, how professional we were.

Colin slipped back into his seat on my right. He was still chuckling but he gave my elbow a nudge with his as if to say, "you'll be all right". All right! My nerves were shot to pieces, but we had a job to do and Ed was already at his position by the sextant, ready to start his first shot.

The aircraft flew serenely on through the night sky on autopilot. We settled into the routine we'd practised many times. The five, or was it six months of specialised training, were paying off. Ed Candlish would rewind the sextant forty or fifty times; there was certainly a lot of data to work on and I had my work cut out to record it all and use it to best possible advantage. We coasted out into the Gulf of Mexico. I looked anxiously at the Doppler indicators, hoping the calm sea below us would still yield strong echoes and therefore accurate groundspeed and drift readout. I looked at my graphs and applied a small correction to my distance-gone counters for 'spectrum distortion' and sea movement. Absolutely nothing could be left to chance. We turned and headed northwest towards Shreveport, Louisiana, towards the NTP. All hands to the pump now for the final eleven-shot sequence – no mistakes! Shots complete, position lines plotted on the soggy chart, final adjustments made to our track and ETA. Tone started....3, 2, 1 – tone off. Exercise complete! Nearly six months of hard work brought to a close.

Now allowed to look at position information, Ed took a quick radar fix. No time for a really accurate one, but the error in the fix seemed quite small, a good sign. But we couldn't be absolutely sure. It was time to descend into the low-level system for a furious hour and twenty minutes of non-stop action. Once again, the radar screen behaved itself and gave Ed nothing to worry about. We climbed out of the low-level system and signalled our intention to air traffic control to return to Barksdale. In their usual efficient way, and it being the early hours of the morning, they gave us clearance to route directly to Barksdale instead of continuing with the ponderous procedural climb to altitude. Colin made a routine call to squadron HQ and passed details of aircraft serviceability. No information on our results was forthcoming; Group Captain Colin King, our detachment CO had given specific information that crews were not to be given results: "Let the crews concentrate on a safe recovery after a long night sortie." Fifteen minutes ahead of us were Flight Lieutenant Peter Perry and his 230 OCU crew. AOC 1 Group had chosen a highly-experienced crew of instructors within the detachment. Flight Lieutenant Roger Morris and his crew from 44 Squadron and Flight Lieutenant Steve Ackroyd and crew of 617 Squadron were equally spaced behind us. My old 45 Squadron mate Spike Reynolds, had knuckled down to his life as a nav radar on 617 Squadron and had earned himself the distinction of being one of the 'selected few'.

Down at Barksdale, our air and engineering staff were leaving the auditorium. They'd been watching results as they came in and got recorded on the large tote board. Now they made their way to 'the line' to welcome us back and see the aircraft safely in. In the air, we'd been completely oblivious to events on the ground. Later, I was to get the whole story from one of our supporting aircrew officers: "It was absolutely nerve-racking. We watched all the results coming in and the highs and lows were intense, all made worse by the tote staff who were up to all sorts of tricks to generate extra excitement. In fact, on one occasion a USAF officer nearly throttled one of the toters for excessive slowness in recording his unit's score! Frankly, we wished we'd been up there with you instead of watching the drama unfold on the ground."

Early light from the east allowed Paddy and Tony to see our ground crew from some distance as we taxied in. Paddy became excited: "They've all got their thumbs up. It must have been a good result!" I sat back in my seat and let out a deep breath, "Well, thank God, we haven't made fools of ourselves."

Some days later, dressed in my number one uniform, standing side by side with my four aircrew chums and our four senior ground staff, I allowed my eyes to wander around the auditorium. Americans certainly did not do things by halves. They'd taken a massive hangar, lined it with false walls and created a very large and very swish theatre. Around the outside of the theatre, yet within the hangar itself, every competing unit had been invited to create a bar in the style of their home state. Ours had naturally been done up to mimic the quintessential English pub. But now the auditorium was absolutely packed and all eyes were on the stage and the massive tote board behind it. The master of ceremonies, a highly-respected USAF colonel, was beginning to call winners up to the stage to receive their prizes. In front of us, the OCU crew proudly stood up as they were called to be presented with the Mathis Trophy for combined bombing and navigation. They'd had a horrendous set of equipment failures in the air, but with sheer dogged determination and drawing on their vast store of experience, they'd fought off the challenge and turned in a performance worthy of the Mathis. Nobody doubted they deserved it. A great roar of applause went up as they received the trophy and their individual 'miniatures'. They turned and stepped off the stage.

Something made me look at Colin on my left. My goodness, he was nervously wringing his hands and looked ill at ease, really unusual for him. "Colin what on earth is wrong?" "Well, this is my third time here and I never expected to be doing this!" I smiled, hardly believing that this laid-back individual could feel nervous right now. He'd shown no nerves in the air when they were justified. Right now I was enjoying myself along with the rest of the crew. I savoured the memory of that meeting with my plotter leader, Squadron Leader Simon Baldwin, immediately after landing. "Eight tenths of a mile – Excellent!" It was certainly better than I'd hoped for and it secured an overall score of 368 points, ten points above our nearest rivals. Top out of fifty-one competing aircraft. Simon had been delighted that all his patient, hard work and scrupulous planning had yielded the desired results.

The colonel by his lectern was now calling up the winners of the navigation trophy. One by one, nine of us in single file, we eased out of our seats and marched up to the stage.

Upon our return to the UK, we landed at RAF Benson and left the aircraft there to be collected by a couple of ferry crews. The commander-in-chief had wanted to show us off to the press and had selected a suitable base near London for this event. An Argosy transport aircraft then took us back to Scampton where our wives were waiting along with both Waddington and Scampton senior officers. They all congratulated us and pressed drinks into our hands. The atmosphere was warm and friendly and then Paddy's and Colin's wives presented them with a couple of blue envelopes. In an act of appalling timing, the air secretary's department had chosen this moment to let them have the bad news, 'Dear Flight Lieutenant, thank you for your valuable service. The Air Force Board regrets that your commission will be terminated next year...'

Anthony Wright took part in the last Red Flag exercise with Vulcans just as the V Force was winding down as a deterrent and just before the Falklands campaign, Operation Corporate.

The Last of the Vulcans and Exercise Red Flag 1982

It was in 1977 that the RAF was first invited to take part in Red Flag. They put forward two Vulcans and ten Buccaneers to take part. It was not the point scoring of bombing and navigation and the award of trophies, as experienced in the Strategic Air Command (SAC) bombing competitions, but involved 'war games' consisting of several aerial combat training exercises per year. It took place at Nellis AFB, Nevada, and still does today. The blue forces (friendly) are made up of various USAF units along with invited allied air forces. The red forces (enemy) are made up of aggressor squadrons of the USAF units which fly the tactics employed by Soviet aircraft along with the associated electronic counter measures.

Also available at Nellis for Red Flag is the Red Flag measurement and debriefing system (RFMDS). This is a computer which, on a huge screen, provided real-tracking of attackers and defenders along with the threats that they were encountering. Those not flying and stood down for that day could watch 'the war' in progress and decide who was winning and losing. Afterwards aircrew of the blue forces, using the RFMDS as a method of debriefing, could see, when the data was played back, where they could improve. Since those early days of participation Vulcans and Buccaneers did not always operate on the same exercise but often took part separately. Furthermore, with the withdrawal of the Vulcans in service, and later the Buccaneers, the newer aircraft, the Tornados, took up the baton. Today, in 2013, Typhoons have also started to take part. Each exercise covers a two-week period with aircrews flying the war games in the Nellis range area of the Nevada desert. The area involved covers hundreds of square miles and is situated just northwest of Las Vegas.

In 1982, the last year that the Vulcans took part, four crews from RAF Waddington, and one from RAF Scampton, were selected each from one of the five remaining bomber squadrons. The crews were namely: Detachment Commander Wg Cdr Mayes OC IX (B) Squadron and crew, Willoughby-Crisp crew 35 Squadron, Montgomery crew 44 Squadron, Macartney crew (my crew) 50 Squadron and the Withers crew 101 Squadron.

Terrain following radar antenna just below probe.
(*Nigel Baldwin*)

Early accounts of Red Flag describe the exercise as being flown by day. However, as time went on they were flown at night. Our Red Flag was different from the others as not only were we going to fly low level at night but, for the first time, I believe for any Vulcan in the exercises, drop practice bombs. Interestingly, this was also to be the last night-flying Red Flag until that element was re-introduced into the exercise in 1990.

We started training in October 1981 for Red Flag 82-2 scheduled in January/February 1982. The sorties in the UK were night low level, using terrain following radar (TFR), normally lasting just over two hours culminating in dropping a 28lb practice bomb on a target at Wainfleet in the Wash Danger Area. We completed six of these before all five crews flew out to RCAF Goose Bay, Labrador for further training. This was carried out over the Strike Command Canadian (STC Can) low-level routes, at night using the TFR, in total darkness without a light to be seen in the miles of uninhabited land of pine forests and lakes. On returning to the UK we continued flying TFR sorties throughout December with the last one completed in the first week in January. Finally, on 6th January all crews flew to RCAF Goose Bay and the next day double-staged to Offutt AFB, Nebraska and then on to Nellis AFB, Nevada for the exercise. We settled in to our accommodation which eventually turned out to be in two Las Vegas casinos during the detachment. Next day we were briefed by the USAF exercise staff at Nellis. Part of the briefing took us a bit by surprise when we were told that while we were there, statistically they expected there would be an aircraft crash or two with the possibility of a crew member being killed and that wasn't just flying on Red Flag. There had been an instance where visiting crews who were staying downtown Las Vegas had opened their hotel room doors unwittingly to strangers, had been robbed then strangled with the wire coat hangers from their rooms.

Our first sortie, before the exercise began in earnest, was to familiarise ourselves with the terrain by low flying across the Nevada desert during the day. It was here that we saw some of the pitfalls and traps to be aware of at night. These weren't the opposing enemy but geographical challenges. There were towering buttes and mesas that we had to fly round and this was when there was excellent visual contact by day. However, it was to be a different story at night; flying in pitch black the pilots were dependent on the nav radars like me to direct them around the obstacles purely by interpreting the radar screen.

Our crew planned for eleven sorties of which two were early returns, one a recall due to atrocious weather and another when a direct vision (DV) seal failed just as it happened later, on the Black Buck 1 sortie, for John Reeve in the Falklands. The sorties, which differed in area and tracks each night; were approximately one hour and fifty minutes in length with a 28lb practice bomb dropped on a target at the end. Each sortie was packed with excitement trying to avoid the enemy and simulated surface-to-air missiles (SAMs) and get to the target. All the crews in the blue forces also had to take a turn at both briefing and leading a particular attacking wave. Along with us in the blue forces were the USAF participants flying the F-111, F-4 and the F-15. The red forces on the exercise were flying the F-15 and the F-16 and were extremely skilled operators. One day, when not flying, I was one of the few Vulcan aircrew who did make the effort to go and see the RFMDS in action. It was impressive at the start. However, after the first fifteen minutes or so it got slightly tedious and the words 'paint' and 'dry' seemed appropriate to describe the scene. Therefore, I left it to those that really were interested.

Because we were operating at low level, at night, flying across miles of uninhabited desert, apart from take-off and landing at Nellis, our pilots were flying practically blind in the darkness and had to trust the navigation teams. It was only on returning from the desert range and climbing to height that sometime later a huge bright area suddenly appeared and attracted the pilots' attention. It was the lights of Las Vegas. Each night on landing there followed the same pattern. First there was debriefing followed by a swift exit to the Nellis officers' club for a wind down, chatting to other American participating crews, including our 'F-16 enemies', and then back to our Casino.

There is one story concerning the F-16 that springs to mind and proves the Red Flag statistics were correct. One evening just as we were about to enter base operations I heard a shout and turned round to see an F-16 on fire, smoke billowing out behind it, flying, or not as the case might be, low across the airfield parallel to the runway and with a bang the pilot ejected. I had my camera on my shoulder and was just able to take a photograph of the aircraft on fire as it hit the ground. It was that quick. We carried on to plan, briefed and eventually walked out to the aircraft on the huge apron with

Vulcan Mk2 at Nellis AFB with F16 taxiing out. (*Bill Perrins*)

smoke still coming from the F-16. When we got into the aircraft and onto intercom we were told by air traffic control that all aircraft crews were to close any hatches, windows and doors and not to venture outside as it was hazardous. We complied and were then told the reason. Unknown to us the F-16 used hydrazine, which is highly toxic and highly inflammable, to fuel the aircraft's emergency power unit (EPU). If the F-16's engine failed then there was no power to restart the engine or operate the flying controls. The EPU was there to try a restart. Failure of the EPU to generate power means that the pilot has no option but to eject. This one did. Once the fire teams and others in breathing apparatus and contamination suits got the situation under control we were cleared for take-off.

Red Flag crew. Left to right: Ian Jeffries – AEO, Chris Lackman – co-pilot, Kevin Weeks – nav plotter, Mike Macartney – captain, Anthony Wright – nav radar. (*Anthony Wright*)

Looking back, the flying on Red Flag was very testing, with much adrenalin used by all concerned. Despite that we learnt a good deal and were extremely satisfied to have completed it. Definitely an exercise not to be missed.

The training of crews in Red Flag proved beneficial when Operation Corporate, Falklands Campaign, occurred three months later. The people in the list below were very much involved with Black Buck and are in the photograph overleaf.

Vulcan Mk2 Red Flag crews 1982. (*Anthony Wright*)

RED FLAG	OPERATION CORPORATE
Dick Arnott	Res BB5/6
Gordon Graham	BB1
John Hathaway	BB5/6
Wg Cdr Mayes	Detachment Commander Red Flag, Waddington BB Ops Cell OC 1X Squadron
Alastair Montgomery	Res BB5/6
Bill Perrins	Res BB 5/6
Hugh Prior	BB1
Bill Sherlock	Ascension Support Staff
Dave Stenhouse	Res BB5/6
Peter Taylor	BB1
Martin Withers	BB1
Anthony Wright	Northwood Vulcan Adviser Waddington BB Ops Cell
Bob Wright	BB1

Chapter Eleven

NORTH AMERICAN SUPPORT

The RAF had support centres at Goose Bay and Offutt to look after the many Vulcans and Victors that visited the States, Canada and flew round the world. In this chapter David Bourne and Adrian Sumner describe working at a United States Air Force Base running an RAF detachment.

David joined the RAF in 1948 when he was fifteen-and-a-half-years old. After spending three years at Cranwell learning to be a ground radar fitter he was granted a cadetship at the college and commissioned in the Equipment Branch in April 1954. However David managed to get an A1 medical category and started flying training at 3 FTS in July 1957. **David Bourne** was based in Offutt from 1975 to 1977 and tells his story here.

Posting to Offutt AFB

In the spring of 1975 I was posted to command the Strike Command Detachment at Offutt AFB near Omaha, Nebraska. I had been to Offutt several times so I was familiar with the operation but, once nominated, I had to have an interview with the AOC. He was renowned for his one-sided lectures. The fact that I had had, previously, the command of two units which were dispersed from their HQs had obviously passed him by and the impression that I was given was that I was barely to be trusted with the Offutt detachment. I was forty-two and had been in the RAF since I was almost sixteen so I was not best pleased with this rousing cheer of doubt from the man who had been AOC and for whom we had won an unexpected prize at the last Giant Voice. I nearly told him to stick his posting but the fact that this was likely to be my only complete accompanied overseas tour before I retired meant that I just swallowed and pressed on.

I was allocated a Western Ranger at the beginning of May. On such rangers we carried a bomb-bay pannier full of spares which might be of use for servicing the aircraft. As we were going through an established base at Goose Bay and then going to another one, I had the pannier pretty well emptied and filled with our household furniture, since married quarters for the USAF were empty of such. The sortie to Goose Bay was planned for 5th May 1975 but Offutt needed certain spare parts in a hurry so we were required to double stage that day to Offutt using Goose as a re-fuelling point. As we approached Offutt at 45,000ft in high cirrus cloud, we received a radio message that there was a tornado watch on in Omaha but no one explained what that meant; however, the landing forecast sounded acceptable. Fortunately for me, the 55th Strategic Reconnaissance Wing Ops came on frequency and said: "If it is any help we have just sent one of our KC135s to Lincoln." I thanked him and initiated our diversion to Lincoln fifty-eight

From left, Flight Lieutenants Mike Feenan, Graham
Yearwood, Nigel Thomas, Andy Ward, David Bourne,
C/T Hamish Brown. (*David Bourne*)

miles SW of Omaha. Almost immediately we came out of the cirrus and we were over a 45,000ft solid north-south vertical wall of cloud stretching down to the ground. It is the only time that I experienced a passing touch of vertigo. We were soon on the ground at Lincoln and parked on the SAC dispersal as the sole aircraft. Unfortunately we collected a piece of brass rod in one of our tyres which meant we were greeted by a hissing sound when we got out.

Brian Cable was the very experienced Vulcan navigator who was to be my deputy. As the USAF Global Weather Centre (GWC) was based at Offutt, Brian had set up all the Olive Branch (low-level, see page 123) routes as Vulcan routes. He then arranged with GWC to put them into their computer so that at the touch of a button the computer applied that day's weather to the route and printed out the sortie navigation details which the crew then picked up and entered on their route form for the sortie. It worked like a charm. We would gather prior to the sortie in the base operations centre, file the flight plan and then repair to the 'greasy spoon' for a pre-flight meal.

The Western Ranger and Olive Branch Training

Western Rangers were allocated to the squadrons by group. The squadrons would then grant them to crews as part of their overall training. The in-bound crew would fly in from Goose Bay arriving normally in the early afternoon. They would have with them a crew chief who was in charge of the Vulcan's servicing with the detachment providing the ground crew. On arrival the aircraft was met by an American customs or immigration official as Offutt was the first point of entry to the USA of the aircraft and crew. The two departments took it in turns to meet the aircraft and they always hoped that it would arrive after 17.30 as they were paid an over-time fee of $100 in that case. Either my deputy, or myself, also met the crew with our staff car which was a nine-seat Chevrolet Estate which was adequate to carry the crew and their kit. Once cleared into the country we would take them over to our headquarters which was in one of the vast hangars. I would brief them on the flying programme which was set for them plus the administrative plan for their stay. There was no accommodation on base so the services of the Ramada motel were used. This was just outside the Bellevue gate of the base and provided rooms, restaurant and bar of a comfortable standard and reasonably priced. One of the great advantages of this motel was that, should the crews need to be kept at a state of readiness to recover to the UK in times of political tension, it provided all that was required under one roof. It was at this point that my briefing went on to cover the temptations this motel also had within it. Remembering that each of these crews carried knowledge of high security war plans in the shape of their war targets, any situation which could lead to blackmail was to be avoided. The motel was also used by USAF personnel and the attraction of all these men under one roof drew many ladies to the bar. But then all our crews were the essence of discretion and responsibility were they not?

On the day prior to the first sortie we would order up the flight plans from GWC. On the day itself we would collect the crew from the Ramada and the flight plans from GWC and take them to base ops. The crew copied the plan and filed their flight plan and we took them over to the greasy spoon. Then out to the aircraft and away into the wide blue yonder. My deputy and I did not control the flying or authorise the sorties; that was all done from their squadron in the UK in accordance with their briefing for the ranger. Our job was to facilitate those UK authorisations. On their return we met the Vulcan and our ground crew serviced the aircraft ready for the next day's sortie. When they had completed the required sorties we set them up for the return flight to Goose Bay.

Although we had no control over the flying, we could advise on action using our local knowledge. For example, one morning we were about to launch two Vulcans. The cloud was low and it was very hot and sticky. I was in the ATC Local when I noticed that there were hundreds of swallow-type birds flying in the first fifty feet right above the runway and not moving away. Any Vulcan taking off would have scooped them up into the engines so I cancelled all flying. The Vulcans returned to dispersal but the swallows took not a blind bit of notice. No one complained about my doing that as it meant that the crews stayed for one more day at Offutt at the lucrative daily local overseas allowance to complete their sorties on a later day.

On one occasion my advice to a Vulcan pilot to land was overridden. The Vulcan had returned early from the planned sortie having declared that it had suffered a bird strike. I went up to ATC Local to see if I could see anything wrong and much to my sur-

prise the aircraft had suffered considerable damage to the leading edge of the port wing. There was a hole of about 18 inches long and almost the whole thickness of the leading edge immediately outboard of the engine intake. It must have been a

Vulcan parked with a Valiant and Victor at Offut AFB early 1960s on the disused runway. (*Adrian Summer*)

massive bird and I could not see how far it had entered the wing. I passed all this to the captain with the suggestion that he land so that the ground crew could have a much closer look. He thanked me for the information and my suggestion but said he would continue in the circuit to complete some continuation training. I could hardly argue as he was a wing commander. When on the ground we found that the bird had smashed through the wing structure to the main spar but fortunately had not damaged a fuel tank. A specialist ground crew came out to assess and do the repairs while the aircrew went home by other means. The only other time that I was 'confused' by a wing commander (but this time one from a Hercules squadron), was during another tornado watch. He was by then ensconced in the Ramada. When the news of the tornado watch got to him he rang me up and demanded that I keep the nose of his aircraft into the wind. As we have said so many times when pressed by events in the RAF, "ruddy rotate it yourself".

General Dougherty greeting AVM Largerson AOC 1 Group with crew,
David Bourne on left. (*David Bourne*)

We also had VIP visitors to contend with. C-in-C Strike and the AOC came to see what we were doing and how well we provided support for the Vulcan crews. On one occasion the AOC, AVM David Evans, asked to be shown around the SNCO's married quarters area. I was set to pick him up at the officers' club at 14.00hrs. I used my own car, which was another version of the Chevrolet estate car, so that it would be inconspicuous, rather than take the staff car. When we came out of the club he automatically went to a compact small car that was at the kerb side. When I directed him to my car he asked if it was mine and, knowing that it made his staff car at 1 Group look like a mini, I took delight in telling him it was and that there were four litres of engine under the bonnet with petrol at forty-five cents a US gallon.

Red Flag

I think it was in the summer of 1977 that the Buccaneer squadrons were invited to take part in the Red Flag training out of Nellis AFB. Marham's tanker squadrons would tank the Buccaneers past us to land at Nellis while the four tankers came in to us. The plan was for half our detachment with half of our ground equipment to go to Nellis for the duration of the Red Flag. In the normal course of events we would expect,

Vulcans at Offut with David's car. (*David Bourne*)

at the most, three Vulcans with us for Olive Branch training, with the odd Hercules transiting through, outbound or inbound to the UK, on the westabout route to the Far East. I was hoping that with half my chaps away the planners at Strike would keep us free from too much traffic.

That hope was rapidly shot down when on the day of the Buccaneers moving to Nellis we were told that we would have to handle two Nimrods overnight on their way to California, plus a Hercules and a Vulcan. The Hercules was bringing the tanker ground crew from Goose after they had seen off the tankers. They arrived after we had put the tankers to bed. The Victor tankers' arrival was also complicated with their deployment of brake chutes on landing. I asked them not to drop their chutes until clear of the runway which, in the event, they all ignored. I was collecting the chutes with the two admin corporals and, as the tankers were landing close behind one another, we had to clear the runway of the discarded chutes quickly and it didn't help that it was a hot afternoon. At the end of the day we had one Hercules, four Victor tankers, two Nimrods and a Vulcan in our dispersal on the dis-used runway. The only advantage I could think of for all this was that we should be able to sell quite a lot of booze!

Positive Vetting(PVT) Clearance

The positive vetting clearance involved a supposedly close analysis of your political leanings. You were also assessed for moral rectitude and your ability to stand up to the possibility of having various temptations placed in your way which could leave you open to blackmail and giving away the secret details of your targets and our methods. You had to provide referees and all your close family details. Only with PVT clearance were you allowed to join V Force. This was why I briefed crews about the temptations that could be lying in wait for them once they stood down after flying. Sadly it would seem that some of the crew members were not listening.

The resulting fall out ended up with the station commander RAF Waddington wishing to cease using the Ramanda as crew accommodation. Back at Offutt I was not aware of any of this until the next Vulcans came in. One of the crews that came in had the AOC 1 Group with them. The AOC asked if we could use another motel but I said that there was not another motel that came close to the facilities that the Ramada gave in such close proximity to the base. I pointed out how we briefed the crews and that they were all responsible grown men, were they not, and I said I did not want to make any changes. He agreed with me but said that the station commander at Waddington strongly recommended against continuing with the Ramada as the supposed temptations there were too great; which was the first that I had heard of it. We were parented by Waddington and I realised that I was on my own personal Titanic with the station commander Waddington in charge of the iceberg! The final outcome was that as the station commander made my annual assessment on my personal report, the dreaded Form 1369, I ended up collecting a less than laudatory report as I prepared to leave Offutt, despite my efforts to preserve the security of our crews.

I was posted home in March 1978 to Strike Command into flight safety. In 1981 I reverted to specialist aircrew and went to 207 Squadron Northolt flying Devons. One of them had been in the RAF as long as I had and I reckoned that I was a new museum exhibit so it was time for me to retire. Which is what I did when I was fifty in 1983 to become the post-master at Winchelsea in East Sussex until 2007, thence to Tenterden in Kent.

Adrian Sumner was appointed detachment commander at Offutt from October 1980 to August 1982 when he had to close the detachment. He tells the story of the closure but includes a few other stories of his career along the way.

The Warmer Side of the Cold War: My First Association with the Vulcan
I started on the Vulcan in February 1970 at 230 OCU RAF Scampton . Two of the three crews on my course were destined for Cyprus. I suppose that I must have bought Wg Cdr Ron Dick the right amount of beer, as I ended up as his co-pilot on IX Squadron at RAF Akrotiri. We were the first IX crew to replace those which had moved there from RAF Cottesmore the previous year.

I remember one exercise when having completed the Cyprus low-level route for some reason going clockwise, the wrong way round on this occasion, we formed up in V formation with two other Vulcans and carried out a simulated bombing run on Akrotiri. After the exercise, the station commander, Air Cdre John Stacey, was shown F95 film of our attack and he noticed a white blob in the centre of the station. "What on earth's that?" was his immediate question and on being told it was his white Land Rover, he immediately ordered the vehicle to be resprayed with a camouflage scheme similar to the Vulcan.

Another recollection was flying back from Masirah in the Oman. Akrotiri had been hit by a severe thunderstorm and there was nine inches of standing water on the runway, so we had to divert to Adana in Turkey, where we were hosted by a USAF fighter squadron. On climbing out, recovering back to Akrotiri, Ron asked me where I had stowed the case of squadron wine which had been kindly given to us by the Americans;

I didn't enjoy telling him that I had left it back in their crew room at Adana and I definitely got the impression that Ron was not best pleased.

Whether or not it was because of this incident but, a short time afterwards, I was ordered to sleep overnight in the crew room with the squadron cat to take my turn to guard the Tirpitz Bulkhead which was on display there. This trophy, part of the boat itself, needed to be guarded as there was a continual battle between 617 and IX Squadrons as who deserved to keep it. That very day a 617 crew had flown it in from the UK and the inter-squadron rivalry between 617 and IX as to who sunk the battleship, and therefore the ownership of the bulkhead, was still very much alive in 1971.

In those days we sometimes deployed to Tehran Mehrabad in Iran for low-level training, and during these sorties we always flew with an Iranian observer on board. On one occasion, the observer was standing between the seats, and in the far distance, Ron and I could see an aircraft trailing a plume of black smoke which appeared to be coming straight towards us extremely quickly. Bearing in mind that we were at low level, the aircraft, an Iranian F4 Phantom, came head on and flew under us, close enough for me to see the helmets of both the aircrew. Having passed, I turned around to check on the observer whose mouth was wide open and his

A celebrity visit in December 1970. Left to right: Wg Cdr Ron Dick – captain, Flight Lieutenant John Fry – AEO, Adrian Sumner – co-pilot, Joyce (Marty's wife), Flight Lieutenant Bob Sinclair – nav radar and singer Marty Wilde. (*Adrian Sumner*)

face was extremely pale. To this day, I do not know whether the Phantom crew actually saw us or not!

My greatest memory from Cyprus days, was our New Zealand Ranger in February 1972. Ron had received a letter from the widow of an ex-squadron commander who had sadly died; he had had a silver bat, the IX Squadron emblem, as a mascot on their car and she wished to present it to the squadron. The only problem was that she lived in Christchurch, South Island NZ. Unfortunately, this was not sufficient justification for a trip 'down under' so a further reason had to be found. I am not sure how it happened, but Ron managed to get an invite to take part in the Hamilton Air Show, south of Auckland, North Island. Our base throughout our stay was the

Part of the Tirpitz bulkhead. A fiercely contested trophy between IX and 617 Squadrons. (*Adrian Sumner*)

RNZAF airbase at Ohakea, just outside Palmerston North.

As it happened, we were the first Vulcan to return to New Zealand since 1959 when a Vulcan B1 XH498 undershot the runway at Wellington damaging the port undercarriage, and crash-landed back at Ohakea. I understand the crew chief remained with the aircraft in NZ for a number of months! Our ranger was not without incident, but of a different kind. During the first evening of our arrival, our aircraft was 'zapped' having kiwis painted within the roundels on either side of the nose. Then, during our flight down and back to Christchurch to pick up the silver bat, we came across an old steam train known as the 'Kingston Flier' which we managed to capture on F95 film. On returning to Ohakea, Ron was handed a telegram which was from the engine driver, a Mr

Glendenning, which read – +++GREAT FLYBY STOP DID YOU KNOW THAT YOU HAD AN OIL LEAK UNDER YOUR LEFT WING STOP+++. Apparently several years later Ron Dick re-visited NZ and found out where Mr Glendenning was living. He knocked at his door and said to him "We have never met,

Kingston Flier going left and Adrian Sumner going right.
(*Adrian Sumner*)

but I have been close to you," to which Mr Glendenning replied, "you're that bloody Vulcan pilot".

Another occurrence was as a result of flying up and down the fantastically beautiful Milford Sound in New Zealand again during our flight back from Christchurch. Months after our return to Cyprus, I was back in the UK on my intermediate co-pilot's course for conversion to the left-hand seat. I was browsing through the flying magazines in Smiths and came across a Vulcan filling the whole of the centrefold picture; on closer inspection, I realised it was our aircraft in New Zealand. The picture had been taken by an Australian professional photographer who was on his honeymoon, and who happened to be fishing in Milford Sound at the time.

Flying back to Cyprus from New Zealand, whilst crossing the Inter-Tropical Front and endeavouring to climb out of severe icing, we had the outer lamination of two of our front windscreens crack. We subsequently landed safely at Tengah in Singapore, and the aircraft remained there for a double windscreen change whilst our crew flew back to Akrotiri by VC10. Some days later the aircraft was recovered back to base by Flight Lieutenant Jon Tye and his crew. Within minutes of it landing at Akrotiri, Ron was summoned to the station commander's office to explain to John Stacey why one of his aircraft had been seconded to the New Zealand Air Force....Ron had forgotten about the kiwis in the roundels!

The End of an Era

My last association with the Vulcan was as the final detachment commander at Offutt AFB from 1980 to 1982. On arrival in the USA, I had to be briefed at the British Embassy in Washington DC before flying down to Nebraska and it was a great delight that my wife and I were able to stay with Ron and Paula Dick in Washington, as he was posted there as the air attaché.

Offutt AFB was the home of the Strategic Air Command Headquarters (SACHQ), and during World War Two the base housed the Martin Bomber Plant, which produced hundreds of B26s and B29s. The most famous being the 'Enola Gay' which dropped the first atomic bomb.

The RAF detachment which was housed in one of the old wartime buildings known as 'Mod B', consisted of myself, my flight lieutenant deputy and twenty-six airmen, who were mainly Vulcan engineers, plus wives and children, which eventually totalled ninety-six souls. I say eventually, as we had two births during my tenure. My immediate boss was the station commander at Waddington, with our annual inspection carried out by AOC 1 Gp, who was AVM Knight at the time. Our primary task was to look after the Vulcans and their crews who were detached to Offutt for low-level training, and also to take care of any other RAF aircraft staging through central USA. The Vulcans flew low-level routes throughout the mid-west states simulating the Russian Steppes, known initially as Oil Burner routes, prior to the fuel crisis. However, following the US government's policy change on fuel conservation under Ronald Reagan in 1980, the name became unacceptable, and so the routes were renamed Olive Branch to retain the OB nomenclature.

There's no such thing as a courtesy visit! (*Adrian Sumner*)

The build-up to the Falklands War happened during this period when we had already started donating Vulcans to various museums around the world. I attended one such handover by AVM Knight of XM605 to Castle Air Force Base Museum in California in September 1981. The air marshal received an engraved clock in return! A short time later, I was requested to recover this aircraft's nose probe for use back in the UK as there was a chronic shortage of probes to equip the Vulcans for air-to-air refuelling to get down to the Falklands. I managed to get a lift for a handful of my engineers in a brand new KC10 Extender across to the Castle AFB on the west coast to remove the probe from XM605, which, by that time had already been placed on display in the museum. The USAF and museum staff were extremely cooperative, and no questions were asked.

Offutt farewell ceremony 12th June 1982.
(*Adrian Sumner*)

With the demise of the Vulcan, I was tasked in June 1982 with closing the detachment which had existed at Offutt for twenty-five years. As part of the closing ceremony, I organised an event on Offutt's disused runway during the day and a cocktail party in the officers' club in the evening. Four Vulcans were flown from the UK, one of which, XM573, was to be given to the SAC museum which was then housed at the end of the disused runway just outside the airfield boundary. The bombing competition trophies were also flown out from the UK to be displayed at the cocktail party. On the morning of the event, it was gloriously hot. However, as the guests, which included twenty-one generals, plus the state governor, started to arrive at the venue after lunch, the clouds were looking ominous. I was just about to commence the ceremony when it started to rain, and being in the middle of the airfield everyone ran for the nearest cover. Luckily I had provided two MASH tents which the USAF had kindly erected for me on the disused concrete runway, from which strawberries and teas were going to be served following the ceremony. However, the rain was so hard that everyone, VIPs and guests alike, had crammed into both tents.

The forecast from SAC HQ indicated that the rain would last for forty minutes, so I decided to serve the strawberries and teas early, which was an extremely interesting exercise in such a crammed space! Meanwhile, there was a B52, KC135 and an FB111 holding over the airfield which were to be part of the formation flyby, as the Vulcans had flown against all three types in the annual SAC bombing competition over the years. Luckily the rain stopped at the appropriate time, the SAC band struck up, and the ceremony began. Following my preamble, four Vulcans were scrambled and took off for a formation flyby in diamond, followed by the USAF aircraft. XM573 then broke off for a full individual display before landing. The aircraft was then handed over by C-in-C Strike Command, Air Marshal Bairstow, General Benny Davis and Governor Thone, the Nebraska State Governor. As the Form 700 was being passed across, the rain started once again! Dare I say the cocktail party went off without a hitch. The following day we moved XM573 to the outdoor SAC museum. Interestingly all of the museum exhibits, plus the Vulcan were subsequently moved a few years later to a brand new purpose-built indoor facility between Omaha and Lincoln. Sadly, I found out earlier this year that the Vulcan has now ended up outside, once again, due to lack of space in the museum.

Adrian's auction of surplus parts. Some good stuff not
going to waste! (*Adrian Sumner*)

The following month, having sent a number of items of ground equipment back to the UK on a C130 Hercules, I was tasked with the disposal of the remaining detachment equipment which was surplus to requirement; this included our vehicles, a Vulcan engine, various Vulcan 'black boxes', a giraffe, a bicycle, tools etc. After some investigation, I found an auction house in North Omaha which was willing to take on the task and so we shipped everything there, but I was told there were to be no reserve prices. Hence, somewhere in the States there are numerous Vulcan black boxes being used as coffee tables! Incidentally, the Vulcan engine was bought by a Rolls-Royce car enthusiast, who wished to display the engine alongside his vehicles, and whom we convinced needed a Land Rover to tow the engine and trolley plus a set of AF spanners to service the vehicle….he paid $1,500. Overall, the auction raised over $21,000. So as I write this if Robert Pleming needs another engine for XH558 he knows where to look!

On the final day of the detachment, in August 1982, all of my personnel, plus families booked out of the local hotel, where we had stayed overnight. We all attended a farewell ceremony on base, during which the RAF ensign was lowered and I handed it to the base commander, Col McCone, as a memento. The local television station filmed the event and the Omaha Pipes & Drums played a lament. However, our final moment at Offutt was not without incident. When the VC10 arrived to take us all home to the UK, the captain declared that his crew would run out of crew duty time by the time they returned to the UK, and, therefore, we would have to stay an extra night in Nebraska. You can imagine my feelings at the time, having just completed the farewell ceremony. In the end, the VC10 captain agreed to take us to Washington where we spent the night before flying back to Waddington.

As a postscript, Ron Dick sadly died in 2008, and it just so happened that I celebrated my retirement in the same year with a trip to New Zealand. Not knowingly, I drove past Hamilton thirty-six years to the day since our participation in their air show, and I also went to see if anything had changed at Ohakea, which had become a RNZAF Huey helicopter base. The only thing of course which was missing was….a Vulcan!

As a post-postscript, in 2013 my wife and I stayed with a couple in Kiev, Ukraine on a friendship force exchange. As it transpired the husband was a retired lieutenant colonel who flew MiG27s back in the 1980s....how times have changed.

Just a small RAF detachment. (*Adrian Sumner*)

After attending the Joint Services Defence College at Greenwich, Adrian became officer commanding operations and Pilot Training Wing at RAF Finningley, where he was chief instructor on the Jetstream. His final tour in the RAF was with NATO at the Supreme Headquarters Allied Powers Europe (SHAPE) in Mons, Belgium. After retiring from the RAF in 1997 as a wing commander, Adrian flew as a captain on the BAe146 for two small airlines, and then worked as a contract pilot and QFI flying Royal Navy Jetstreams at RNAS Culdrose. He is also a qualified hot air balloon pilot. During his forty-one-year flying career Adrian amassed over 9,500 flying hours, of which 2,300 were on the Vulcan.

Chapter Twelve

OPERATION CORPORATE

During my time at Avros as a test pilot I helped develop the Vulcan, the Nimrod and the Victor K2 and when the Falklands campaign took place I was in the United States on the Aerospace Board of Smiths Industries. Watching the story unfold on the television the whole thing seemed unreal and I couldn't help thinking that it was amazing that all my three aircraft were actually being used in their combat roles.

So far I have been very lucky to have been able to write books about the Nimrod and the Victor describing their roles in the campaign. This book contains the missing link as far as I am concerned, the Vulcan involvement, told in the main by the people who took part which gives an air of authenticity which a third-hand account can never achieve. A breakdown of the actual sorties and analysis of the Black Buck 1 fuel plan is in Appendix 2.

The first narrator is **John Laycock**. Group Captain commanding RAF Waddington at the time where the Vulcans were based.

John Laycock (left) presenting the South Atlantic medal to
Dave Castle Black Buck 4, 5, 6. (*Dave Castle*)

Waddington April 1982 – a Prelude to War
Between the first and last days of April 1982, RAF Waddington's mission changed from having four squadrons of medium bombers assigned to NATO in the strike role, to starting combat operations in the South Atlantic with ten aircraft converted to the low-level attack role, one squadron disbanded to become a Tornado squadron and the remainder on standby to support operations in whatever way the Air Staff decided. The only part of these changes which had been planned was IX Squadron's conversion to Tornado.

On 1st April, nobody at Waddington, reading the bizarre story of an Argentine scrap dealer raising the national flag over Leith harbour, South Georgia, would have thought that it was anything other than a good April Fool's day story. However, the next day, when news of an Argentine invasion of the Falkland Islands focused the world's attention on the South Atlantic, the initial surprise turned to serious consideration of what the RAF, and the Vulcan in particular, could do in response to such an unexpected development.

In the next week, the word from Downing Street was increasingly of an armed response and a Naval Task Force being assembled for despatch to the South Atlantic. The word from our parent headquarters, HQ No 1 Group, was that not too many people should stray too far from the station over the approaching Easter weekend. Then, on Good Friday morning, 9th April, the order came to generate ten aircraft in the conventional role and reactivate their air-to-air refuelling systems. Although the order was expected, it was unusual: it had not been practised by Vulcan crews for fifteen years and, to prevent fuel leaks, the system had been made inoperable by inhibiting the two non-return valves immediately aft of the refuelling probe. Reactivating the system would require fitting new valves to the ten aircraft. Not surprisingly, there were no valves held in store at Waddington for a system so long out of use. However, a rapid trawl through RAF maintenance unit stocks revealed some twenty of these critical items held at RAF Stafford and an immediate demand was made for their delivery; the valves arrived at Waddington the next morning.

Conventional bombing, although still a capability, was unpractised. The 1974 decision to spend no further money on this role for the Vulcan, nor indeed on its ECM equipment, resulted in the aircraft being withdrawn from assignment to NATO in the attack role. Some of the bomb carriers for 1,000lb weapons had been stored in various places and some had been scrapped. Similarly, the bomb aimer's ninety-way selector panel, needed in the cockpit to replace the nuclear weapon release panel, had been given no priority for preservation.

The thirty-two Vulcans still at Waddington were a mixture of aircraft powered by the two types of Olympus engine in service, the 200 series and the more powerful 300 series. The latter powered the aircraft which came off the production line modified for the USAF Skybolt missile fit. The missile was never acquired, but the prospect of our flying with maximum fuel plus 21,000lbs of conventional bombs made the aircraft selection easy. Within two days, ten of the 300 series powered aircraft were declared operational in the conventional role with activated air-to-air refuelling systems.

First thoughts about crew selection were that up to ten crews should be identified to match the ten aircraft. However, it soon became clear that crew training would put a huge demand on the Victor tanker and their air-to-air refuelling instructors (AARIs), who would have to fly in the Vulcan right-hand seat. HQ 1 Group decided that captains would require two day and two night-receiver sorties, under instruction, and the task simply could not stretch beyond a maximum of five crews. Also, as information came in about the operating base at Ascension Island and the number of refuelling operations that could be required just to take one Vulcan to the Falklands and back, there would have to be ten Victors at Ascension leaving ground handling room for only two other large aircraft. On Easter Monday, I asked the available squadron commanders to nominate their best crews. OC 50 Squadron came in later. The next day five were selected: Squadron Leader Montgomery, 44 Squadron; Squadron Leaders Reeve and McDougall, 50 Squadron; Flight Lieutenant Withers, 101 Squadron and Flight Lieutenant Gardiner, IX Squadron. In February 1982, Montgomery, Withers and Gardiner had taken part in the final Vulcan Red Flag exercise as had the OC IX Squadron, who nominated two of his crews. Montgomery, Withers and Reeve were the first to prepare for air refuelling training.

As the size of the training task clarified, so the organisation to support the task evolved. Operation Corporate aircraft and crews would need the support of operations and engineering personnel on a scale similar to earlier detachments for Red Flag and the SAC bombing and navigation competition. Personnel were drawn from across the station and some postings were put on hold. Command was invested in OC 44 Squadron, Wg Cdr Simon Baldwin, and the flight's headquarters established in operations wing. The engineering support, with the four primary aircraft, was placed on Alfa dispersal, immediately adjacent. Additional aircraft were placed on Bravo dispersal, just being vacated by IX Squadron.

Bombing and navigation training began for the selected crews on 13th April. The first task was to reacquaint them with the handling and release of live 1,000lb weapons. This was achieved by dropping 1,000lb retarded bombs on weapon ranges in Scotland and the Isle of Man. It was assumed that attacks would be made at night, so releases were made by radar alone and this provided an early opportunity to assess the accuracy of the aircraft bombing systems. The navigators practised astro-navigation over lengthy stretches of the North Atlantic. All the results were closely analysed.

Air refuelling training started from scratch. Under normal circumstances training would begin with crews attending ground lectures at the Victor OCU at Marham. There was no time for such luxuries. While HQ 1 Group was coordinating the availability of tankers, air and ground instructors came to Waddington to brief the crews. Daytime receiver training began on 14th April and was completed by the Montgomery, Reeve and Withers crews on the next day. By then it became clear that the limited availability of tankers would restrict the initial conversion to three crews. They completed their night training on 16th and 17th April but although Squadron Leader McDougall's crew completed day receiver training on the 17th, night training was delayed because of lack of tankers. Also it became clear that there was little chance of training Flight Lieutenant Gardiner's crew and they were released to normal duties. The Operation Corporate flight, with crews from 44, 50 and 101 Squadrons, quickly adopted the unofficial title '195 Flight'.

Realisation that possible targets would be vigorously defended by Argentine air defence forces led to a study of Argentine equipment and capability. Much of their weapons and radars had been acquired from western sources but the Vulcan's ECM equipment was arrayed against Soviet systems. The current fit would not suffice. Similarly, navigating the aircraft accurately over 4,000 miles of open ocean to a run-in point over the sea to attack an island target could not be done, except by using long-range search radar at high level to fix the aircraft's position, thus giving its presence some unacceptable advertising. New ECM and an accurate navigation system were required.

Vulcan flying over Lincoln celebrating the anniversary of Waddington being granted the Freedom of the City. (*Aviation Historian*)

Response to this request was rapid and led to some innovative engineering solutions.

Sometime earlier the RAF had purchased fourteen surplus VC10 aircraft from British Airways, primarily for their Rolls-Royce Conway engines. However, the VC10 navigation system included inertial navigation equipment. These were removed and fitted to both Vulcans and Victors. They worked well and solved the over-water navigation problem. The type of ECM equipment required was available from RAF sources, but existed in the form of underwing mounted pods. Faced with how to attach the Buccaneer AN/ALQ 101D or 'Dash 10' ECM pod to the Vulcan, Waddington's engineers located and examined the old Skybolt underwing mountings. They then built and fitted a mild steel beam to the mountings and attached the Dash 10 pod to the beam. Additional modifications to the 300 series aircraft had included cooling ducts for the Skybolt missiles and these allowed for the wiring for the Dash 10 to link back to the cockpit. The system was declared operational on 19th April. The following day crews began to operate the pod against ground equipment, hastily installed at the Spadeadam range in Cumbria, which simulated the emissions of air defence radars known to be operated by the Argentines and capable of being deployed to the Falklands. At a later stage, the Skybolt mountings were further modified to carry both Martel and Shrike anti-radar missiles.

Starting the second week of training the three primary crews had completed air re-fuelling conversion and were flying simulated combat sorties. These comprised climb-ing out to rendezvous with a tanker, topping up to maximum all-up weight (AUW) then completing a high-level navigation leg over the Atlantic, descending to low level over the sea and attacking island targets on the west coast of Scotland. In case there would be some flight to the target at low level over land, the crews practised night low-level navigation using terrain following radar (TFR) and released live 1,000lb bombs at low level on bombing ranges. Navigation, bombing and ECM training pro-gressed well, but major difficulties occurred in the air refuelling training as the Vul-can's refuelling probe suffered persistent leaks. All manner of devices were added to solve the problems which persisted right to the end of the second week. Only at the last minute was the Victor's refuelling valve stripped down alongside the Vulcan's no-tionally identical valve and it was found that the Victor had a small modification not carried out on the Vulcan valves because the system was out of service. Valves on the Vulcans were modified and most of the subsequent refuellings were achieved without significant leakage.

As international shuttle diplomacy ebbed and flowed from London to Washington and Buenos Aires, the atmosphere at Waddington was unlike anything previously ex-perienced. A part of the station was involved in the intensity of preparing to go to war, while the remainder was preparing for major peacetime ceremonial events or even clearing from the unit for new tours elsewhere. On Saturday 24th April, led by the No 1 Group Pipe Band, the four flying squadrons, with bayonets fixed, would escort their squadron standard parties through the City of Lincoln to celebrate the anniversary of the granting of the Freedom of the City to Waddington. Aircraft from each squadron would fly overhead. On 29th April IX (Vulcan) Squadron would disband with due cer-emony and, reviewed by the AOC-in-C RAF Strike Command, hand over the squad-ron standard to the newly-forming IX (Tornado) Squadron from RAF Marham. In the longer term, preparations were being made for a major ceremony to take place at Waddington on 1st July 1982 to disband the remaining three squadrons and formally end the era of the V Force as a chapter of RAF history.

On Monday 26th April we were informed that the chief of the Air Staff, together with AOC-in-C Strike Command, AOC 1 Group and the air commander of Operation Corporate, all RAF assets in the South Atlantic, would visit Waddington to brief the crews the following day. Then we would learn which target CAS wished us to attack. This decision would determine the type of attack profile. The options available were limited to low level, by day or night to deliver a stick of 1,000lb HE-retarded bombs, or, medium or high-level attacks by day or night releasing 21 x 1,000lb free-fall bombs. In any event, to give the best chance of a surprise attack, a descent to low level and an approach to the target area below radar cover would be the preferred option.

If the CAS wished us to target the runway at Port Stanley, the best form of attack against the now significant array of air defence radars, missiles and guns would be to climb from low level over the sea to medium altitude to release free-fall weapons to crater the runway. In the event, this is what he wanted. The plan, therefore, was to approach the target area below radar cover in complete radio and radar silence. At a point indicated by the INS the radar would be switched on to acquire the target area. Once the aircraft was aligned with the target it would climb to the chosen altitude where release of the free-fall bombs would guarantee a high enough velocity for the bomb to penetrate the runway before detonation. To achieve the maximum cratering effect the release height needed to be a minimum of 8,000ft above the target. CAS wanted us to prevent the Argentine air force fast jets from using the runway at Port Stanley. Thus the attack profile was determined.

By this time it was clear that diplomacy was unlikely to prevent the outbreak of hostilities and an attack by a Vulcan would take place as soon as the task force was ready for action. This could happen by the end of April. To prepare for this eventuality Squadron Leader Montgomery was appointed detachment commander in Ascension and his crew and an advance party of engineering personnel were selected, equipped and put on immediate standby to travel. The following day they deployed by VC10 from Brize Norton and arrived in Ascension on 28th April.

The Action Plan

The plan was to deploy two Vulcans to Ascension on 29th April. Three aircraft were prepared with 21 x 1,000lb HE bombs and maximum fuel. Squadron Leader Reeve and Flight Lieutenant Withers would deploy to Ascension rendezvousing with three Victor tankers over southern England. Squadron Leader McDougall, freshly qualified in air refuelling the night before, would accompany the formation to the completion of the first refuelling and, if that was satisfactory, return to Waddington. The entire departure, rendezvous and refuelling was to be carried out in strict radio silence, a procedure as yet unpractised and unfamiliar to the Vulcan crews. These same restrictions would apply to the combat operations except that the departure and refuellings would take place at night with up to ten tankers together with the primary and reserve bombers. It was quite clear that, if these complex procedures were to be achieved successfully, all of which was beyond the experience of the Vulcan crews, the expertise of the tanker AARIs would be required again and they would have to deploy as part of the Vulcan crew. Three somewhat surprised Victor AARIs accepted their fate and served with distinction as Vulcan crew members.

On 29th April IX (Vulcan) Squadron disbanded with due ceremony at a parade reviewed by the AOC-in-C Strike Command. As well as the parade in No 3 hangar, the day would include a reception in No 2 hangar and a formal luncheon in the officers' mess. A final ladies' guest night would be held the following evening. These, essentially peacetime, events ran in parallel with the bombing up and final engineering preparation of the three combat aircraft and the final briefing and flight planning of the crews. The C-in-C and AOC 1 Group took the opportunity, between ceremonial events, to have a final word with the crews and wish them well. In the early afternoon I slipped away from the mess and went to air traffic control for the departure. The three aircraft took off at about one minute intervals and climbed slowly to the southwest to rendezvous with their tankers. Some fifteen hours and forty-five minutes later, after a series of refuellings, the Reeve and Withers crews landed at Ascension. Word came through that the two aircraft had landed with no significant unserviceabilities and were being turned round ready for launch the following day. Final preparations for action were complete.

'Money is No Object' – The Vulcan in the Defence Suppression Role
Even as the first attacks were going in, the Air Staff was exploring all possible ways of improving the capability of the aircraft which could operate in the South Atlantic. Air Vice-Marshal Ken Hayr, assistant chief of the Air Staff, operations, visited Waddington to brief us on plans to enhance the Vulcan's capability. For the first and only time in my thirty years in the Royal Air Force I heard the phrase, 'money is no object'.

All manner of weaponry was considered, but what was to engage our engineers and aircrew over the next month were the anti-radiation missiles. The task force commander had become very concerned about the early warning (EW) radars which the Argentines had deployed to the Falklands. These were thought to be capable of guiding hostile aircraft towards the British ships, and the aircraft carriers in particular, by tracking the flight paths of the Harriers. Thus we began a remarkable period when several weapons, never before considered appropriate for the Vulcan, were fitted, trialled and, on two occasions, fired in anger in the Falklands.

The first such weapon was the anti-radiation missile. Already in service with the RAF, this missile was used by the Buccaneer in the anti-shipping role. For the Vulcan to carry this weapon, a second underwing attachment point would be required. Our engineers constructed a more robust underwing pylon than the one used for the Dash 10 pod and fitted it to the opposite wing Skybolt mountings. The more complex cabling was again routed through the existing ducting in the wing to a control panel at the AEO's station. As well as the firing mechanism, the panel contained the instrumentation to allow the AEO to interpret the signals received from the missile after target acquisition. The AEO would then direct the pilot to point the aircraft, and thus the missile, directly at the target, a process known as 'bore sighting'. The Argentine EW radars were made by Westinghouse and their operating frequencies were known. With this information the crew would be aware when they had acquired a radar transmitting in the anticipated frequency band. Martel was first flown on 4th May, by Squadron Leader McDougall and his crew, and test fired on Aberporth range the next day. The AEO firing the missile was Flight Lieutenant Rod Trevaskus.

By mid-May, the task force commander considered the threat to his ships so serious that efforts to destroy the radars should be made immediately. He could attack the radar locations with Harriers and naval gunfire but he had no anti-radiation missiles within the task force. Waddington was tasked to mount an attack using Martel as soon as possible. Two aircraft were prepared and deployed to Ascension on 16th May. They were ready for an attack on 18th May with Squadron Leader McDougall as primary and Flight Lieutenant Withers as reserve crew. In the event the attack was cancelled by the War Cabinet at the last moment. They could not accept the risk of civilian casualties from the Martel's large warhead. One EW radar was thought to be located very close to civilian housing in Port Stanley and one source even suggested that it was in the governor's back garden. On 19th May, the decision was taken to enlist the aid of the United States to use a smaller anti-radiation weapon, the AGM-45A, codenamed Shrike. Ac-

Shrike missiles fitted to a Vulcan at Waddington.
(*Anthony Wright*)

tion, resulting from dialogue between the Air Staff and the Pentagon, followed the next day. US technicians were flown to Waddington from the US Naval Air Station at China Lake, Nevada and the missiles arrived from USAF bases in Germany, where they were assigned to the F4 Phantom in the defence suppression role against Soviet radars. It was quickly established that both the Argentine EW radars and their Skyguard AAA control radars operated in frequency bands that the missile could acquire. Once again our engineers, together with their US colleagues, designed and built the fittings and modified two of the Corporate aircraft, XH593 and XM597, to carry the Shrike missile. On XH593 a double carrier was fitted to the new mounting allowing two missiles to be carried while retaining the Dash 10 pod. However, the attack profile for the weapon ensured that if attacks were made at night, thus avoiding any possibility of interception by Argentine fighters, the height of the aircraft during acquisition and pre-attack manoeuvring was above the operating altitude of any ground defences and the Dash 10 was no longer required. XH597 was further modified to carry four missiles, two on each carrier.

Attack Profile

A severe limitation with anti-radiation missiles is that the target radar has to be transmitting for it to be able to achieve acquisition, launch and homing to the target. Also, Shrike was an early design of this type of missile. We were soon made aware that to achieve a successful launch the missile had to be very accurately bore-sighted and released at a range between seven and four miles from the target. To achieve these release parameters the aircraft had to acquire the target while flying at heights of around 20,000ft, turn to aim the aircraft and missile directly at the target then enter a dive, still pointing directly at the target until reaching the release range. In practice, this meant setting up a fighter-bomber-type dive attack which, happily, the Vulcan was able to accomplish. However, the pilot had none of the information necessary to perform the manoeuvre, so a method had to be devised using information from both navigators and the AEO.

As the precise location of the radar was unknown, the aircraft had to approach the target area with the missile in acquisition mode. When radar signals were received the AEO's instrumentation would show whether the target was left or right of the aircraft's heading. The AEO would then direct the pilot to turn towards the radar until the aircraft was pointing directly at the radar head. The navigators would thus have a position line to the radar. The aircraft would then turn away from the radar and approach from a different direction, preferably 90° from the first approach. With a second position line to the radar, the navigators could fix the target's position. Then, using a combination of INS and the aircraft bombing radar, the navigators could direct the pilot to a position from where the dive attack could commence. This, at least, was the theory devised by the US weapons experts and our weapon testing specialists from Boscombe Down.

The pressure to launch an attack was so intense that there was no time to test either the weapon or the delivery method in the UK. Squadron Leader McDougall and his crew deployed to Ascension in XH593 just a week after the Martel mission was cancelled. A Boscombe Down weapons specialist, Flight Lieutenant Harper, flew to Ascension with the crew to familiarise them with the weapon and operating techniques while on route. One major advantage of a missile attack over a bombing mission was that two large fuel tanks could be fitted in the bomb bay giving the aircraft extended range and significantly reducing the number of air refuellings to reach the target area, even though there was a requirement to loiter over the Falklands for up to forty-five minutes. Also, the Vulcan crew was sufficiently practised in air refuelling procedures not to require the assistance of an AARI. The combat crew for the attack carried a third Vulcan pilot.

Remarkably, Black Buck 4 launched at dusk on 29th May, just ten days since Shrike became the preferred weapon. Some four hours down route, a rare HDU failure in one of the accompanying Victor tankers caused the mission to be aborted. Black Buck 5, the first missile attack mission by a Vulcan bomber, XH597, was flown on 31st May.

One of the most remarkable and unexpected parts of John Laycock's account of how RAF Waddington prepared for war was that IX Squadron was being disbanded at the same time and there was an important 'bonding' ceremony with the City of Lincoln. John had to ensure that Waddington coped with war and peace at the same time, a truly remarkable feat. He delegated operational control to Wing Commander Simon Baldwin who immediately arranged for Mel James, senior engineering officer of 101 Squadron, to put a team together with necessary spares to fly to Ascension.

John Laycock mentions the Skybolt and the need to amend the original provision to carry the missile so that the Westinghouse jammer, the Martel and Shrike missiles could be carried. **Mel James** explains how this was done.

The 'Pye' Pylon

Critical to the success and safety of operations on Black Buck sorties was the selection of aircraft which had been modified to carry the Skybolt 11,000lb missile in the 1960s. The Skybolt was big and the heavy fittings, still installed in the wing on the six aircraft available to carry the missiles, included two large steel lugs near the leading edge of the centre wing, and a further large steel lug several feet aft. All the lugs had been blanked off by simple metal-shaped panels. The forward lug cavity allowed space for missile control cables to pass through ducting in the wing to an operator's panel in the cockpit. Missiles and externally-mounted electronic systems in those days were self-contained with their own dedicated analogue controls, which had to be installed with hard wiring in the space available. The wiring and control switching required precise tests to ensure they would be reliable and function when needed and, in peace-time, this would mean many months of ground and flight trials to match the equipment with the plethora of rules and regulations surrounding installation of new and complex role equipment.

There would also be a need to conduct compatibility checks to make sure the new system or systems did not interfere with those existing on-board. But that was peace-time. There was only time now for a check to guarantee that the necessary electrical power for operation was available and that if weapon release was required, the firing sequence would not cause damage to the host aircraft. But perhaps even more important, there was a need to install a pylon on which to mount the weapon or mission equipment. In the 1980s it had been normal practice to design and install a pylon unique to the particular underwing store. The days of common carrier pylons, adaptable for a number of stores, were still some years away. What was needed first was a basic pylon attached to the wing, which could then have a dedicated attachment which would be delivered with the specific weapons or stores. Under a fighter aircraft, this would be a tall order; such a structural combination would probably touch the ground, but under the Vulcan wing, there was plenty of room. How to design and build such a basic pylon? Enter Squadron Leader Chris Pye, OC mechanical engineering (aircraft) squadron at Waddington. Chris was a graduate aeronautical engineer and in the late 1970s, had undertaken with me, at the RAF's expense, a masters degree in aircraft design at Cranfield University. That course had prepared us, under the RAF's advanced pre-deployment training system, to take on very high level engineering design activities on RAF aircraft.

Chris and his squadron were given the task of designing and building a basic pylon to fit under the Vulcan wing. Keeping artistic flair to the minimum, he used forged and cast steel plates and fittings to assemble a basic pylon structure which could be attached to the Skybolt mounting lugs and have the necessary stiffness and strength to support any of the stores being proposed for the Black Buck sorties. After initial weapon trials the pylon would be 'tidied up' somewhat and made aerodynamically smoother by the installation of a metal casing around the front. Whilst Chris' design skills were not in doubt, at least at station level, it was decided from 'on high' that the pylon should be checked by representatives from the stress office at Manchester where all the original aircraft design information was available. Two stress engineers duly arrived at Waddington and checked over the pylon. They left Waddington, satisfied with what they saw, within the day.

Ken Kendrick, the senior engineering officer on 44 Squadron who dealt with the aircraft at Waddington while Mel was in Ascension tells his story below.

Operation Corporate Engineering Support

In January 1981, I was posted to 44 (Rhodesia) Squadron at RAF Waddington to be the senior engineering officer and flight commander ground. This was my first foray into Strike Command and the Vulcan; it was to prove to be the most illuminating of my career thus far. I soon became familiar with the routine of managing the eight aircraft and the ground crew through the necessary training to keep the aircrew combat ready. The Vulcan aircraft had some unusual vagaries: one was that it had a propensity for blowing a complete set of electrical fuses for no apparent or discernible reason and to be completely serviceable when all the fuses were replaced; it also had a tendency to sit on its tail, if the fuel was incorrectly distributed within the airframe. There had been quite a few recorded instances of this phenomenon, and we had a very narrow escape one day on Alfa Dispersal.

The management of the fuel system was the responsibility of the occupant of the right-hand seat in the cockpit – normally the co-pilot. On the day in question, the co-pilot had been allowed by his captain to fly in the left-hand seat and on taxiing in, the captain had overlooked the requirement to pump fuel to the forward tanks; he was the last person to leave the aircraft and he suddenly became aware that he was not able to reach the ground as the bottom of the ladder was slowly moving upwards. Quickly realising what was happening, he directed that those of us waiting at the foot of the ladder should stand on it as a matter of urgency while he re-entered the cockpit to pump the fuel forward. Thus a very embarrassing occurrence was prevented.

All routines changed when General Galtieri's Argentinian troops invaded the Falkland Islands and, overnight, our postings were stopped. That Easter weekend in 1982 saw a level of professionalism and devotion to duty quite remarkable considering that only a few days earlier we had been running things down. Aircraft selection for the task of conventional bombing, AAR and long-distance flights were made and the necessary preparations begun. There were three squadrons remaining at RAF Waddington: Nos 44, 50 and 101 were each tasked to produce three aircraft to the required standard and the second line recovered one aircraft from maintenance so that by the late afternoon of Easter Monday, ten aircraft were complete and ready for operations. Reinstating the AAR systems was not without its problems and some more light-hearted moments. To prove that the systems were working and leak-free, the aircraft were first defuelled and then refuelled through the AAR probe. The driver of the refuelling tanker pumping fuel into an aircraft reported that he had pumped into the aircraft more fuel than the aircraft's tanks could hold and it was not long before fuel was seen leaking from the aircraft's radome. Investigation revealed that the AAR probe was leaking and that the radome was full of fuel.

Trials of the aircraft in its new guise were undertaken in short order to ascertain such details as oil consumption over extended periods, handling at heavy weights and bombing with 1,000lb bombs. Initially a trial with the Martel air-to-surface missile was performed but for reasons described earlier, the Martel was abandoned in favour of Shrike. The AUW at take-off was to be the heaviest the Vulcan had known and advice was sought from Rolls-Royce on the effects of increasing the maximum rpm of the engines and, since most of the engines' power is developed at the higher end of the rpm range, the fuel systems were adjusted to give a maximum rpm of 103%.

There followed a period of intense work and installation of additional equipment to improve the survivability of the aircraft and enhance their effectiveness. Although RAF Waddington was concentrating on the Vulcans, assistance was received from various other sections of the Royal Air Force. The Dash 10 ECM pod had a cooling system that required deionised water and RAF Honington provided the necessary deionising equipment, which was installed in the officers' toilet on Alfa Dispersal. Personnel from RAF Marham helped install the Carousel inertial navigation systems; Jetstream and Dominie aircraft from RAF support command were available and ferried parts and people around the country. When modifying the aircraft to carry an ECM pod and the Shrike missile, it had not been possible in the time available to introduce a 'clear aircraft' system switch to enable inert jettison of the stores. Hence, the underwing stores could only be fired in anger or downloaded on the ground; this shortcoming explains why the aircraft that was forced to divert to Rio de Janeiro when the refuelling probe snapped off during an air-to-air refuelling, did so still armed.

1,000lb bombs about to be loaded into bomb bay.
(*Mel James*)

Throughout this period of activity, it became obvious that the normal shift pattern of ground crew work was not compatible with the task. As a result, 44 Squadron ground crew went to twenty-four-hour working: twelve hours on and twelve hours off, with the two engineering officers overlapping both shifts. The station's commitment to provide aircraft for flying displays, passing-out parades and the delivery of aircraft to museums at home and overseas did not diminish and was completed alongside the operational flying and trials. It was noticed that every take-off and landing was monitored by a team based in a white van, which was parked in a lay-by on the A15 road adjacent to the threshold of runway 21. As the aircraft approached, a door in the side of the van would open, a camera would appear and, after the aircraft had passed, the procedure would be reversed. At the same time, a Soviet 'trawler' was in the North Sea in line with the runway's extended centre-line just outside the UK's territorial waters, a situation with which the aircrews were aware.

On the night before the deployment south, the chief of the Air Staff visited the station, met personnel and viewed the aircraft. He was highly amused by the graffiti that the armourers had painted on the bombs and expressed his gratitude to the troops for all they had achieved in such a short period of time. The aircraft deployed and flew into the history books.

In fact, the now famous Vulcan XM607 was there by a stroke of good fortune. Early in February 1982, during the implementation of a servicing instruction (SI), which involved a non-destructive testing technique (NDT), a serious crack was found in the aircraft structure, which was declared as Category 3 damage – i.e. damage beyond the capability of the station to repair. It was considered then that owing to the forthcoming run-down of the Vulcan fleet, the aircraft should be declared 'beyond economic repair' and should therefore be one of the first to be scrapped. However, XM607 was well liked by the aircrew and was a remarkably 'good bomber' and it had sufficient fatigue life remaining to allow it to continue flying until the squadron disbanded. Representation was made to the engineering authority (EA) at HQ Strike Command for a stay of execution for XM607 and for the funds to effect the repair. Fortunately, the previous SEngO of 44 Squadron was by then employed in the Vulcan office of the EA and a personal plea was made to him on behalf of XM607. He used his powers of persuasion to obtain the necessary authority for the work to be undertaken and in the following week, a team of airframe technicians from the maintenance unit at RAF Abingdon arrived at RAF

Farewell formation over Rutland Water after Operation Corporate. (*John Laycock*)

Waddington to restore XM607 to airworthiness. This was indeed fortunate because the aircraft met all the necessary criteria for modification to Operation Corporate requirements and was the first to be so modified.

When the aircraft landed at Rio on Black Buck 6, the captain was determined that the local authority should not impound the aircraft. He had already jettisoned into the sea, through the entrance door, all the paperwork and documents referring to the aircraft and its sortie and then, after landing, he taxied the aircraft to the front of the terminal building and parked it nose onto the grass to avoid it being towed away. The forthcoming visit to Brazil of the Pope encouraged the Brazilian authorities to cooperate with the release of the aircraft, obviously not wishing His Eminence to see a British war machine as he stepped from his aircraft. However, without the necessary manuals and paperwork the Vulcan could not be prepared for flight; hence, a complete set of aircraft manuals and a Vulcan towing arm were sent to South America by a RAF VC10.

After all the aircraft and crews had returned safely to RAF Waddington, they were attached to 44 Squadron for the remainder of its life: the squadron was disbanded on 31st December 1982. The aircraft took part in the Victory Parade in the City of

London forming an integral part of the flypast. A four-aircraft formation flew over the bases in the UK where Vulcan aircraft had been housed since their introduction to service.

The disbandment parade was held before Christmas 1982 and an early decision to conduct the parade in a hangar was sensibly made. Earlier in the year, the ground crew had watched with increasing mirth the attempts by the station warrant officer (SWO) to bring their counterparts on IX Squadron up to a reasonable standard of ceremonial drill, with countless rehearsals and extra drill. 44 Squadron personnel were briefed that we would do it right first time, which they did, much to the chagrin of the SWO, who thought there was a conspiracy to deny him his big day! So after just one working dress rehearsal and a full dress rehearsal, the squadron was reviewed by the C-in-C STC and, once again, performed brilliantly. At the last minute, and much to the SWO's disgust, it was decided to have one of the aircraft as a backdrop to the parade. By a complete and unknown coincidence the aircraft selected had been collected from the AVRO factory at Woodford by the reviewing officer when he was a flight lieutenant. The parade and ceremonial followed by a formal lunch for all ranks was a fitting conclusion for a squadron that had achieved so much in its sixty-five years of service to the country.

> As mentioned **Mel James** was engineering officer on 101 Squadron but had been chosen by Simon Baldwin to lead the support team at Ascension Island. His account of how he got everything organised and packed up at Waddington in record time is incredibly understated and he deserved a medal for the brilliant decision to take his Land Rover out in the transport aircraft despite being told it wouldn't be necessary.

It was Easter 1982 and I had taken the opportunity to take the family to Cornwall for a short holiday and to visit friends. Of course, we had been watching the news and developments in the South Atlantic as the Argentinian forces occupied South Georgia and made noises about recovering Las Malvinas. Even as the invasion appeared inevitable, it was nothing to do with us. We were running down and why would a heavy bomber be of use; it was a navy operation, surely?

I was washing the car outside my parents' holiday home near Polperro when the police car pulled up.

"Squadron Leader James?"

"Yes, what can I do for you?"

"Would you phone your squadron, sir. It sounds like they need you."

A quick phone call and a six-hour drive later the family was back at Waddington.

I had been asked to report to Wing Commander Baldwin, OC 44 Squadron and the station commander for a briefing. I couldn't imagine what the boss of 44 would need me for but, to be prepared, I diverted via eng ops to get an engineering perspective first. OC eng ops filled me in with as much as he could.

"We've been tasked with supporting the operation to recover the Falklands and OC 44 is in charge. The operation has been given the name Black Buck. Chief of the Air Staff is involved, C-in-C Strike and our AOC. To all intents and purposes, Scampton is already shut, so we're the only unit with bombs and the legs to get to the Falklands. Wing Commander Baldwin is putting together a team of specialists to work out the role we can undertake, and as far as the engineering detachment is concerned, you're it!"

The legs to get there? How are we going to bomb Argentinian forces from Wadding-ton? The answer soon came as I discovered that we would detach to Ascension Island, a tiny blob in the Atlantic Ocean about seven degrees south of the equator. The island had an airfield, named Wideawake (I bet it would be now), built during World War 2 by the Americans to assist with deliveries of aircraft to European and other theatres of war. The runway had been extended, along with several others in remote locations around the world, to act as a possible landing diversion site for the NASA Shuttle pro-gram. What facilities did the airfield have? No information yet, but an advance detach-ment of Nimrod and Victor aircraft would arrive soon. Was the American military in residence? Yes, but only a small detachment party from Patrick Air Force Base, Florida, which supplied their rations. The Americans were in charge of all movements on the apron but there was no engineering support.

The station was al-ready in full swing iden-tifying the aircraft which could be used for the operation. It had been decided to use Vulcans which had been modi-fied in the 1960s to oper-ate the Douglas Skybolt, a wing-mounted missile. The attachment points were blanked off, but the access ducting in the wings was still there.

Westinghouse Jammer ready to be loaded on to the Pye pylon with Corporal Pete Webb from RAF Honington. (*Mel James*)

Trials were in progress with Martel missiles and virtually every other weapon in the UK military inventory was under consideration. The flight refu-elling system, blanked off many years before, had to be re-instated. The engineering problems were soon fixed, in spite of fuel seals cemented up and badly fitted and in-stallation tools long lost! But getting crews up to an operational capability with refuel-ling was another thing – but that's a story for the pilots.

My task was to decide how many men I needed in what roles, how much detach-ment equipment I required, what spare parts I would need and how long it would take to get ready. Whatever numbers I came up with, there would be a maximum of two Hercules, maybe three, aircraft available to fly us to Ascension Island. I worked out that for engineering activities 7/24, I needed a deputy and twenty-eight technicians covering all technical trades including crew chiefs. If weapons new to the Vulcan were to be fitted I would need specialists from the weapons home units. I also had the pick of the best men from the three squadrons still active at Waddington – 44, 50 and 101.

My deputy would be Flight Sergeant Al Packer from 44. I would send him ahead of the main party to check out the airfield and prepare for our arrival. With one crew chief, an electrician and two mechanics he left Waddington on 27th April 1982 in an Andover aircraft with the nominated detachment operations crew, led by Squadron Leader 'Monty' Montgomery, to join a VC10 at Brize Norton heading for Wideawake airfield. The remainder of the ground party, including me, would depart Waddington later that evening with the ground equipment and spares.

Members of the Vulcan engineering detachment on Ascension Island. Far left is Corporal Webb who carried out urgent repair work on XM607's Westinghouse Jammer before its successful flight on Black Buck 1. (*Mel James*)

The Hercules duly arrived and we started to pack the aircraft as meticulously as possible to make good use of the space, each batch of equipment having been carefully 'chalked' on its pallet by the station movements staff. However, the first item to be taken on board was my squadron long wheel base Land Rover. I had been told not to take any MT; adequate MT for detachments would be provided on Wideawake airfield. I didn't believe a word of it. In the melee of setting up facilities for detachments of Nimrods, Victors and goodness knows what other aircraft types, someone was bound to lose out – and it wasn't going to be me. Having put the Land Rover in first, with pallets quickly surrounding it, it was impossible for anyone to demand that it be removed without causing undue delay to the aircraft's departure.

Personal equipment finally packed – including my camp bed, sleeping bag, mess tin and cutlery – and goodbyes for an unknown detachment period said, we were on our way in Hercules call-sign Ascot 4216 at 2230 local time. Eight hours and forty minutes later we arrived in a sultry Dakar airfield in Senegal, West Africa. We had already consumed the limited supply of rations on the Hercules so, although we were asked to stay with the aircraft while it was refuelled and the new crew took over, I decided to slip over to the terminal and stock up on sandwiches and drinks from the Air France catering department using cash from the local RAF movement officer's imprest fund. As I approached the airport building from the ramp, I was confronted by a very tall black security man in traditional Senegalese clothes. I'd heard the West Africans were tall, but this guy was big. Needing the toilet first, I rustled up my best schoolboy French.

"*S'il vous plaît, ou est la toilette?*"

"Down there, sir, on the left", came the reply in broad cockney.

"You're a Brit."

"Yes, sir. RAF police, but I thought I'd dress the part."

An hour or two later, we were airborne again for the second and last five-hour leg to Ascension; boredom was relieved somewhat by a pleasant chat on the flight deck with captain Squadron Leader Ron Tidball of 70 Squadron. Ascension certainly looked tiny and vulnerable as we made our approach.

The arrival brief was basic to say the least. Here's your pay book in case you need cash down at the American Volcano Club or in the Exiles Club in Georgetown. The Post Office has a stock of 'blueys', the blue folded air mail letter forms which would be sent free of charge back to the UK. The admin office was manned by personnel from RAF Scampton, control of the whole base site was under the command of Captain Bob McQueen RN, and the senior RAF officer was Group Captain Jerry Price, station commander at RAF Marham. Although RAF flying had mainly been restricted thus far to training and familiarisation, the Fleet Air Arm were omnipresent with a constant stream of Wessex and Sea King helicopters bringing stores from ships offshore. Until their operational presence was needed with the next phase of the deployment south, thirty-four marines from SS *Canberra* were put at our disposal for guarding our armed aircraft. Third battalion Parachute Regiment were also regular visitors but they had to be requested not to cock and check their live weapons while seeking shade under the Vulcan bomb bays!

Personnel accommodation was in the village of Two Boats, about half way up the major surviving volcano on the island known as Green Mountain. The increased altitude at Two Boats provided welcome cooler air, particularly for the airmen and SN-COs who were accommodated in six-man tents. Officers were housed in three line-astern single-storey blocks, similar to RAF SECO huts, named after planets. The ops crew, Monty and co, and I duly took over Mars Block which was mostly empty but for a dusty lino floor, but it had a shower and wash basins. From the block, we had a superb view of the bay off Georgetown which, at the time of our arrival, accommodated SS *Canberra*, SS *Elk*, HMS *Intrepid*, two hospital ships (SS *Uganda* and HMS *Hecla*) and a couple of Type 21 frigates.

As the owner of a Land Rover, I became very popular as the promised MT did not exist. The Nimrod detachment had found an abandoned American school bus, recovered it to a serviceable state, and christened it the 'Maggie T'. Two Sherpa mini-buses eventually arrived by Hercules and were used as crew transports. The only other vehicles were modified Land Rovers used by the SAS, as I soon discovered. If my detachment chaps were using the Land Rover, the technique for moving around the island was to stand by the road and hitch a lift. Soon after arrival, I stood on the road by Mars Block awaiting a ride to the airfield. The road above was unsighted because of the steepness of the terrain so it was not possible to know what vehicle might turn up. Minutes later, a Land Rover came over the rise, all wheels some three feet in the air as it leapt over the hill. It screeched to a halt beside me and the two occupants, in face-covering balaclavas in spite of the heat, invited me to join them.

The only available seat was a small bench in the back facing backwards and surrounded by a machine-gun turret. I clung on for dear life. A typical journey from Two Boats to Wideawake airfield took about twenty minutes. Ten minutes later, as we arrived at the airfield boundary, the SAS offered to let me go, most corners along the

Ground crew Vulcan servicing tents.
(*Bill Perrins*)

route having been ignored.

Thursday 29th April at about 1800 hours saw the arrival of Vulcans XM607 and XM598. The bomb bays and bombs on both aircraft were saturated in condensation due to the cold soak at altitude followed by a rapid descent into semi-tropical conditions. To my surprise XM598 was serviceable. XM607 needed a can change on the X-Band Jammer suite in the tail; otherwise it was also serviceable. A good start as we received a signal stating that operations would start the next day.

By 0300 on the 30th, XM607 was also serviceable and I sent a message via the DSSS[6] secure phone that both aircraft would be ready for operations that day. In view of the heat, both aircraft were fuelled to 90%. If the tanks had been filled to the top, there was the risk of fuel venting in the heat – we had already experienced a daytime temperature of 95°F. We would fill the tanks to 100% as evening fell. Since XM598 had arrived serviceable, it was prepared first and all functional checks completed. XM607 also suffered from a problem which was only apparent when a full fuel load was critical. The capacitors which provide an indication of fuel contents were often difficult, if not impossible, to calibrate exactly at the full and empty points. My procedure was to calibrate the system so that a zero indication meant the tanks were empty; this could mean that when tanks were full, and incapable of taking on more, the fuel indicator might read low. In 607's case, the indicator was reading 300lbs low but the tanks were definitely full. Squadron Leader John Reeve, the primary crew captain, was not happy with this so elected to take XM598 as his aircraft. 55 and 57 Squadrons had the lion's share of problems preparing their aircraft. Fourteen of their Victor tanker aircraft were prepared for flight and positioned for their exact location during the departure sequence. XM598 and XM607 were also pre-positioned on the ramp so that they were in the right location for taxi and take-off. All these movements were coordinated with the American ramp manager, Lonny, or his assistant Benji. With no markings at all on the ramp, and an inexperienced tug driver, the concept of spacing aircraft accurately so that they did not interfere with each other, either in terms of actual contact or causing jet blast damage, was a major problem. In fairness to the American ramp personnel, who were used to receiving and parking one C-141 cargo aircraft once per month, the problem of ramp spacing seemed insurmountable. My offer to drive the tugs was nevertheless rejected!

While the operational crews for XM598 and XM607 were getting dressed and ready,

---

[6] Direct-sequence spread spectrum communication system.

Monty's crew carried out Carousel navigation system checks and bomb release checks from about 2100 hours. John Reeve and Flight Lieutenant Martin Withers, captain for XM607, were then briefed by my engineering team on the additional checks we had carried out to prepare the aircraft for what could be a sixteen-hour flight. My avionics technicians had been working closely with the nav radars to ensure the navigation bombing system was tweaked to near perfection. The X-Band jammers, which should protect the crews from enemy radar detection, were working properly but, even on the routine peace-time training sorties of around five hours, were subject to glycol leaks which might cause overheating and cause the systems to shut down. The aircraft would have a very high take-off weight in the conditions present on the airfield with a full bomb load and wing-mounted stores, so landing gear and engines were given a final once over.

At 2200 hours, formal 'crew in' took place. Noise levels on the apron were already at a peak, with ground electrical power generators and cabin coolers operating on fourteen Victors and two Vulcans. At 2230 all engines were started and the pan was now a cacophony of engine noise, generator noise and anti-collision lights. XM607 had a crew-in snag; the Westinghouse ALQ-101 ECM pod, borrowed from the RAF Buccaneer fleet and attached to the port pylon, would not run up. Corporal Pete Webb, on loan from RAF Honington, quickly re-set the offending circuit breaker, and all was well. Telephone and Telex transmissions on the island were blocked at 2100 hours but it would have been impossible to use either on the airfield. At 2250 hours, the taxi sequence commenced. XM598, followed by a Victor, followed by XM607 were the last three aircraft away from the apron. XM607 became airborne at 2310 hours. The apron was now totally silent. The crew chiefs from 598 and 607 and I looked at each other without saying a word. That was the most incredible sight we had ever seen. All we could do now was wait.

The first event following the departure of the combined Victor and Vulcan fleet has been well documented. John Reeve returned in XM598 after trapping the seal of his cockpit direct vision window and suffering unacceptable noise levels. After burning off fuel at 20,000lbs per hour and flying at 5,000ft with airbrakes out, XM598 was light enough to land, two hours fifteen minutes after its departure. The crew also reported a couple of minor snags, but the aircraft was soon serviceable and ready to fly again. So Martin Withers and crew in XM607 had now moved up to the primary bomber slot. My team and I stayed on the ramp, watching the sequence of Victor tanker operations as they returned to refuel and fly again to rejoin the complex refuelling plan. I eventually stood down at 0630 but was woken by Monty's AEO, John Hathaway at 0815. He reported that the operation had been successful and XM607 was returning.

At 1445 hours on 1st May, the Victor 'mother' ship which had accompanied Martin Withers and crew to the target touched down, followed by XM607 at 1452 hours. After a brief welcome back to the crew, they were whisked away for an intelligence debrief before we started our engineering debrief. No 2 frequency changer needed replacing. The X-Band jammer would not run up, but the Westinghouse ECM pod had worked successfully and jammed an Argentinian Fledermaus radar which had illuminated the Vulcan as it approached the target. Not bad for a fifteen-hour sortie, but as we always used to say, the more you fly them, the more serviceable they stay!

Life on Ascension followed a similar pattern with the inevitable panics, shortage of spares, refuelling probe catastrophes, continuing fights for space on the ramp and even a fire in my Land Rover, until a planned lull in operations allowed me to return to Waddington for a well-earned break on 24th May.

The most noticeable difference I saw on my return was the effect of the pressures experienced by the Victor tanker fleet. Trials were well established for converting some Vulcans to the tanker role which became the responsibility of 50 Squadron. I spent a short detachment with 50 but my formal role as senior engineering officer on 101 Squadron ended with disbandment of the squadron in August 1982. Looking back, I suppose my time on Vulcans was very short, when compared with the long operational service of the crews, but it was definitely a very busy and rewarding time – and certainly unforgettable.

> **Mel James** told me one or two stories that confirm that some things never change whatever the circumstances. Not all were printable but I managed to choose one.

The Fridge

The arrival of hundreds of new operators, technicians and several new aircraft on Wideawake airfield meant we had to be creative when it came to domestic arrangements for those tied to the airfield during the working day and night. Being unprepared somewhat for the increasing fleet of aircraft on the airfield, the Royal Navy had set up a field kitchen on the ramp between the two lines of Victor tanker aircraft and the small base hangar, well away from the Nimrod aircraft on the opposite side of the ramp. The arrival of two Vulcans disrupted their plans. The dust blown up by a Vulcan manoeuvring into its parking position, between the field kitchen and the base hangar, was too much to bear. The navy duly moved their field kitchen well away from any aircraft. When they had gone, a lone refrigerator was noticed standing idly in the dust in the 100 yards or so between the Vulcans and the Victors. It had been left behind presumably because it was faulty. I and my technicians watched the fridge for the rest of the day; it did not move. As dark fell, I rallied my troops.

"Go and get that fridge. It's obviously unserviceable but if you electricians can't fix it you shouldn't be working for me."

The fridge was duly recovered – much to the annoyance of the Victor engineers who had also been watching it – and brought back to my tent. It was often said in the Falklands that the man who has corrugated iron is king (he can now keep dry). On Ascension, the man with a fridge was king (he now had a source of cold drinks in the searing heat). The fridge still had some food in it, albeit now somewhat 'past it' in the heat, but it was also pretty scruffy. As my old Nan would say, it needed a good fettle. The fridge was duly fixed and we had our source of cold drinks for the Vulcan techs on the ramp. In the late afternoon of the next day I was returning to my tent on the ramp when I noticed a burly Royal Navy warrant officer and young leading recorder seaman talking to my avionics trade manager, Chief Tech Parkinson. I broke into the conversation.

"Can I help you?"

"Nothing for you to be concerned about, sir."

"But you appear to be interviewing my airman, and your young assistant is busy writing something. What's it about?"

"We're writing a Summary of Evidence, sir."

"A Summary of Evidence in connection with what?"

"In connection with the theft of a refrigerator, sir, being the property of Her Majesty's Navy. We're taking a Summary of Evidence for a Summary Hearing and, I expect eventually, a Field Court Martial."

"Well, I told my guys to recover that fridge and I have quite a few comments to make about its general condition, as a food storage device, so when you've finished with Chief Tech Parkinson, you'll find me in that tent over there so you can take my evidence. If you're planning to court martial my men, you can court martial me!"

"That won't be necessary, sir."

"I insist!"

Some twenty minutes later, the warrant officer duly arrived in my tent – alone.

"Where's your recorder. I've got quite a bit to say."

"As I said, sir. That won't be necessary."

"I've been thinking about this situation while I've been waiting for you. I don't remember seeing you on the airfield or around Two Boats."

"We arrived on the VC10 today, sir. Sent by the Provost Marshal's office. But I think I can sort this out."

I reported the 'interview' to the senior RAF officer on the island, Group Captain Price, but heard nothing more about the proposed court martial and we kept the fridge. However, the corollary to this story is interesting.

Exactly twenty years later, at a time when I generally spent my holiday periods lecturing on cruise ships, I was giving one of my lectures on a popular cruise ship somewhere in the Pacific. I was telling the story of the fridge in my presentation on life on Ascension Island during the Falklands War. I had just finished telling the story when a voice from the back of the lecture theatre shouted, "I was that warrant officer". It transpired he had eventually retired from the Royal Navy and had taken up an appointment as the cruise ship's security officer. We became firm friends for the remainder of the cruise.

A fascinating account of how the Vulcans were got into the air and kept serviceable. Mel had a twenty-seven-year career in the RAF, during which he specialised in equipment reliability and safety and was the final OC Eng Wg at Cranwell. He retired as a wing commander in 1997 and continues his career as an aviation consultant, specialising in airworthiness and logistics.

While it was all happening at Waddington and Wideawake, **Tony Wright** was sitting in Northwood watching all the activity.

Operation Corporate – HQ RAF Northwood

As remarked elsewhere my flying on 50 Squadron was unexpectedly interrupted by the Falklands War. I was on leave but hearing that we were going to war over the Falklands certainly got my immediate interest. I reckoned that if the Vulcans were going to be involved then I would have a good chance of going, as our crew had taken part in Red Flag the previous year. However, when I returned from leave I was highly disappointed, to say the very least, to find that our crew wasn't going. The reason was that some of our crew already had posting notices. Other crews, including volunteers, had been selected and training had already started. This was imperative as three out of the four captains had never tanked before and three out of the four nav radars had never used a 90-Way conventional bombing panel to drop a stick of conventional bombs. As to the latter there were only a handful of us nav radars on the station that had.

At the time there was no indication that there would be anything more than one Black Buck raid. Considering the distance involved, Ascension to Port Stanley and return, and the Victor tanker involvement it was after all a huge gamble. However, in the end there would be seven raids planned of which I was involved in six. An Operation Corporate Black Buck cell at RAF Waddington was set up in liaison with the Vulcan detachment of aircraft, aircrew and ground crew already in situ on Ascension. The cell planned the raid Black Buck 1 which was carried out by Martin Withers and crew on the night of 30th April/1st May 1982.

However, after the success of Black Buck 1, with 21 x HE bombs, it was decided to mount another raid and, at the same time, to send a 'Vulcan man' down to RAF Northwood, from where the war was being directed, to be close at hand as the Vulcan advisor. As our crew had missed out taking part and I knew the Red Flag crews down on Ascension I was sent to Northwood just in time for Black Buck 2.

Our working conditions were rather ad hoc and chaotic to say the least. We worked on decks, in naval parlance, and physically down 'the hole', a massive underground bunker. I believe that I was on Deck Three. However, we were not able to use the large rooms, offices and briefing room because it was all NATO funded and NATO wasn't part of the war. Therefore, we had to make do with small rooms and offices, often with three specialist advisors sharing. I was with a Harrier pilot, an ex-student of mine at RAF College Cranwell, and a Victor tanker navigator. When it came to major briefings these were given in a larger office, only by comparison with people crammed in the majority standing and some sitting on the top of tables and filing cabinets. I therefore knew what the situation was with regards to all aspects of the war as it happened, apart from submarines where there was a separate briefing to only a select few elsewhere.

Black Buck 2 was carried out again on the night of 3rd/4th May using 21 x HE bombs. My group captain at Northwood, who reported to Chief of Staff AVM Chesworth and Air Marshal Sir John Curtiss the air commander, wanted me to hazard a guess as to the success of the attack. No one else could give a definitive answer as cloud was covering the target area during the next day and therefore no photographic evidence was readily available. I could only say how experienced the nav radar was, whom I knew well, and leave it like that. I was in regular contact with my colleagues Monty Montgomery and Bill Sherlock on the Vulcan detachment on Ascension. This was via an RAF secure computer system and a classified, secure, telephone passing armament changes and decisions, made both by Waddington and Northwood.

Unfortunately, Black Buck 3 on 16th May was cancelled due to poor weather and on Black Buck 4, the night of 28th/29th May, all aircraft, Vulcan and Victors, returned to base due to a Victor tanker's hose drum unit (HDU) that had failed five hours into the sortie.

Certain things always stick in my memory. The first was of one poor officer who had the unenviable job of writing the diary on the war as things happened. This involved wandering from office to office asking people what was going on in their sphere. As everyone worked on a need to know basis he was politely told that they couldn't tell him anything. I had visions of no diary ever being written. Each evening at the end of my shift I went to Watford as I had elected to stay with my parents rather than in the mess. After an intensive few hours of experiencing war, knowing ships such as HMS *Sheffield* had been blown up and people killed, it felt surreal to drive out of the gates of Northwood along a calm, tree-lined country road, then along through Watford High Street with people shopping, chatting and leading a normal life.

Soon after the invasion on the 21st May I was recalled to Waddington as I was needed to be part of the team working in the Black Buck cell. Therefore, I handed over my duty at Northwood to another nav radar.

Black Buck 5 on the night of 30th/31st May employed new tactics which should have happened on the earlier Black Buck 4 mission. The Vulcan's bomb bay load of 21 x HE bombs was changed for four Shrike missiles to be carried on pylons, under the wings, two on each side. It was the first anti-radar mission on the Falklands during which three Shrikes were launched.

Black Buck 6 on the night of 2nd/3rd June, again an anti-radar mission, was launched carrying four Shrikes. Once airborne and on their way no further communication was made as briefed. I stayed in the cell for some time and then eventually drove back home. Little did I know what was going on in the air but just after 6pm I was greeted by my wife saying that my mother had just telephoned to say that while watching the six o'clock news on TV there were pictures of a Vulcan that had just landed in Rio. I dismissed this saying that my mother probably wouldn't know what a Vulcan looked like and that it couldn't be true. When I turned on the TV and saw another bulletin I knew that she was absolutely right. I had to return to Waddington and then started speaking to the RAF air attaché in Brazil by telephone, to negotiate the return of aircraft and crew. As a result the crew were detained, and spent a week in Rio. Neil and crew, minus Shrike, flew the Vulcan back to Ascension and then returned to Waddington. The proviso from the Brazilians was that both the crew and that particular Vulcan were not to be used again in the conflict. As to their homecoming, the only person to meet them on arrival at the pan on shutdown was me! No other senior aircrew officer was available. So after greeting the grinning, sun-tanned crew and exchange of a bit of banter we all went off to the operations block where I'd arranged champagne and for the families to be there awaiting them. The crew were appreciative of my efforts and handed me a bottle of Brazilian, Cerveja Antartica, beer. I've still got the bottle. It's now empty of course.

Black Buck 7 on the night of 11th/12th June was flown by Martin Withers who had carried out the first attack. The armament was switched back to 21 x HE Bombs to target airfield facilities. This was the last of the Vulcan sorties as the Argentinians surrendered on 14th June.

On 12th October 1982 I was in one of the three Vulcans that took part in the Falklands War Victory Parade flypast over the City of London. The salute was taken by the Lord Mayor of London, accompanied by Prime Minister Margaret Thatcher, outside the Mansion House.

> These accounts demonstrate what can be done in an incredibly short timescale if the situation arises. There is a tendency to remember the names of people at the spearhead of this amazing campaign but, as the above accounts makes clear, there were an enormous number of people all over the UK and in Ascension that worked very hard to make the Black Buck raids so successful.

Chapter Thirteen

WIDEAWAKE AND PORT STANLEY

An enormous amount of work had been done by the planners and the engineers to prepare for the Black Buck sorties but in the end it was the crews who carried out the operations. This chapter explains and describes how these very risky flights were carried out flying in uncharted regions.

The first account is by **'Monty' Montgomery** who was detachment commander at Ascension and was very much involved in the preparation and flight testing of the aircraft. He and his crew flew reserve on Black Buck 2, 5, 6 and 7.

In early 2007, Martin Withers and I were invited by the MOD to pay a visit to the Falkland Islands with a group of veterans during events to recognise the twenty-fifth anniversary of the Falklands War. Flying back to Ascension Island was a strange sensation which was not improved by finding that we were travelling aboard the oldest flying 747 in the world operated by an airline of which neither of us had heard.

'Monty' in front of one of Martin's craters on the Falklands,
now excellent duck ponds.(*Alastair Montgomery*)

Stepping out onto the tarmac at Ascension, everything had changed and yet nothing was different. In the dark, the wind from the hidden sand blasting machine blew across the ramp straight out of the same furnace it had all those years ago. There were now a few fancy buildings and a lot more tarmac; but, as the light spilled over Green Mountain and the other delightful ochre volcanoes of Ascension, old déjà vu was creeping up on us. Was it really twenty-five years since I had stood just a few yards from here on the edge of what had then been bundu? Twenty-five years since I watched, in awe, the noise rolling out of the dust, the heat and the dark as Victor after Victor roared off down the runway, disappearing out of sight over that dreadful hump (as an added aid to concentration there was a rather large hill on each side of the runway, blessedly hidden by the dark) and appearing again as they sought the safety of height. Then, the quite different noise of four Olympus as first one and then a second very overweight

Vulcan set off on the mission that was to start one of the strangest wars in our history.

Hindsight is always a gift and the number of pages written about Black Buck could probably stretch from Ascension to Stanley and back. The run up to Black Buck 1 following the selection of three, later four, crews has been dealt with in many books and articles not least Rowland White's stirring book *Vulcan 607*; and, much of the difficulties of the early days recorded in the interesting and fascinating (if not always entirely accurate) film: The Falkland's Most Daring Raid. The achievement of the Vulcan and Victor crews and, in particular, the remarkable fortitude of those on BB1 – and specifically Martin Withers and Bob Tuxford – has rightly been recognised. However, not enough attention has focussed on the remarkable work of the engineering and ground staffs at both Waddington and Marham: the dedication of the planning teams, at RAF Waddington, overseen by John Laycock and led by Simon Baldwin; and, of course, the triumph of the Vulcan airframe.

Apart from all the problems surrounding providing the crews with the specific training they needed to undertake whatever the mission eventually was to be, a great deal was required of the Vulcan itself. Three sets of issues were fundamental: identifying and solving the basic engineering problems set by the nature and length of the likely missions; identifying and matching logistic requirements; and, finally, managing, in every sense, the fuel.

Six airframes, modified to carry Skybolt — a stand-off weapon designed in the 1950s —were quickly identified and this allowed the fitting of an initially rather crude and a later little more refined pylon known, after its designer, as the Pye pylon. This allowed the carriage of critical ECM and, later, Shrike and Martel missiles. Harold Macmillan probably did not have us in mind when he made his agreement in 1960 with President Eisenhower; however, without the availability of these modified aircraft with their up-rated 301 series engines, the mission would probably not have got beyond the planning stage. As an aside, it is a fact of the Falklands War that every type of aircraft that took part – all judged fit to face the Soviet Union – was extensively modified and the Vulcan was no exception.

Less controversial for engineers was the fitting of a twin Litton Carousel navigation system. This box was bolted on behind and below the first pilot's seat and was therefore directly accessible by the plotter. On our third night flight, the first with this BA-style kit fitted, someone from the depths of MOD announced that this would require 'at least' one year of trials before being authorised for use. We were duly able to report that it worked just fine after the first flight and it performed better thereafter as inertial platforms do! In fact, on the next sortie, it was good enough to use to carry out an 'internal aids' approach to land[7]. Indeed, this inertial platform was key to operating over the long distances in the South Atlantic.

Much work had to be done to restore the functionality of the conventional bombing system. This was not inherently difficult – it just took time to complete on the small number of airframes that three crews were also trying to fly and, of course, no

---

[7] Nav radar gives runway distance/runway deviation/nominal height info to the pilot instead of a ground radar controller.

one had any idea of how much time was available. To cloak this with the perspective of hindsight, the very first AAR intro sortie was flown on 14th April and we deployed to Ascension Island on 28th April.

For many years, AAR had been a black art only able to be mastered by fighter pilots and a few and therefore superhuman Victor pilots. While something of an aerial joust, it was not only challenging but eminently enjoyable. Some of our early efforts were none too impressive; indeed, with some aplomb, it was possible to get the basket almost into the starboard engine intake whence it banged off the fuselage next to the nav radar's window. This did little for the morale of the rear crew or, indeed, those in the watching Victors who were more used to the supermen mentioned above. But enough about my own efforts. I should add that Martin Withers claimed a 'first time' success, much to the chagrin of his air-to-air refuelling instructor (AARI), Dick Russell, and this was long before 'hindsight' even turned up.

While we might not have mastered the art, thanks to the patience of Victor AARIs, who, now and then, peaked out between fingers, we soon reached an adequate skill level – by day. However, the fact was that the probes leaked. There was some concern that our, okay then my, somewhat agricultural skills were not helping and may have been weakening joints within the probes. A mix of solutions was tried: the first two involved simple mechanical barriers on the probe and upper nose to deflect the fuel. Simple, and simply ineffective. The pilots then suggested fitting vortex generators to the nose to mix the airflow to evaporate the fuel: clever, and entirely useless. At this stage, the engineers went back to first principles and examined the probes internally, to find that, in almost every case, an internal seal had been fitted back to front.

This had all taken time and used up probes. I did not help by knocking the end off one on what was meant to be a routine test flight of other systems. It is worth reflecting on what took place as it had something to say about our training. It was late on a Saturday evening and we flew as a four-man crew. We met up with a Victor somewhere over east Lincolnshire and everything was absolutely normal as we carried out two dry prods. On the third approach, as the probe hit the basket, merry hell broke loose: the windscreen disappeared under a flood of fuel; more warning lights flashed up than I thought existed; and no immediately useful advice came from the back of the aircraft. My concern was to miss the Victor and I turned down and to the left. Eventually, everything was sorted out.

Various engines and electrical systems were started up and we set off for Waddington and the stern stares of selected engineers who were now going to have to spend what little was left of Saturday and most of Sunday sorting out the mess. And it accelerated the hunt for serviceable probes which was taking place in the most unusual places. Ask Castle Air Force Base who took the probe off their static display Vulcan and sent it back to the UK!

In addition to the engineering conundrums around the fuel system, and the need to bring three crews quickly up to an adequate standard to refuel day and night as part of a complex sortie, there was looming a much greater fuel issue that would only really become apparent during the transit of the two armed bombers from Waddington to Ascension Island.

In the final days prior to deployment, the crews had built up to a composite night sortie. This consisted of a series of refuelling tracks; releasing 7 x 1,000lb bombs at Garvie Island just east of Cape Wrath; a low level route through and around the Western Isles followed by a pop-up attack on Jurby range on the Isle of Man. The sortie concluded with another refuelling exercise and recovery to Waddington. All of this was fairly challenging but far from being exceptional. Crews had been chosen for their breadth of experience, particularly at night and low level, and two had recently undertaken a Red Flag exercise in Nevada. The real demand was getting the engineering requirements and the crew training to come together in a workable timeframe. All of this was played out to a political backdrop which, while not of an immediate concern to the flying crews, was certainly ever present. Additionally, tiredness amongst air, ground and planning teams was an issue. Excluding the nine-hour transit to Ascension, the three crews each flew around forty hours, most in relatively short, high intensity sorties, in fourteen days. Ground crews and engineering officers worked untold hours while the planning team at Waddington, with others at group and MOD, game-planned out what seemed an ever increasing number of options. It was the same at Marham.

As crews, we spent time on target study and, in particular, on considering attack tracks and threat dispositions; however, much of this was left to those led by Simon Baldwin. Nevertheless, one area was not, at this stage, given enough attention: fuel consumption. There was a fairly pragmatic reason for this. The urgency had been to make sure machines and crews were capable of attempting the sort of mission envisaged by the air staffs. By the time that point was reached, time had run out and the crews had to deploy, so some issues had to be left until Ascension.

Crew selection has been dealt with elsewhere and I was bitterly disappointed not to be chosen as the lead crew; however, it was an honour to be made detachment commander with the understanding that our chance would come. Little did I know, this new found status would often lead me to face up to the wrath of Captain Bob McQueen, the commander of Ascension Island and the most terrifying man in the world whose contribution to events have never fully been recognised! There was still a great deal to do to translate what had been learned in a few short weeks of training into an operational mission: but we were on the move. I could write a book about Bob McQueen – he was remarkable and an absolute dead ringer for Trevor Howard. Captain Bob's opening words were along the lines of: "What the **** are you here for?" In truth, without him, the place would have collapsed. It was he who insisted that when McDougall and crew landed by VC10 that I put them straight back on the same AC! I did, but only after feeding them a lot of beer.... I have never been quite forgiven. But Captain Bob really was a tiger with a heart of gold. He wrote a short book called *Island Base*.

Ascension opened up a new experience in every way. Much time was lost sorting out accommodation for the air and ground crews. The latter were in a tented city near the airfield; by various means that I will deny, an almost derelict half Nissan hut/barrack block was found at Two Boats. This paradise – christened the Delta Hotel and with a hand-painted signpost showing a severed right arm dripping blood with eighteen camp beds and a Hercules crew next door – with one toilet and wash basin – was probably much better than many of our predecessors had in their day. However, it was about 4km from the flight line and this distance and lack of transport caused innumerable difficulties. The first imperative, however, was to integrate as closely as possible with the Victor detachment.

The Victor teams were superb. They were dug in and they were well equipped. In addition to a full air ops and eng ops team they had a modern marvel: a photocopier. And most importantly, they had experience. It should also be added that, having been just about the first to land on the island, they had grabbed all the best rooms. Indeed, their block even had a toilet. However, the five-star accommodation, showers, toilets and within 500 metres of a bar, had been nabbed by the Nimrod crews – *as they had been to ASI before!*

Two Boats village and the Delta Hotel with Bill Perrins. Normally a school room. Delta for Vulcan and DH for direct hit. (*Bill Perrins*)

The first step was to set up Vulcan ops; as this consisted of an empty desk and two chairs, it was not a time-consuming process. As quickly as possible, we settled down with the Victor crews to sort out the flight profile required to get a Vulcan from the island to Stanley. At this stage, none of the three tanking-qualified crews had flown in a formation of more than three aircraft. The experience of the Victor teams during long-range MRR missions – and their long familiarity with deployment planning – highlighted the scale of the problem; in particular, the number of tankers that would be required to get a Vulcan onto the target while retaining enough fuel on the transit down to return to Ascension and, post target, to have sufficient endurance to reach a recovery rendezvous point.

Readers should not be fooled by some of the rather simplistic diagrams that have appeared in books and articles over the years that claim to show the refuelling plan for Black Buck 1. In most cases, the author has been trying to make understandable a very complex plan. Managing the movement of this cargo of fuel down the South Atlantic was extremely difficult for those in the air: a paper plan, no matter how good, was one thing; translating that into a fleet of aircraft in the dark and under radio silence was quite another. And it was here that the addition of the AARIs to the Vulcan crews, particularly in the early sorties, made a crucial difference; these pressed men actually understood those diagrams where – for the moment – we did not. And their key role was to choreograph the Vulcan into its part of the aerial 'pas de many' that was about to take place.

The broad outline of 'The Plan' was that Victors would depart Ascension first with the two Vulcans at the back of the stream. As the formation moved down the Atlantic, Victors would top up Victors and the Vulcans at various refuelling 'brackets'. At some stage, one Vulcan would return while the Victors would use their fuel to get a 'Long Slot' Victor to the final refuelling point with enough fuel in that aircraft to allow it – somewhat further down the line – to give the Vulcan enough fuel to get to the target and, crucially, back to a rendezvous point to be met by a further clutch of Victors. As a plan, it was reasonably understandable if potentially challenging.

The first question asked by the tanker team at the initial planning meeting was fairly simple – "what will be the average fuel burn per hour of that thing?" Good question....

Our team, expected to answer quickly, was pilot, co-pilot, navigator on occasion, and a very worn copy of the Vulcan ODM. Those not familiar with this tome – which pre-dates programmed calculators far less computers – should know that it was a fairly large book containing graphs and charts to allow crews to work out vital flight data: take-off distance required; un-stick speeds; safety speeds; and, of course, fuel consumption for various aircraft weights and at different altitudes. Simply put, thanks to much careful work by development crews (people such as Tony Blackman) before the aircraft entered service, putting in one set of data allowed an output to provide the desired figures. Or, in our case, not!

In the case of the fuel consumption graphs, the matrix is small and any attempt to enlarge on the now vital photocopier only built in inherent errors. More importantly, with all the stuff added on, we were well beyond the weight scale shown on any diagram. The Vulcan maximum – and maximum did mean *not to be exceeded* — take-off weight was 204,000lbs. Normally, after take-off and a climb to 40,000ft plus ten minutes, the weight would be around 185,000lbs and, at this altitude, the fuel burn would reduce with weight from around 11,000lbs an hour to about 8,000lbs an hour.

With 21 x 1,000lbs bombs in the bay and the considerable extra weight on the wing pylons, the Black Buck bombers would take off at a weight of around 208-210,000lbs. Moreover, AAR is very difficult in the upper air due to decreased density; consequently, much of the transit would be around 28,000ft. And, as the aircraft would be manoeuvring in a large formation, additional fuel would be used just to maintain position. More crucially, with regular refuelling brackets to allow recovery to Ascension, the weight of the aircraft until the start of the last refuelling bracket was unlikely to be below 195,000lbs. No Vulcan had ever refuelled at these weights. Also, at some stage, a contingency was required for the notoriously bad weather that inhabited the tropics. So, "what is your average fuel burn in that thing" was a *very* good question indeed.

In the first instance, we did our best to interpolate the charts to come up with a figure. The Victor team then used their own mystical charts to work out just how much fuel had to be delivered to each bracket; the skill and patience of the Victor planners,

Barry Ireland and Colin Haigh, in ensuring final success was as remarkable as it was unsung.

We were very aware of the inherent danger of coming up with a figure 'to make the plan work'. There were, after all, a limited number of Victors and enough had to be retained for the recovery of the Vulcan after the attack. So, while the initial figures looked workable – we recognised we did not have real data. With hindsight, we should have asked Waddington to trial an aircraft at these weights and height – although I suspect the answer might have been more benign than turned out to be the case. I later found out that work was going on in MOD and at HQ 1 Group to try and calculate representative figures; if so, nothing came to us. This, of course, does not mean it was not sent. It is probably difficult now for many to realise how limited communications were in 1982. The age of mobiles and email was a long, long way off. The only secure – without resorting to teleprinters – link to Waddington and MOD was via a somewhat superannuated and rather strange link known as DSSS. Now, in the rush to deploy, I had been told nothing about this fancy piece of kit and had no idea of the voice gymnastics involved in using it. So, when I hitched a lift (the only way to do this) from Two Boats down to Wideawake to the shed where air ops was located, as opposed to tanker ops which was in a tent, and asked to speak to Waddington, the ops officer sensibly asked if I knew how to use the kit. Now, no-one wants to appear an idiot especially when they have just arrived as a precursor to the Mighty Bomber that was certain to sort out the Argies in one fell swoop... so (stupidly) I said:

"Oh yes, of course."

There followed some mumbo jumbo with tapes being inserted into various orifices which only confounded my confusion somewhat. Where, I thought, do I speak into this thing? "Ok, sir," he said, smiling, I thought, just a little too wisely; "You can go ahead." Luckily, he nodded in the direction of what can best be described as one of those booths that lucky contestants used to occupy in quiz shows in the 1970s. So, I made my way to the booth, rather ridiculously wondering if I knew the name of the highest lake in South America....and bravely spoke into the machine: "Waddington PLEASE."

Donald Duck answered: "Yoo a wanta waddowheresir?" "W-A-D-I-N-T-O-N" I answered in Duckspeak. "Ah, WADELINGTOWN" she appropriately answered, still wearing the bucket over her head. I was getting the hang of this. Eventually, I got Waddington or, Wadlingtown as seemed much Duck and Disney like. Amazingly too, I reached John Laycock, the station commander. Not so amazing really, as the support staff at Waddlington, I mean Waddington, were working as long hours as we were and had been patiently waiting for a word. However, the 'conversation' was a farce. It was all but impossible to inject any opinion or views at all; instead, the conversation had to be limited to the basic facts. And maybe that was no bad thing: the time for argument or discussion was long gone, I needed simple orders and I got them. It was dawning on me that what I would get now would, thankfully, be instructions and it was up to me to execute them; I could wish for no more.

Later, we had access to a secure word data system known as ASMA which transformed communications. However, this beast was at the airfield while we slept at Two

Boats. Unsurprisingly, every time it went off, one of us was called for; and usually, it was of no importance. Indeed, the stream of well meaning but irrelevant traffic – almost always from MOD or Northwood and not Waddington — was to become one of the banes of my life at that time. Best of all perhaps was the useful message, top secret of course, authorising me to allow crews to 'exceed 250kts at low level'. Not a mention of the fact that someone had noticed our take-off weight! Anyway, that was for us to fix.

There is a side story to the arrival of the bombers which highlights how little there was on Ascension Island and just how naive about the whole thing I was. As I have hinted, we were not quite in the Costa Smeralda-style accommodation of the Nimrods or even the more Magaluf standard of the tanker boys; there is a degree of exaggeration and perhaps jealousy here. About two hours before the bombers arrived, I realised that I was tired, a trifle hungry, constipated and probably smelt quite bad. Our rushing around the island since arrival had not allowed for any activity to tackle the issues raised above. However, I knew that I would shortly be off to air traffic control to oversee the arrival of the aircraft and, from my long experience of that branch of the armed forces, I knew the tower would be well equipped with shower, toilets, a generous kitchen and a welcoming team. In the picture section there is a photograph of the absolutely basic Wideawake air traffic control tower at Ascension Island: The 'tower' was managed by a US Air Force sergeant whose only real role was to pass the wind speed. It is worth remembering that for a few hours just one day later, this would be the busiest airfield in the world. Wideawake indeed!

Back at the Victor tent, we were still struggling with identifying a workable plan. Our inability to come up with a consistent fuel usage figure was not helping. We had been hoping for real figures from the two transit aircraft. However, their departure had been delayed and, at any event, we needed a figure now to get on with planning. Inevitably, tempers were frayed: the Victor crews were quite understandably aghast that we did not know our expected fuel burn while we could not explain that we just did not have enough data and did not know why more fuel could not be added to the party. The reason for the latter, of course, was that there was a limit to the number of tankers on the island – which already comprised almost all of the Victor fleet. All of this may seem unimportant now, long after the event, but the stresses and strains were evident long through the evening as calculation was followed by recalculation and re-thought plan was followed by another re-jigged diagram.

Some sense was brought to the proceedings by the calm counsel of Group Captain Jerry Price, Marham station commander and the air element detachment commander at Ascension Island. After a lot of discussion and many visits to the 'Penguin Phone', we discovered that the Vulcans were delayed twenty-four hours by the same problem: lack of fuel or, more specifically, lack of tankers, after all, most of them were on the island. However, the delay gave time for careful thought and, just as important, some rest.

The new day brought a new impetus and a plan was finalised. It was not risk free. The number of tankers now planned into the formation for the outbound transit meant that tankers off-loading at the first bracket would need to be recovered, turned and launched to generate the recovery tanker force. Perhaps most significantly, the fact that we just were not sure of the burn rate in the Vulcan meant that those tankers going furthest south could be almost as stretched as the Vulcan. Consequently, it was decided to turn one of the recovered first wave tankers into a contingency – a terminal airborne tanker (TAT) ready to recover the

The fuel supply to Ascension and Wideawake came by pipe from the tankers to the shore and then overland. (*Alastair Montgomery*)

long stop Victor if it became short of fuel. With all the hindsight now flapping about, this decision should have brought two people – Jerry Price and Trevor Sitch – the Seer of the Century Award.

When the bombers arrived, the crews, and Martin and John in particular, were surprised at the brevity of our (genuine) welcome. We wanted our hands on their fuel figures. At that moment, BB1 was less than twenty-four hours away and we had to get much more serious about our consumption figures to ensure we could get the right amount of fuel to the right place. Unfortunately, one crew had used the time-honoured chinagraph pencil on plastic method of recording the figures and these had been wiped clean except for the last three-hours worth of data. The second crew had more information but not enough to allow a really confident review of their consumption. Neither crew had realised how important this would be and, like me until a few days previously, retained the view that there would always be a tanker available! However, by careful questioning of the AARIs and the pilots and some recalculations of how much fuel had been exchanged, it was clear that our assessment of a fuel burn of around 12,000lbs/hr fell short: 14,000lbs/hr – or even higher, was more likely.

With pride, the crews were delivered to the Delta Hotel which had been scoured clean during the day and were shown their luxury camp beds. One navigator brought us down to earth with his pre *Trip Advisor* viewpoint: 'What a Sh*thole.' Ah well.

Thus, a plan was built and the next evening the Victor and Vulcan crews crammed into the tent for what must have been the most surreal operational brief for many years. There were still nagging doubts that the plan might be a bit short – and, as it transpired, it was not quite good enough. Despite all the contingencies built in, these were not enough to cope with the additional factor of appalling weather in a key section of the march down the Atlantic well described elsewhere including the difficulties of RV join-up at night and the sequential positioning for paired refuelling at Bracket 1. It was the fortitude of crews and the bravery of individuals that accepted risks well beyond the normal that made the mission a success. And that too was well beyond the normal.

Of course, lessons were quickly learned and the fuel planning for subsequent missions was much more effective. The key innovation was splitting the tanker waves and, if I close my eyes now, I can look up from the front of a Vulcan cockpit as if back on Black Buck 7 and see the final wave of tankers – passing over 8,000 feet above us on their way to the long stop and saving fuel with a higher level transit. The exploits of the McDougall crew on Shrike missions, long inadequately recognised by commentators if not those in the know, is well described in David Castle's piece elsewhere in this book.

All in all, the aircrews, the planning staffs, the ground engineers and support staff got the very best out of the airframe. That the airframe was capable of accepting and integrating all the modifications rushed onto it in just a few weeks left many of us wondering what kind of weapons platform we could have had if only a fraction of the funds expended on upgrade programmes on the B52 had been spent on the Vulcan. Even the Americans ask that.

Black Buck briefing.
Right to left: Nick — intelligence, Group Captain Jerry Price, Neil McDougall, Monty, Peter Ford hidden behind OHP, and two Victor crew 'Footy' and Terry Anning. Note loud hailer on table used to ensure everyone was heard. It was also used to somewhat break the tension. (*Alastair Montgomery*)

All these years later, Vulcan and Victor crews from Ascension look back in some surprise and much pride at what was achieved on the Black Buck and other sorties. We have the odd debate, considerable banter, do not agree about everything we think we remember and drink, perhaps, less beer than used to be the case. Most importantly, amongst all those who took part, whether in the air or on the ground on ASI and in the UK, there is a bond that will last.

In dragging this from my brain, I was particularly amazed at how many fuel consumption charts my then co-pilot Bill Perrins had kept; however, if I have got my fuel figures above wrong, then the fault is mine not his. Virgin Atlantic passengers are in good hands!

Above: Ascension Island. Wideawake airfield on left. (*Bill Perrins*)

Below: Wideawake ramp with packing cases, Vulcans and USAF C5. (*Bill Perrins*)

Left: The luxurious Wide awake Air Traffic Control (*Bill Perrins*)

Centre: Wideawake runw from Green Mountain. (*Perrins*)

Below: Wideawake airfie from engineers' servicing tents. (*Bill Perrins*)

Opposite top: Vulcan at V awake with Shrikes loade

Opposite bottom: Vulcan XM607 touching down a Black Buck 1. Tail numb visible on fin with Victor tankers on ramp behind. *Perrins*)

Top: Vulcan XH558 on 50 Squadron as a tanker.
Above: Vulcan K2 with HDU and 'tanker paint'
markings. (*Chris Lumb*)
Opposite top: Vulcan K2 tanker with ground crew
loading the refuelling hose. (*Chris Lumb*)
Opposite bottom: Vulcan refuelling from a Vulcan
tanker. The probe is hidden from the pilot.

Top: Vulcan K2 tanker refuelling a Vulcan Mk2.
Above: Tornado refuelling. Note special paintwork for the tanker. (*Chris Lumb*)
Opposite top: 27 Squadron Vulcan flies over a Soviet helicopter carrier.
Opposite bottom: The final V Bomber formation, 18th December 1982, 44 Squadron Wadding-
ton, touring all No 1 Group former Vulcan bases. Captains Monty Montgomery, Martin Withers,
John Reeve, Neil McDougall with John Laycock in the right-hand seat. (*John Laycock*)

Top: Vulcan XH558 in 1989 when it was in the RAF Vulcan Display Flight. (*Charles Toop*)
Above: Martin Withers once more showing us what the Vulcan can do.

By the way, Black Buck 1 did not exist. I had 'misheard' the instructions issued by the DSSS Duck described above. Thus, I wrote up the authorising sheet as Operation 'Black Bull'. And, hence, the Victor control linked by HF was known as Red Rag! I re-wrote the authorisation sheet the next day and, if you do not believe me, I still have the original. Such is history.

Monty mentions the weight of the Vulcan and the fact that the aircraft were operating over the maximum take-off weight of 204,000lbs which was de-termined by an operational aircraft having full fuel of 72,000lbs and twenty -one 1,000lb bombs giving a dry tanks weight of 111,000lb. The fuel chart[8] for Black Buck 1 shows 136,000lbs dry tank weight which gives an actual take-off weight at Ascension of 208,000lbs but the operators felt the weight was nearer 210,000lbs. It was just as well the aircraft had the higher power Olympus engines given an outside air temperature of around 30°C.

Monty went on to command RAF Manston and retired from the Service at 50 as group captain operations at Strike Command during the Balkan campaigns and the Iraq no fly zone.

Jim Vinales became a nav plotter instructor at the Vulcan OCU at Scamp-ton the year after his success in Giant Voice, and in September 1977 he was posted to RAF Brüggen as an ops officer. He went back to Vulcans in No-vember 1980, on his return from Germany. Here he describes Black Buck 2.

4th May 1982 – Vulcan XM607
With the last refuelling bracket complete, the Victor tanker started reeling in the fuel hose and commenced a turn to the north, away from us. In Vulcan XM607, we start-ed the long 'under-the-radar' letdown to low level, at that stage about 180 miles to the northeast of Stanley airfield. The ponderous 'radar descent' soon had us all im-patient and we increased the rate of descent to get down quickly to the relative safety of low-level flight. One thing worried me, however. I'd been anxious to know the task force's expected position at 0400 hrs, the time we would be in the local area, but that information was not received before our departure. Now, as we flew at 300ft ASL di-rectly towards Stanley airfield, I was worried we'd blunder through the centre of the fleet. And, blow me down, we did! Unable to switch on our radar prior to attack for fear we'd give ourselves away, we were blind to what lay in the ocean ahead of us. Sud-denly, an audible bleep! I looked at the radar warning receiver (RWR) to my right, in front of the AEO and realised we were being looked at by somebody's radar. That had to be one of the ships. Soon, there was a plethora of bleeps and flashes on the RWR.

Using the directional flashes on the RWR, Barry and I did our best to get the air-craft weaving away from all responses on the nose, hoping to avoid directly overflying any ship. We earnestly hoped all the operators down there had been briefed about us coming. The last thing we wanted was a missile coming our way from one of our own ships and thoroughly ruining our day. Fortunately, we soon left the bleeps and flashes

[8] Appendix 2.

behind us. We could now concentrate on the attack. Still over a hundred miles to go, I now hoped that the Carousel inertial twin nav systems that had been hurriedly fitted to our Vulcans had behaved themselves over the last eight hours of flight. Fortunately, the two indicators were showing positions fairly close together. I halved the distance and took that as my working position. Sixty miles to go. Fingers very tightly crossed. At forty miles, we left low level and climbed up to 16,000ft, our ground-mapping H2S radar now switched on. Within seconds we had a clear radar picture of the northeast corner of the Falkland Islands. I was greatly relieved to see that we were pretty well on track. Thirty miles to go.

I could hardly believe what we were about to do. Just over five weeks' earlier I'd been on 50 Squadron, having just returned from a Ranger to the centre of Strategic Air Command's nerve centre, Offutt Air Force Base. From there we'd performed a couple of low-level exercises as the Vulcan Force had been in the habit of doing since well before my arrival on Vulcans in 1970. Perhaps the one thing uppermost in all our minds was where we'd end up as our squadron faced disbandment within the next few months, together with all the other squadrons in the Vulcan Force. But General Galtieri and his military junta had other ideas.

Air Vice-Marshal Michael Knight, AVM, AOC 1 Group had come down from group HQ at RAF Bawtry and had joked about possible Vulcan involvement. He, frankly, did not expect that it would come to anything, believing the whole thing would be exclusively in the hands of the Royal Navy, but he urged the crews who'd been nominated for the task of specialist training to enjoy the flying. In the event, it turned out not to be a joke and within a week he was down to see us again, this time with a somewhat more serious look on his face. On 50 Squadron, the Reeve crew had been selected for the task. But the crew had a small problem. Their nav plotter, Flight Lieutenant David Harthill was about to leave for the States to meet up with his heavily-pregnant wife. It was planned that the child would be born in the US and this was not a plan that David wanted spoiling. So he asked the boss to be allowed to continue with his trip and for somebody else to be nominated in his place. Since at the time of asking, the whole business of Vulcan involvement was pretty nebulous, the boss agreed to let him go. I was sitting in the planning room with a few other fellow aircrew. Squadron Leader Bill Burnett, one of the two flight commanders, was looking for somebody to replace Harthill. Squadron Leader Neil McDougall (who would himself later feature prominently in the South Atlantic effort), let it be known that I'd been heard to say that I'd gladly volunteer. Bill, who was my regular crew captain, looked at me and asked whether I was keen. "Of course!" I could hardly say anything else!

Group Captain John Laycock, RAF Waddington's station commander, realised that a combat cell would have to be set up to oversee the station's involvement in Operation Corporate, as the Falkland Islands shindig soon became known to the UK military. He selected Wing Commander Simon Baldwin, CO of 44 Squadron, as Operation Corporate commander and a support staff of experienced operators was soon put together to get things moving.

There followed two to three weeks of intensive training for the crews, especially as the tempo intensified when it was confirmed that Vulcans would definitely be involved.

Three crews were initially selected for the job. Ours consisted of Squadron Leader John Reeve as captain, Flight Lieutenant Don Dibbens as co-pilot, Flight Lieutenant Mick Cooper as nav radar, Flight Lieutenant Barry Masefield as AEO and myself as nav plotter.

We had all sorts of problems with the air-to-air refuelling systems but slowly, almost imperceptibly, they were resolved. However, it was appreciated early on that our pilots were far from ready to take full responsibility for the massive amount of air-to-air refuelling that would have to be undertaken on the mission, whatever that was. Moreover, most of it was to be done at night. The decision was therefore taken that experienced Victor captains would fly in the Vulcans and take responsibility for all aspects of air-to-air refuelling; our own pilots just did not have the time to get up to speed. It was a wise decision. Our Victor pilot turned out to be Flight Lieutenant Peter Standing, an excellent chap whom we, on our crew, took to very quickly.

Black Buck 2 fully loaded with 21 x 1,000lb bombs. (*Mel James*)

The next problem to be tackled was the business of accurate navigation. It was conceivable that celestial navigation could be employed on the long, eight-hour leg from Ascension Island to the Falklands but it soon became evident that celestial navigation would be impractical as a lot of manoeuvring would have to be undertaken as the refuelling effort kicked in, and celestial nav required long straight and level legs. Out of nowhere, it would seem, came the order for some aircraft to be sent to RAF Wyton for the fitting of Carousel inertial navigation systems. These were duly installed and aircrew familiar with the equipment were despatched to Waddington to teach us how to use it. A morning's instruction, an afternoon's practical in-flight, and we were all hot-to-trot on Carousel! Things happened very fast indeed in the build-up to the Falklands War.

Deployment of two aircraft, each fully loaded with 21 x 1,000lb bombs, to Ascension Island, was set for the evening of 28th April. However, problems were encountered in the fuel plan and AVM Knight took the decision to delay departure until the following morning. I went back home and said hello to my wife, Jean, who was not expecting me back that night. Next morning she drove me back into base and I kissed her goodbye, not sure when I'd see her and the two boys again.

We crewed into XM607 and took off, with Martin Withers' crew in loose formation. At Land's End we joined up with several Victor AAR aircraft and headed off under limited radio silence into the Atlantic. Nine hours later, having experienced our first tanker trail, we landed at Ascension Island. The place was buzzing with movement. Aircraft, mainly Victors, everywhere! Tents everywhere! I spotted an old, very good friend of mine, Mark Ingham, Victor nav plotter. "Jim what are you doing here?" he cried. "Not entirely sure." I lied. Too early to tell him we were here to bomb Stanley airfield, with his help. Mark was an old friend from Singapore days. Later, after both of us were posted to Vulcans at RAF Waddington, we'd shared a house and I had been best man at his wedding. It was good to see his ever-smiling face.

At the Victor/Vulcan ops tent we were met by Squadron Leader 'Monty' Montgomery. He and his crew, our third Operation Corporate crew, had been despatched a few days earlier to set up our Ascension HQ. He gave us a quick arrival brief and got us moving in the way of our accommodation. We'd be busy next day, he averred. The great accommodation we'd been promised turned out to be a big empty shed of a place, with a number of camp beds spread around the vast empty space. But we were too tired to do anything other than flop into the beds. In due course we'd sort ourselves out some better digs. For now this would have to do.

The next morning, 30th April, together with the Withers' crew, we made our way down to the airfield. The executive order was in: the target was confirmed as Port Stanley airfield and we were to put a stick of 21 x 1,000lb bombs at an angle of 30 degrees across it. Our crew were nominated as the primary crew and Flight Lieutenant Withers and his crew would fly as reserve crew. The Vulcan operation was to be known as Operation Black Buck, but this was not entirely clear in the signal I'd looked at and I entered the name as Black Bull in my flight plan (as 'Monty' did). Some eleven Victors would assist us on our way. I sat myself down in the planning tent and started working on my upside-down Mercator plotting chart. Throughout the day, Victor operators kept coming at me with bits and pieces of revised AAR refuelling plan. By the end of the afternoon, I was totally and utterly baffled by what I was supposed to be doing. I just hoped that Peter Standing, our Victor chap, had a good grasp of what was required.

A slip of paper was passed to me, marked 'Top Secret'. What on earth was this, I thought. Oh My God! It was the Met forecast for Port Stanley airport at 0430 the following morning: favourable conditions, not that it mattered as we'd be bombing on radar. But the Top Secret classification on a Met forecast tickled me. Of course, it was fully justified. It was certainly important at that stage not to broadcast our intentions to the world; war was about to break out and we'd be firing the first shot. I still have that slip of paper. It sits in a box of papers right next to that coffee-stained chart from Giant Voice 74.

Air Vice-Marshal George Chesworth had flown in from HQ Northwood to oversee the execution of this mission. At briefing, the AVM stood up and stated: "The purpose of this exercise is to put a stick of bombs across Stanley airfield – let's get on with it!" An hour later, briefing complete, we walked out to the aircraft. Thirteen aircraft to be manned up – a massive formation of large aircraft was to take to the skies. I stood under our aircraft, Vulcan XM598, and changed into my immersion suit. We were close to the equator, and climbing into an immersion suit in this heat was tough, but we'd be flying for eight hours into the depth of winter in high southern latitudes, and I wanted to be ready for the worst.

One by one, the large formation of aircraft took to the skies, with the two Vulcans towards the end. John had had a problem on the ground shutting his DV panel on his windscreen and, as we passed 10,000ft, the pressurisation warning horn sounded off, very loudly indeed. It did not take long to realise that we were not going anywhere in this condition. The aircraft was suffering a leak of pressurisation, probably at the DV window. The decision was therefore taken to hand the mission over to the reserve crew, Flight Lieutenant Martin Withers and his team.

In our aircraft, John had detected another fault, this time with his inner helmet. He asked Peter Standing, flying in the co-pilot's seat to take over the controls as he changed his helmet. Peter, being a Victor captain and not fully conversant with the lightness of touch of the Vulcan flying controls, was surprised that the controls were beginning to feel even lighter and unresponsive. I looked up at my airspeed indicator and saw that the airspeed was dropping alarmingly. Our regular co-pilot, Don Dibbens, and I immediately realised that the aircraft was entering the stall envelope and both shouted at him to get the nose down, pronto, and gather up airspeed. Barry Masefield, our AEO looked at me, "this is all going terribly wrong", I said nothing, quietly cursing the turn of events.

We landed somewhat overweight and taxied to dispersal. The rest of the crew decided they'd head for their beds but I could not. I was determined to stay up and watch unfolding events as the formation headed south. I wanted to be there when the bomb release codeword, 'Superfuse!' was transmitted back to base. We should be the ones doing it but things had not turned out that way.

In the Withers aircraft, Vulcan XM607, there was a stunned silence as they heard our message. It took a couple of seconds to absorb the unbelievable and then they got on with it. They flew on through the night. The fuel plan was not working altogether to their advantage and a deficit was beginning to build up through the formation. Crews were pushing on beyond what was prudent, aware of the importance of the overall mission.

In the back of XM607, Flight Lieutenant Gordon Graham looked at his chart and followed the progress of the overall formation. At this stage, his involvement was passive as navigation was in the hands of the lead Victor crew. He would not need to take over until after the last refuelling bracket and start of descent towards the Falklands.

Some six or seven years earlier, Pilot Officer Graham had been a first-tour navigator going through the OCU. I was one of his instructors. A quiet Scot, you could nevertheless sense that he was highly motivated and anxious to do his best. My colleague, Flight Lieutenant Roly Grayson had set his course an exercise, a classroom 'plot' where they would mimic a flight in the contemplative atmosphere of the classroom. To this end, Roly had issued all the navigators with a blank Mercator plotting chart. Gordon was not used to the Mercator projection, having always used a Lambert's orthomorphic at nav school, a chart with different characteristics. Having completed his exercise, he handed his chart in for marking. Roly checked his work and noticed that virtually everything had been done correctly as per the book, but he was puzzled to see that Gordon's fixes of position had all ended up in the wrong places. He called me in and asked for my assistance. Eventually, we discovered what he'd done wrong. He'd used the blank chart upside down with the expanding Mercator scale to the south instead of the north!

Now he looked at his Heath Robinson of a chart. The support staff back at Waddington had had a hell of a job trying to find a suitable chart of the South Atlantic. Eventually the senior navigator had decided to take a Mercator of the North Atlantic, turned it upside down, re-entered latitude as 'south,' and offered it to us as the chart to use. In other words, Gordon was now obliged to do, in active service, what he'd been mildly rebuked for as a student except that, as he was now in the southern hemisphere, it would work perfectly.

The final refuelling brackets were performed in turbulent weather, with flashes of lightning illuminating the night sky. Scary stuff, as fuel was transferred from Victor to Victor and Victor to Vulcan – not at all healthy. Martin's crew realised they were 10,000lbs short. As the final Victor turned on the red lights, indicating no more fuel, he broke radio silence to ask for more. But there was no more. Flight Lieutenant Bob Tuxford had passed more fuel than he could afford and now faced the prospect of ditching his aircraft south of Ascension. Together with the rest of his crew, they'd taken the courageous decision to give as much as they could, and certainly more than was prudent.[9]

Back at base operations, we were aware of the drama unfolding in the South Atlantic. The station commander, Group Captain Jerry Price, was furiously ordering the refuelling of the early returning Victors and sending them back into the air. Their mates further down the line were desperate for the extra fuel.

Martin and his crew put the fuel business behind them and got on with the job. They'd been briefed to bomb from 8,000ft but they reckoned that was dangerously within the range of the air defence artillery on the airfield, so they agreed between themselves to 'up' the bombing height to 10,000ft.

At Ascension, we waited for developments, some of us, including myself, smoking ourselves hoarse. The young HF operator looked quite calm as he read a book, waiting for somebody to speak to him. Eventually at about 8am, Ascension time, the radio crackled into life, "Superfuse, Superfuse! 10,000lbs of extra fuel required!" Massive joy and relief. The mission had clearly not gone entirely to plan and the evident shortness of fuel across the formation had been a great worry. But the job had been done and action had been taken to ensure returning Victors would be met and safely recovered to Ascension. A stick of bombs had been delivered as required at Stanley airfield and the Argentinians had been left in no doubt as to the intentions of the British government to recover the Falkland Islands. It was time to get to bed for a few hours. Later we would welcome Martin and his crew back at Ascension, but that would not happen for another eight hours.

Now it was the morning of 4th May and we were smack in the middle of Black Buck 2. Don Dibbens had replaced Peter Standing in the co-pilot's seat. John Reeve contemplated his instruments, alert to instructions from the back of the aircraft. John was a friendly, chatty character and had a boyish enthusiasm for everything concerned

---

[9] For full coverage of this extraordinary story see *Victor Boys* by Tony Blackman.

with aviation. He was always joking and had put in a lot of work to help improve the Vulcan's AAR effort. After all, it had been at least fifteen years since the Vulcan had last engaged in AAR. Don Dibbens was a pretty calm character and seemed not a bit fazed by the situation we found ourselves in. Flight Lieutenant Barry Masefield was the AEO. A short, very friendly chap, he was keen to do his bit for the crew and the mission in hand. Alert now for Argentinian radar signals and ready to counter with emissions from our electronic counter measures pod, slung under the wing. Mick Cooper, nav radar, had a powerful reputation as an operator and had won numerous prizes in bombing competitions. He'd temporarily left the RAF but had returned a few years before.

The force had learned from the problems in the Black Buck 1 refuelling plan and the AAR effort from Ascension to the cast-off point, allowing the Vulcan two extra refuelling brackets and an additional 20,000lbs of fuel, had worked superbly so far. We now had as much fuel as we could expect, and we'd be meeting a couple of tankers on the way back anyway, so, hopefully, we'd be all right.

Twenty miles to go. Mick was now concentrating deeply on his radar offsets, bombs already selected on the 90-Way conventional bombing panel. I was doing my best to ensure all inputs into his bombing computer were correct. Don chirped up, "I can see Port Stanley!" "Great! Can they see us from down there?" (On radar or whatever.) We'd be bombing from 16,000ft. It had been decided since Black Buck 1 that the range and altitude of the air-to-air missiles at Stanley might be able to get up to 14,000ft, so let's allow ourselves something of a margin.

Ten miles – bomb doors open, all switches made.

3-2-1 bombs gone!

One by one, the bombs left the aircraft at just under half a second interval apiece. Once they'd all gone, we turned to the north. The crump of the bombs hitting the ground was amazing. We were already climbing away, putting as much vertical and horizontal space between ourselves and Stanley airfield as we could.

We'd been instructed not to speak to the task force. Instead we were to sector scan our radar in their direction. This would indicate to the ships that we'd completed our bombing run. It was a mistake. A thousand fire control radars, it seemed, opened up on us and we quickly turned our radar transmissions off. Whose silly idea was it to sector-scan the task force? They must have thought we were threatening them.

It seemed as if we were flying parallel to the Argentinian coast for ages, but, eventually, we were well clear. Half way back to Ascension, we were met by our two Victors. A maritime Nimrod vectored us towards each other. Refuelling was completed with no further drama. Peter Standing, our excellent and affable AAR expert, now back in the co-pilot's seat, was very grateful for the fuel. "That tasted good!"

There'd be three more Vulcan missions against Port Stanley. Two of those would be Shrike anti-radar missions, with the aim of destroying the Argentinians' ability to search the skies. The last mission would occur shortly before surrender and was designed to shatter Argentinian morale completely.

It had been impossible to mount large-scale Vulcan operations against the enemy forces on the Falklands. The refuelling effort required was just too great. But the effect of the use of the Vulcans on Argentinian morale had been significant and we were proud we'd done our bit towards bringing things to a speedy conclusion.

February 1983

At the end of the Falklands War, Her Majesty's government was unsure how events would play out in Argentina. Among other defence measures, it was decided to retain 44 Squadron in its operational bomber role until the end of 1982, an extension of six months or so over the squadron's original out of service date. Morale in the squadron was high, and useful training and interesting detachments helped to keep spirits up and engender a sense of purpose. But, bit by bit our squadron aircrew were learning of their new postings and those hoping for the fast jet force or other desirable options were focused on the future of their careers. In late summer and autumn, the question of postings was the prime subject of conversation in the crew room. In due course, I

Martin Withers (left) talking to Jerry Price and George Chesworth after Black Buck 1. (*Mel James*)

received my own posting: Buccaneers! I smiled. I'd had to wait thirteen years to get the posting I'd so desired in late 1969. Ironically, at that stage, the RAF had moved on and I'd been hoping for a posting to the shiny new Tornado. But no, thwarted again. However, the Buccaneer still retained a powerful operational reputation and I was not in a position to make a strong complaint. So Buccaneers it would be.

In December the squadron held its disbandment parade in front of the chief of the Air Staff – an emotional moment in the life of the squadron and the Vulcan Force. Following its formal disbandment on 31st December, there remained the 'trivial' domestic issues of dispersing the squadron's aircraft and equipment and I found myself flying on several sorties to deliver Vulcans to enthusiasts across the UK. To this day, many of these Vulcans remain as prized show-pieces in sundry airfields. Slowly the number of squadron aircrew disappeared to their new appointments and the number of faces on the squadron dwindled to a few. In the end, as February 1983 drew to a close, I found myself in empty squadron accommodation with just one other officer. We shook hands and he departed, on his way to the Nimrod Force at RAF Kinloss, by the Moray Firth. I was left to round up the few papers I needed to keep and that done, I locked up and left the building for the last time. As I walked towards my car I looked to my right and saw that the squadron flagpole was still flying the CO's pennant. No longer appropriate, I thought. So I lowered the pennant and saw that it was showing its age and a bit ragged. Not worth keeping, I thought. I spotted a nearby bin and, without ceremony, I dumped the pennant in the bin and walked away

Several weeks later, during a quiet moment, I reflected on that last day at the old squadron building. 44 had been the last operational bomber squadron. Across the pan, 50 Squadron would continue as a Vulcan squadron for some more years, but in the air-to-air refuelling role together with the Victor squadrons of RAF Marham. What's more, it had been decided to retain a couple of Vulcans as display aircraft. Their 'airships' at the MOD appreciated the value of the Vulcan as a display aircraft in front of an adoring British public. But with the passing of 44 Squadron, the Vulcan was finished as an operational bomber. And, of course, it had been the last of the three V aircraft in the bomber role. It occurred to me that that simple lowering of the pennant and its disposal in the nearest bin had been the very last act in the life of the formidable V bomber Force.

I wish I'd kept that raggedy old pennant!

In Monty's narrative he describes the problems in calculating the fuel plans and the decision to have reserve tankers ready to recover returning aircraft short of fuel. Jim in his splendid account also mentions the Victors and their complicated refuelling plan to enable Black Buck to be supported. What I did not mention in my book *Victor Boys* is the way these very complicated plans were produced. For Operation Corporate, Group Captain Jerry Price charged Squadron Leader Trevor Sitch, nav plotter, to form a team from RAF Marham operations staff and HQ 1 Group Victor staff, take them to Ascension and support all the flight operations. It should be remembered that the seventeen Victors based on Ascension had many more tasks than just supporting the Black Buck sorties; there were the initial Victor maritime reconnaissance sorties ahead of the task force progressing towards South Georgia, the deployment of additional Harrier ferries to the task force, the Nimrod reconnaissance sorties down the Argentinian coast, the continual Hercules logistical parachute supply to the task force and the logistical support of aircraft ferries between UK and Wideawake.

Trevor's team consisted of five other aircrew officers all with many years of Victor air-to-air refuelling flying experience and one non-aircrew NCO; they were working flat out, as were the Victor aircrews.

Specifically on Black Buck 2 it was imperative to improve on the fuel plan for Black Buck 1 but Trevor said that after some twelve hours planning leading up to just minutes before crew briefing time it was deduced that there was still not enough fuel within the entire formation for the mission to be flown that night. Clearly to both Trevor and his team a complete review of aircraft resources, their utilisation and fuel performance figures needed to be thoroughly scrutinised again and the sortie was delayed until

Planning ops room above (left and right).
Trevor Sitch is right at the back of the long room and giving briefing
with Chris Morffew to his left.

the fuel plan was satisfactory.

All the Black Buck sorties were teamwork but inevitably it was the aircrews that got the limelight. However, none of the sorties would have been
successful without the Victors, their aircrew and ground crew, the Victor
operations staff and their fuel planners, the Vulcan ground crews and so
on; the list is almost endless but we should never forget what an amazing
and enormous task the Wideawake operation was, how many people were
involved and how it was planned and carried out in such an incredibly short
time.

Chapter Fourteen

SHRIKING, RIO, AND RETURN

The story of Vulcan XM607 and Black Buck 1 and its mission to bomb the runway at Port Stanley has been told and re-told many times before but very little is known of the three missions that were detailed to attack radar sites on the Falklands Islands to remove a serious threat to the UK task force that was, in May 1982, coming under increasing hostile air attack from Argentine fighter-bombers. This is the story of those three missions, Black Bucks 4, 5 and 6 told by the nav radar of the crew, David Castle.

This account of the Black Buck sorties to the Falklands using the Shrike missiles and the diversion to Rio is absolutely spellbinding. We are very lucky that **David Castle** has taken the trouble to write this story down so that people will know what really happened.

Rio de Janeiro, the Corcovado and the Sugar Loaf Mountain
but the crew only saw it all on their last night!

Rio is a Long Way from Huddersfield
"MAYDAY, MAYDAY, MAYDAY. This is a British four-jet approximately 500 miles east of Rio de Janeiro at Flight Level 430 with an in-flight emergency and very short of fuel. We require an immediate diversion to the nearest suitable airfield."

"This is Brazil control; please say your call-sign, your country of departure and your destination."

"This is Ascot 597, a British four-jet with 6 souls on board, critically short of fuel and with no cabin pressure. We request immediate assistance and permission to divert to the nearest suitable airfield."

"Ascot 597, NEGATIVE. You do not have permission to enter Brazil airspace. Please state your country of departure and final destination."

"Dave, I can't move the escape hatch handle out of the locked position. There is no way we are going to be able to close this hatch and re-pressurise!"

"Try this Brian." I detached my aircrew knife from its sheath on my right thigh and handed it to Brian Gardner, the spare pilot of Vulcan XM597. Brian had been seconded to our crew to assist with the final and most critical AAR procedure after an epic twelve hours of our third and, as it turned out, our final Black Buck mission.

"Try and lever the handle out of its 'detent' position using my knife."

"What?…What did you say? I can hardly hear you…say again…"

Brian and I endeavoured to communicate with each other over the maelstrom of cabin noise as we both straddled across the wide open escape hatch revealing a cobalt blue expanse of the South Atlantic ocean below us. With no cabin pressurisation, oxygen was being force-fed into our lungs under pressure from our oxygen regulators making us sound like characters from an episode of the Looney Tunes cartoon 'Daffy Duck'. But this was no laughing matter. We both had parachutes on and I had my arms wrapped around Brian's waste as he struggled with an obstinate escape hatch lever that was refusing to co-operate. How many times has a Vulcan escape hatch been opened at 43,000ft before, I wondered?

"MAYDAY, MAYDAY, MAYDAY" continued Rod Trevaskus our AEO, this time on UHF 243.0.

"We are a British four-jet, 480 miles east of Rio at Flight Level 430, we are critically short of fuel and require immediate diversion assistance."

"NEGATIVE, NEGATIVE, you must turn away. You do not have permission to enter Brazil airspace. You must identify yourself. What is your departure airfield, where……?"

"Brian, you need to force the handle out of the locked, detent position before the hatch will close again," I interrupted. "If we can re-pressurise we may be able to hear ourselves think," I said with just a hint of irony. By now the cabin temperature was starting to drop. It was minus 54 degrees outside and we were losing a lot of heat through the open hatch. My fingers were starting to tingle and I felt the on-set of potential frostbite. Adrenalin was pumping. I was really scared! 'I must not release my grip on Brian's waist', I kept reminding myself. Neither of us can afford a slip or a stumble otherwise a long, very long parachute descent into the ocean below beckons.

"British four-jet, identify yourself and state your destination." A second Brazilian controller with an American accent now appeared over the R/T. "British four-jet you must…."

"Oh for fuck sake Rod," I screamed. "If he won't be quiet tell him we're from Huddersfield. Now Brian let's have another go," I added in a rather less stressed tone!

"Brazil control, this is Ascot 597 at Flight Level 430, inbound Rio International, from, er-Huddersfield," proffered Rod to help the controller with his stubborn and persistent line of enquiry.

"Ascot 597, roger, standby………"

Brian gave me another nervous glance. We hadn't been taught this procedure on the

OCU and we certainly never practised it in the simulator. I could read Brian's mind. 'We don't get paid enough through the X factor for this sort of thing,' I am sure he was thinking as we eye-balled each other one more time.

"That shut them up," said our nav plotter, Barry Smith. "They won't have a clue where Huddersfield is."

"There is only a light aircraft landing strip in Huddersfield and I doubt if it appears in any of their flight planning publications," I spluttered over the intercom in an accent more reminiscent of Donald than Daffy Duck this time.

As a school boy from Huddersfield, my father would on many occasions take me to a vantage point on a hill overlooking a small light airfield on the outskirts of the town armed with a flask of coffee and an amateur VHF radio receiver. It was this introduction to the exciting world of aviation, along with regular visits in the summer to the Church Fenton and Finningley air shows that propelled me towards a career in the Royal Air Force. My teenage ambition was always to fly Buccaneers. I never dreamed I would find myself one day as part of the crew of an air defence suppression sortie, somewhere over the South Atlantic – and in a Vulcan bomber at that.

There was no way the Brazilian military authorities would ever know that we were the crew of a Vulcan bomber based out of Ascension Island and returning from an attack against a surface-to-air missile fire control unit on the Falkland Islands; a mission that was now close to ending in total disaster with the crew considering abandoning its stricken bomber short of fuel off the coast of Brazil, thousands of miles away from its home base in Lincolnshire. But a mission that would eventually lead to the award of a Distinguished Flying Cross for the captain of XM597, Squadron Leader Neil McDougall. Or did the Brazilians really know who we were and where we had come from and, if so, what would be their reaction if we ever made land-fall and then Rio? If only we could close the escape hatch...

It was Easter 1982 and I, with my wife Chrissie and our new-born beautiful daughter, Elisa, was taking a weekend break at the coastal resort of Filey in North Yorkshire. We were watching the BBC nine o'clock news in our cosy B&B.

"Will the invasion of the Falkland Islands affect you, Dave?" Chrissie enquired.

"I doubt it very much; the islands must be over 7,000 miles away, not much we can do from here."

We didn't practise air-to-air refuelling or conventional bombing and the only weapon we were trained to deliver was the WE-177 tactical nuclear bomb from low level against target sets east of the Urals.

"No, this is a job for the Royal Navy," I added. "If only they still had the *Ark Royal* though with its complement of Buccaneers and Phantoms, their task would be much easier."

Just a week before the invasion, I had sat on the duty officer's desk of 50 Squadron at RAF Waddington and witnessed outside the systematic dismemberment of Vulcan airframes by a local scrap metal contractor. The Scampton squadrons had already gone and IX Squadron was about to disband in three weeks time, leaving the remnant crews of 44, 50 and 101 Squadrons until, they too, were expected to disband in August that year. I was approaching the end of my first tour as a navigator (radar) and was hoping for a posting to the Buccaneer, the aircraft I had dreamed of flying since I first witnessed a display of that awesome jet at RAF Finningley with my father in the sixties. I had performed well as a nav radar and had gained the respect of my fellow crew members despite a shaky start on the OCU course at Scampton. Our crew had shone this year and had come third in the Strike Command Double Top bombing competition, and I had worked extremely hard to be recognised as one of the squadron's more capable navigators. But it still came as an enormous surprise to me to be selected, along with my crew, to be part of an Operation Corporate work-up programme in preparation for a deployment to Ascension Island.

My feelings and emotions were a little confused. Only four crews had been selected. On the one hand, I was elated and proud to have been chosen ahead of many more experienced navigators on the squadron. And yet I felt apprehensive. We all did. Our first child had just been born and Chrissie was going to need me around over the next few months or so. Disappearing off to war did not really feature on her or my list of 'things we must do on our first tour'. The Cold War had presented a different kind of challenge to the military. This event had been rather unexpected and no contingency plan existed in the V Force to cater for a scenario such as this. Nevertheless, this is why we were here, to respond to the unexpected and put our extensive training now into practice. The pace of life was just about to accelerate beyond anything I had experienced so far in my short service career.

Our work-up programme began in earnest. None of the Waddington pilots had practised air-to-air refuelling in a Vulcan, with the exception of the captain of our crew, Neil McDougall, a rather dour Scotsman with a dry sense of humour. All of a sudden, No 1 Group Air Staff orders were relaxed and peace-time flying regulations went out the window. A different, more operational set of safety criteria was applied in our work-up. After two weeks intensive flying practice, a typical sortie would involve a climb to high level, a night transit navigating by periscopic sextant and the stars, including AAR from a Victor tanker, and a let-down to low level over the Outer Hebrides. A low level ingress at 300ft AGL over the Inner Hebrides and west coast of Scotland using terrain following radar, the H2S radar and night vision goggles, culminating with the release of either twenty-one 1,000lb live bombs at the Garvie Range near Cape Wrath or seven inert bombs at Jurby Range off the Isle of Man.

The Vulcan's analogue and archaic navigation and bombing System (NBS) relied entirely on continuous radar fixing to keep it updated and the bomber on track. But Port Stanley airfield lay some 3,800 miles south of Ascension Island and the first radar fix would not be available until the coast of East Falkland Island came into radar line-of-sight. So we would have to perfect our night astro skills to give us a chance of being anywhere near our target when we descended to low level for the ingress under enemy radar cover. This would be an enormous challenge.

I enjoyed night astro; I considered it an art as much as a science. I practised crewing-in to the aircraft wearing an eye patch so that one eye was already accustomed to darkness and that the dimmest star, the one that would provide the most reliable

Martel anti-radar missile at Waddington prior to test firing. (*Dave Castle*)

position line for a fix, could be recognised quickly. To get a good star shot required a calm, stable air mass to fly through and the activity would have to be de-conflicted with AAR. It also required four members of the crew to work in harmony with intense concentration for over ten minutes to obtain a reliable star fix. One hiccough in this sequence by any member of the crew could jeopardise the accuracy of the NBS and our ability to navigate successfully over such a vast distance. However, in practice we consistently achieved an accuracy of about four to five miles over a three to four-hour sortie. As a crew, we were really proud of this achievement.

Fortunately, common sense prevailed and the four designated Corporate Vulcans were each fitted with a twin inertial navigation system (INS) robbed from VC10s in storage in a hangar at RAF Brize Norton. On subsequent sorties our navigation accuracy was now in the order of three to four miles over an extended eight hours flying time. Good enough to slave the H2S towards its radar bombing offsets on the ingress to the target. Well that was the navigation sorted. But we would still need to make a successful RV with a Victor tanker, not once, not twice but four or five times outbound and then make a final RV with another tanker on our return to Ascension Island. None of us had previously practised with live or inert 1,000lb bombs and, with the exception of Neil McDougall, not one pilot had any previous tanking experience.

My own weapon effort planning calculations revealed that in order to achieve a 75% probability of cratering a 4,000ft by 150ft runway, using a navigation and bombing system with a CEP[10] of 1,900ft, it would require up to seventeen sticks of twenty-one 1,000lb bombs. As my grandfather would have said if he were still alive today: 'You have as much chance of striking a match on wet tripe!'

No sooner had our crew, Neil McDougall, Chris Lackman the co-pilot, Barry Smith

---

[10] Circular Error Probable.

the nav plotter, Rod Trevaskus the AEO and myself got into its stride than our station commander, John Laycock, took Neil to one side to reveal that John Reeve's crew had been selected for Black Buck 1. Our crew was to remain behind in the UK to conduct extra training for another type of mission; a mission that no one in the RAF had ever done for real before and one that only the Maritime Buccaneer Wing had any knowledge or experience of.

The Royal Navy task force commander had become increasingly concerned about the ability of the Argentinian search radars on the Falkland Islands to provide tactical direction to its Sky Hawks and Super Étendard fighter-bombers. Aircraft that were having a dramatic and damaging effect on our surface ships such as HMS *Sheffield*, *Coventry* and *Ardent*. There was intelligence that a mobile Westinghouse AN/TPS-43 was providing such a capability and Admiral Sandy Woodward was keen for it to be suppressed or even neutralised so as to remove the serious threat it posed to his task force.

"I need your crew to report to ops wing tomorrow morning Neil," said Wing Commander Baldwin, the boss of 44 Squadron. "You are to get a brief on the Martel anti-radiation missile from Flight Lieutenant Phil Walters who has come up from Honington. You are going to convert to the SEAD[11] role and you are going to have to learn it fast! In the meantime, here is an excerpt of the Martel check list from the Buccaneer flight reference cards. Get your crew to inwardly ingest and learn the cockpit checks before tomorrow morning. 0800 hours prompt in wing weapons please."

"They want us to do what!?" exclaimed Rod Trevaskus. "Strap a 1,200lb Martel missile onto a Skybolt pylon, fly 4,000 miles to the Falklands, loiter for thirty minutes in the overhead of Stanley, be shot at, and then attempt to lock up and destroy a mobile TPS-43 radar without knowing its precise location. You're having a laugh!"

Again, this was no laughing matter. This was a serious proposition and Phil Walters briefed us enthusiastically about the missile's capabilities, strengths and foibles. The big problem with the Martel was that weapon effort planning revealed only a 60% probability of kill (PK) for a single shot missile launch, and with intelligence reporting that the TPS-43 changed its location each day, there could be a high probability of failure, let alone the risk of collateral damage on the outskirts of Stanley town from its powerful 350lb blast fragmentation warhead.

I recall being summoned to the squadron hangar on a Sunday morning to assist with cockpit and power-on checks to a Martel arm hanging from some Heath Robinson pylon assembly, and by the Wednesday of that same week we had launched the missile live at Aberporth Range – but what a disaster that nearly turned into. Martel had a number of safety breaks and so, naturally, we disabled the warhead and took the extra precaution of disabling its sustainer motor. Only the booster motor would fire so we could demonstrate that the missile could be launched from a Vulcan and that the radar homing head would guide towards a target radar emitter. The plan was for the missile to fall short of the radar by about two miles or so into the sea. However, when the booster motor ran out of fuel the missile continued to porpoise like a laser-guided bomb towards its target and caused sufficient consternation and panic in the range

[11] Suppression of enemy air defences.

hut for the range safety officer to shut the radar down and evacuate his position. The missile fell short by only a few hundred metres and impacted on the beach. Phew.

"Well that worked chaps," I said to the crew in our debrief. "But what about its PK? 0.6 isn't very good, despite that impressive performance at Aberporth."

"And what about the target's proximity to Stanley?" Barry reminded us. Perhaps Martel was going to be too risky.

The following day we were introduced to Flight Lieutenant 'Herm' Harper from the Aeroplane and Armaments Experimental Establishment at Boscombe Down. The US government had secretly agreed to supply the MOD with a batch of AGM-45 Shrike missiles that had been used to great effect by F-4s and A-6s during the Vietnam War, and 'Herm' had some knowledge and insight of the missile's capability from his trials work both in the US and at Boscombe Down.

"The good news," Herm opened with, "Is that Shrike can achieve a PK of up to 0.9."

"And the bad news?" I asked.

"Well you would need to launch two in quick succession and you will need to get as close as seven miles to the target."

Group Captain Laycock took Rod Trevaskus and me to one side to see what we thought and whether we could come up with an improvised tactic. How would we locate the TPS-43? Would we be able to achieve a firing solution? What were our chances? John Laycock needed to know and needed an answer quickly.

"Well, if we were able to obtain an intercept bearing on the radar warning receiver (RWR) from the TPS-43," suggested Rod, "And then from Dave's interpretation of the H2S radar we were to manoeuvre the aircraft to obtain another cross-cutting bearing, we could in theory obtain a two-position line fix on the TPS-43."

"I could then drop my radar markers over this location so as to ascertain our range from the TPS-43," I concluded.

"A bit of a long shot," suggested Rod but we both believed with a bit of further refinement we could get it to work. On the planning table in front of us, Herm unfolded an A3-sized sheet of graph paper depicting the missile's engagement parameters in a series of concentric circles and parabolic curves.

Two shrikes on the Pye pylon. (*Mel James*)

"Look at this footprint," said Herm. "If you launch from precisely 6.9 miles in a ten-degree dive, whilst bore-sighted against the radar head you can achieve a PK of 0.7. If you were able to ripple fire two Shrikes in quick succession in a twenty-degree dive, that figure rises to 0.9. However, you can see that if you over-run by just 0.1 mile, the PK drops off a cliff to as low as 0.2 and to zero by six miles. How confident are you of your radar skills Dave because you will have to determine the launch point; the INS will not be accurate enough."

"It all depends on whether the radar is mobile or not and how certain of its location we can be. I can use radar offsets to help me fix its geographic position but the radar will still need to radiate for the missile to guide and home in. OK, I may be able to determine a range from the H2S radar but Rod will still need to give the pilots a steer so as to bore-sight the missile before launch and give the Shrike's homing head a good chance of seeing the emitter within its narrow field of view. Barry, you will need to call down the range-to-go from the output of my radar markers, and the handling pilot, Neil or Chris, will need to make sure we have achieved at least a ten-degree dive before the launch point."

"I'm going to have to 'bunt' the aircraft to achieve a dive like that, a tip-in manoeuvre is out of the question," said Neil.

"Any dive is better than a level release," replied Herm. "But it's the release range that is absolutely critical to achieve a kill. And of course, this is all predicated on the assumption that the Argentinians will switch their radar on. Good luck chaps, you're going to need it!"

John Laycock was impressed with our enthusiasm and was content to recommend our tactic to group for their authorisation.

There was no time for in-flight trials of the Shrike missile, let alone a live firing at Aberporth this time. On 10th May our crew was alerted and told we were to be collected at 0500 and taken by road transport to RAF Brize Norton where we would embark on a VC10 for Ascension Island. There was no spare ramp space on Wideawake airfield for another Vulcan, so the Shrike missiles would be airlifted there also. Now the following tale may have been told many times before and some would say it is anecdotal if not apocryphal. However, I can vouch for its authenticity because I was there as a witness. The VC10 had been re-rolled for freight with just a half dozen seats remaining in its tail section. Amongst all the ammunition crates and supplies were two open racks of Sidewinder AIM-9L air-to-air missiles destined for the task force and eventually the Sea Harriers embarked on HMS *Invincible* and *Hermes*. Each AIM-9L had had its safety pins removed and when I enquired of the corporal air load master where on earth they were she pointed to a cardboard box on the cabin floor where she had gathered them all.

She explained, "The red flags on the pins said 'REMOVE BEFORE FLIGHT', so I pulled them out and kept them in this box for safe keeping."

"What the?"....I was suddenly rendered speechless. But fortunately not Neil who bellowed at her to put the pins back in before we got airborne! I was not yet a QWI[12] in 1982 but even as a Vulcan nav radar I knew how important the pins were to the safety and reliability of those precious missiles.

"What the hell are you lot doing here?" demanded Squadron Leader Bill Sherlock as we tried to disembark the VC10 at Wideawake airfield following a laborious eight-hour flight from Brize. "You tell us Bill," pleaded Neil as the rest of the crew gathered its kit and was about to disappear across the tarmac for an ice cold lager in the Volcano Club.

"I'm sorry Neil but the base commander, Group Captain Jeremy Price does not want you here. He has told me to send you straight back to Brize. There is no accommodation for you all and your mission has been put on hold as a result."

[12] Qualified Weapons Instructor.

"What – you must be joking." He wasn't! "If you don't allow us just one beer before this jet is refuelled and turned round you are going to have a mutinous crew on your hands Bill," protested Neil.

A six-pack of South African Castle lager and thirty minutes later we were airborne once again, this time en route back to RAF Brize Norton, only nine hours after we had departed from that same airfield.

We were to return, nevertheless, to Wideawake airfield under our own steam in Vulcan XM597 on 26th May, this time equipped with two AGM-45 Shrike missiles suspended from two Heath Robinson makeshift pylon assemblies under each wing.

Whilst we had trialled the Martel missile and achieved a successful live firing at Aberporth, we did not have the same luxury or opportunity for Shrike. The only test we were able to make was to check the homing head sensitivity against RAF St Mawgan's ATC radar as we coasted out over the Cornish peninsula. But would it fly off the rails when Rod Trevaskus pressed the firing button in anger, and would it guide? Only time would tell.

Later on in my career with 12 Squadron in the maritime strike-attack role, I experienced many an encounter with Soviet intelligence-gathering ships masquerading as fishing trawlers off the Scottish coast. But my first introduction to this Soviet capability was at Ascension Island where one such vessel, decked out with a sophisticated array of aerials and sensors, was positioned some ten miles to the south of the island. It was assumed that the trawler was just gathering routine intelligence but in reality it may well have been alerting the Argentinians to our formation's launch out of Wideawake. This only came to my attention when I recently read a report posted on an internet forum by a former member of Grupo de Artillería Antiaérea (GAA) 601 that revealed the unit had been receiving tip-offs of the take-off times for Black Bucks 4, 5 and 6, and could therefore calculate our ETA over the Falkland Islands.

Black Buck 4 launched at midnight on 28th May with the task of neutralising the Westinghouse TPS-43 radar, located 'somewhere' on East Falkland. This was not a suppression of enemy air defences (SEAD) mission where we would be required to 'suppress' the radar site whilst another formation conducted simultaneous attacks on other designated targets. There was no coordinated Harrier GR3 attack planned for that morning and so this would be more a DEAD than SEAD mission (destruction rather than suppression). Intelligence reports indicated that the TPS-43 was being constantly rotated through three locations: one on Mount Round, one on Sapper Hill and a third close to Stanley on the outskirts of the airfield. Our aim was to locate the TPS-43, fix its position, get a lock on and ripple fire two Shrikes in quick succession in a twenty-degree dive from a sanctuary height of 12,000ft and at the all-important range of 6.9 miles. As both Skybolt pylon positions had been taken up by the Shrike missiles we would not be able to carry the Westinghouse ALQ-101-10 ECM pod afforded to both Black Bucks 1 and 2 for self-protection in order to jam any fire control radar that threatened us.

Intelligence told us to expect Roland surface-to-air missiles and Oerlikon 35mm guns capable of engaging targets up to 10,000ft with their Skyguard fire control radar.

But this was not a covert mission; we would not have the element of surprise and we were not going to jam their radars. We would have to announce our presence, remain in the overhead in a search pattern, locate and identify the sites and entice the TPS-43 into illuminating us. We should be safe from the triple A and Roland as long as we remained above 10,000ft.

Just before midnight, pre-flight systems checks were completed, including a short burst of H2S radar, away from the Soviet trawler, to confirm its serviceability. An unserviceable H2S was clearly a no-go item. Take-off in total R/T silence was followed by an uneventful climb to 33,000ft, that is until I continued with my NBS system checks. To my horror I found that I had no radar markers. Without a range and bearing marker there was no way I could mark and locate with accuracy the TPS-43 radar. Or was there? I suddenly recalled my OCU training and the tips Squadron Leader John Williams had given me at an early stage of my squadron work-up programme. Now I was going to have to earn my flying pay and improvise more in order to generate some radar markers to enable me to call an accurate release point for our Shrike attack. The only way of generating alternative markers was by drawing out some long-winded trigonometric equations and by winding the calculated coordinates, in yards, onto the radar offset potentiometers. I didn't have a slide rule let alone a pocket calculator and so I was going to have to do this by long hand.

"What's your problem, radar?" enquired Neil our captain in his usual Scottish dulcet tone.

I explained our situation. It was not ideal but I offered him a crumb of comfort.

"We will have to abort the mission if you cannot guarantee a satisfactory targeting solution," said Neil. "How long do you need before I call an abort?"

"Give me twenty minutes and I will let you know if it is feasible or not," I said enthusiastically.

Well I didn't need to apply my physics degree to this task but I now understand why the minimum requirement from the Biggin Hill aircrew selection process was for at least five O levels, one of which had to be maths.

After about twenty minutes or so I piped up: "Happy. I've calculated the offsets for all three of the possible locations at Sapper Hill, Mount Round and Port Stanley, and Barry has checked my figures. I am confident we can still do this; there is no need to abort Black Buck 4."

Four hours into the sortie, just as we prepared for the final fuel transfer, our accompanying Victor tanker broke radio silence to announce that his hose drum unit was unserviceable. He would not be able to transfer any fuel to us and therefore the mission would have to be aborted after all. The sense of disappointment and deflation was overwhelming for us all. We were sixty minutes from our descent position and only 700 miles from the Falklands. All that hard work getting here, all the preparation and planning, all the time spent developing an improvised tactic to defeat the Argentinians' search radar capability, all my impromptu trigonometry, all of it would now go to waste. The DNCO (duty not carried out) entry in the Form 700 and authorisation sheets following our return said it all!

Our disappointment was short-lived. The following evening on 30th May we launched yet again at midnight, in darkness and in total R/T silence with a formation of ten Victors. Chris Lackman our co-pilot popped his two Temazepam pills to help him sleep and he snuggled down over the escape hatch in an air ventilated suit and sleeping bag for warmth. 'Snuggle' isn't quite the right word as the escape hatch door was not the most inviting or comforting place in the cockpit to grab a nap but there was no other space available; the visual bomb-aimer's position in the nose section under the pilot's ejector seats had been taken up by a crate on which were mounted the Carousel INS gyros and integrators. Meanwhile Brian Gardner, the third pilot who was seconded to the crew to assist with air-to-air refuelling, took his place in the right-hand seat. The refuelling brackets passed by without serious incident this time. Thirty minutes prior to our descent to low level I clambered down over the escape hatch to awaken our co-pilot, Chris. Chris was already wide awake. The tablets hadn't worked. Or had it been adrenalin that had kept him alert with eyes wide open for the past seven hours. Brian and Chris exchanged positions again for the descent. Chris had to switch on quickly; we were just about to enter a dragon's den.

"Top of decent checks please," requested Neil. And down we went, some 240 miles north of East Falkland.

"Flight Level 300," I called passing 30,000ft in a cruise descent. "Flight Level 200....100, 90, 80, 50. Set the regional QNH....1,000 feet. TFR checks!"

"500 feet, 300, 200 steady." I cross-checked with our radio altimeter. Bang on the money. We accelerated to 300 knots for the ingress.

"This is it guys!" The plan was to penetrate under the radar horizon and then car-ry out a steep climb to 12,000ft with about fifty nautical miles to run. Has our navigation been ac-curate enough? Will the H2S radar work when I switch on the transmitter? Will my markers work? Will I be able to identify the radar offsets? Will we be safe at 12,000ft or is there a Roland missile system in the vicinity? So many questions on my mind. So many un-

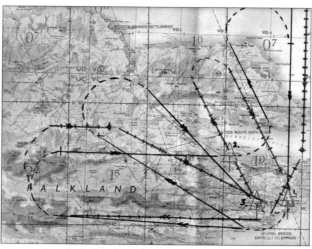

Tactical planning plots to discover the location of the radar. (*Dave Castle*)

certainties. Too many things to go wrong.

With fifty miles to run on the Carousel INS, we initiated our climb to height. This is the moment of truth, I thought. Tilt set correctly, sector scan selected. I switched on the H2S for a couple of sweeps and, lo and behold, Cape Pembroke was only three miles off my radar markers. Fucking brilliant, I thought. Now, let's update the NBS.

But there was silence over the R/T and intercom. No bleeps, no burps. No search radar, no fire control radar, absolutely nothing!

And then, just as we levelled out, there it was in the E-H band of the spectrum, the TPS-43 had burst into full voice like a skylark in spring. We set off on our improvised race track to the west above the possible locations of our adversary radar in an attempt to fix its position. We then opened out to the north of Stanley to get a cross-cut bearing and turned 180° south to fly a menacing run towards the airfield. Perhaps they will think we are a bomber and will try to engage us. And then, as if they had just heard our protestations, suddenly there was a 'spike' on the RWR about 20° left of the nose but in the I-band of the radar spectrum this time.

"Think that's a Skyguard," exclaimed Rod enthusiastically over the intercom. There it was again, this time for five seconds or so, a very distinctive rattling sound. "They're not daft," added Rod.

From our pattern of triangulation and by using a process of elimination, some mental arithmetic and a big dose of intuition, we deduced the location of the TPS-43 and I selected my radar offsets. Having triangulated its location I could now refine my radar markers and provide the pilots with a steer to their flight director, and with range information for Barry and Rod. Neil pulled 597 into a tight turn back on to a recipro-cal heading. We opened out to the north once again. We had sufficient fuel for about two more patterns and two more attempts to engage the radar. Surely they don't know we are ARM equipped. Why won't they keep their radar switched on? If they thought we were a bomber they would try and engage us surely. They won't want another stick of twenty-one 1,000lb bombs raining down on their heads, I thought.

"There it is again," exclaimed Rod as we turned inbound; an E-band spike appeared on the RWR once again. "Come left twenty – roll out. That's a good steer. What's our range Dave?"

"Standby….zero demand, HRS to central," I called to the pilots as I refined my ra-dar mark to deduce the range to go. Chris had now recalculated that we only had fuel for this one attempt. We had to get it right. We had to nail the parameters. Suddenly the TPS-43 went silent again.

"Range Nav?"

"Eighteen miles to run. Fifteen, fourteen….," Barry replied.

A burst of E-band energy appeared again on the RWR.

"Come right five degrees, roll out, that's it, steady." Rod's voice was now reaching a crescendo.

Neil pushed on the stick and bunted 597 into a dive.

"Ten miles," cried Barry. "Nine, eight, standby…..FIRE!" Barry hit the stopwatch almost immediately.

Rod pushed the fire button, waited for a jolt, re-selected the pylon and pressed it once again. A second vibration indicated that both missiles had fired off the rails. This was confirmed to us in no uncertain terms when the cabin was suddenly filled with the smell of cordite. What an enticing aroma, I thought. Suddenly the sky was lit up like Guy Fawkes night as the Super Oerlikon guns opened fire on us with the assistance of their Skyguard fire control radar. The smell of cordite now evoked a different, rather less comforting sensation. The RWR was ablaze and the TPS-43 was in full voice.

"Ten seconds," called Barry. "Fifteen. That's twenty. Twenty-five, six, seven, eight, nine, thirty seconds."

Then silence. The RWR went totally quiet.

"Yes. It's down. We've hit it. We must have, surely! I'll do a BIT (built-in test) check just to make sure the RWR is still serviceable," said Rod. It was.

The predicted time of flight of the missile based on the release parameters was thirty seconds. It would have to be an enormous coincidence for the GAA 601 crew to switch off their radar at this precise moment.

"Right, let's get the hell out of here." Neil pushed the throttles wide open and pulled 597 into a steep climbing turn from 10,000ft. Full power was applied. The sound and vibration from the four Rolls-Royce Olympus engines had never been so comforting and re-assuring. No one was going to catch us now, not even a Mirage if there had been one in the vicinity; we were safe – for a while at least.

We debated at length the chances of our success on the long transit back to Ascension. Was it a coincidence that the TPS-43 operator had switched off his radar at thirty seconds on the stopwatch? Without instant battle damage assessment (BDA) we would not know with any certainty until long after we had landed, and possibly not even then.

Then it dawned on us. We still had to make our final RV with a Victor from Wideawake and successfully tank from him otherwise our perceived success could soon become a failure.

The final RV was made with our lone tanker, courtesy of a radar operator in a supporting Nimrod who helped us to locate and converge on each other without too

much of a fuss. Fuel was transferred without a glitch and we flew into aviation annals having completed the longest combat mission in the history of air warfare; precisely sixteen hours – five minutes longer than Vulcan 607 and Black Buck 1.

We celebrated with a few more Castle la-

Vulcan bomb-bay tank housing 9,250 imperial gallons.
(*Flickr.com*)

gers back in our accommodation at Two Boats village but our celebrations were short-lived. Intelligence had reported the following day that the TPS-43 had indeed been damaged by the Shrike's 150lb blast fragmentation warhead impacting a few metres away from the radar head but a spare wave-guide assembly had been flown in that same day from the mainland and it was back up and running once more. So we would have to go back and do it all over again.

On Black Buck 5 we had spent around thirty minutes in the overhead of East Falkland allowing me time to interrogate the same radar offsets that had been used for Black Bucks 1 and 2. Radar significant points such as a coastal feature, TV mast or corner of a building were used to engage a target that did not show up well on radar. The coordinates of these offset points were calculated in relation to the impact point required for the bomb load. An internal offset was preferred to an external offset due to its closer proximity to the target, thereby minimising the radar aiming errors. On passing over the airfield I had identified the Stanley ATC tower as the internal offset used for Black Buck 1 with a high degree of confidence and so for Black Buck 6, I pleaded with the ops staff and mission planners at Ascension Island to allow us to carry a bomb load in the bomb bay in addition to our Shrike payload on the wing pylons. I was utterly convinced of my ability to deliver a bomb and crater the runway and felt we could do it with only a stick of seven; there was insufficient space in the bomb bay for twenty-one 1,000lb-ers with a bomb bay fuel tank fitted and our loiter plan would benefit from the fitment of a second tank. My request was rejected but I suppose common sense had prevailed again. The priority now was to neutralise the TPS-43 and not crater the runway.

Our down-time lasted a little longer this time, which included an extra day's relaxation and time to modify the Shrike tactic based on our experience and lessons learnt from the day before. We had of course detected a Skyguard fire control radar operating in I-band of the radar spectrum and so elected to take a total of four Shrike missiles on Black Buck 6; two optimised against the TPS-43, our primary target, and two optimised against Skyguard should they attempt to engage us again.

That evening I played the best game of snooker ever in my life in the Exiles Club in Georgetown. Never before in all my misspent youth in the snooker hall at Liverpool University, and never again since in an officers' mess, have I ever made a break of

sixty-seven. I was on fire. Perhaps all the adrenalin flowing in my body had heightened my senses to enable me to pot so many blues, pinks and blacks with such consistency. Then again, perhaps it was just a big dose of luck. I hoped the good fortune would remain with me and our crew just a little longer. We were going to need it over the next forty-eight hours.

Crews for Black Buck 5. From left to right: Rod Trevaskus, Neil McDougall, Barry Smith, Monty, Chris Lackman, John Hathaway, Pete Ford, Dave Castle, Dick Arnott, Dave Stenhouse and Brian Gardner. Bill Perrins must have taken the picture and crew details are in Appendix 2. (*Dave Castle*)

On the evening of 2nd June a small crew

bus arrived to collect us from our accommodation at Two Boats village. We asked the driver to detour via the NAAFI in Georgetown as we wanted to supplement our in-flight rations with extra cans of Coke and fruit juice for our next mission. Much to our chagrin, the NAAFI store manager refused to serve us. "These supplies are for Georgetown residents," the manager said. "You guys are depleting our stocks, go away." All we wanted were a few cans and choccy bars as the detachment supply of in-flight rations was inadequate for a sixteen-hour sortie. Our pleas fell on deaf ears and so for the next ten years I boycotted all NAAFI shops in the UK. They clearly didn't need my business and I didn't want theirs.

Crew-in, start-up, taxi and take-off at Wideawake was now a familiar routine to us. Power on and systems checks were completed with no-go items fully functioning, particularly the Shrike cockpit indicator, H2S radar, RWR and Carousel INS. We launched in total R/T silence again with ten Victors at thirty-second intervals. In daylight it would have been a very impressive spectacle. At night it was just an incessant wall of noise.

Black Buck 6 followed an almost identical profile to that of Black Buck 5. There was only one way to ingress; we had insufficient fuel to push further south and approach from a different cardinal point. At fifty miles we pulled up from our run-in height of 200ft above mean sea level and initiated a climb to 12,000ft where we settled down into another racetrack pattern to try and entice the TPS-43 into action.

Again nothing. Not a single bleep or single burp on the RWR. As we predicted, they suspected our motives and their radar stayed stubbornly silent. They had learnt a valuable lesson from our previous encounter and were, sensibly, leaving their radar in standby mode. Had that Soviet trawler tipped them off? Are they unaware of our presence? I can't believe that, I thought.

Suppression of enemy air defences is a mission or capability that most modern-day air forces possess and practise. The USAF first employed SEAD to good effect in Vietnam with Shrike and in Gulf War 1 with HARM. The principle is to suppress or deny the enemy his use of surveillance and fire control radars so as to facilitate other capabilities carrying out attack missions such as air interdiction or an airfield attack. For a SEAD mission to be successful, all it had to do was ensure the enemy's radar stayed silent. The arrival of Black Buck 6 overhead Port Stanley airfield was timed to coincide with an airfield attack by RAF Harriers launched from HMS *Hermes*.

The aim of the Harriers' attack that morning was not to crater the runway but to destroy soft targets such as static Pucará aircraft and airfield buildings. To crater a runway required a high-explosive bomb with a forged steel casing to be dropped from sufficient a height to impact it with a terminal velocity capable of penetrating concrete. As the minimum stick spacing between two bombs dropped by a Vulcan was equivalent to the width of Port Stanley runway, the optimum attack angle would need to be between thirty and forty degrees to the runway direction to have any chance of scoring a hit, otherwise two adjacent bombs in a stick could straddle the runway without impacting it.

One of my most abiding memories from Operation Corporate was attending a brief in the main briefing room at Waddington during the final stage of our work-up programme in April. A senior air ranking officer had visited to wish us good luck prior to our deployment to Ascension. At the close of the brief this senior officer rose to his feet, coughed and then posed a question to the crews gathered in front of him:

"I have just one final query gentlemen. Can you just explain to me why you haven't chosen to fly at night down the centre-line of the runway at low level so as to drop a neat pattern of twenty-one 1,000lb bombs down its full length to crater it and put it out of use? After all, we have sourced some night vision goggles for you."

Our station commander, Group Captain John Laycock took him to one side and politely explained the principle to him once again. The rest of us just looked at each other in total amazement and shock.

The reason for our attack profile on Black Buck 6 was to simulate yet another bombing mission in the hope that the TPS-43 would switch on and illuminate us. Well the concurrent GR3 attack probably confused the enemy rather than clarified the situation for them. But still the TPS-43 refused to play.

"Right, we are going to have to go completely naked and bare all," said Rod. "Keep your radar on Dave, let's see if we can entice them to come out and play."

"Come on guys, switch on. Here we are again, come and get us! You must be able to hear these thundering Olympus 301 engines, even from our perch at 12 000ft."

Suddenly we heard a bleep on our headsets. "Missed that," said Rod, "but it sounded like I-band. There it is again, I-band, definitely." We continued with our game of 'cat and mouse' for almost another twenty minutes attempting to triangulate the position of the TPS-43 but the Argentinians were playing hard to get. Chris Lackman interrupted our conversation. "Hey guys, we have enough fuel for one more circuit before we need to bug out."

We were becoming increasingly frustrated when Neil announced "I'll be beggared if I have come 4,000 miles just to listen to electronic bleeps and burps on that RWR."

Flight Lieutenant Herm Harper from Boscombe Down had informed us that, as a last resort if the radar did not emit, we could always launch the missile ballistically in a dive but the chances of scoring a hit would be extremely slim. Again, that assumed we knew the precise location of the mobile radar beforehand.

Radar pictures. *Left*: quarter million scale of East Falkland. *Right*: one-eighth million scale of Stanley including airfield. The town of Stanley can be seen as a bright return and, to a trained eye, the runway and air traffic tower are also visible. (*Dave Castle*)

"Dave, can you ascertain the location of that radar?" enquired Rod.

"From what I can deduce, it looks like a Skyguard emitter close to the airfield. I've got my markers over its possible location so we could prosecute an attack if we have enough fuel."

"Ten minutes to Bingo," Chris interrupted.

"OK," proposed Rod. "Let's give it a go. The airfield attack is probably complete. They may feel they are now safe. Let's assume it's on the airfield then."

Neil tipped 597 onto its wing-tip and opened out to the north one last time. We knew we only had one shot at this. But we needed the enemy radar to emit.

"Twenty-five miles to run," said Barry.

I was confident of my radar mark. "Come on, come on, switch on, switch on, I pleaded." Nothing!

"Twenty miles, nothing on the RWR," confirmed Rod. "Captain, we are going to have to assume the Skyguard is on the airfield and launch one of the Shrikes in its ballistic mode," he added. "Perhaps if they see an explosion on the airfield they might decide to switch on the TPS-43."

"Right, we are going down," said Neil, as he bunted 597 into a steep dive from 15 nautical miles.

"10,000 feet, 9,000!" exclaimed Barry.

Suddenly the Shrike cockpit panel meter detected a faint signal. "Come left ten," screamed Rod. "Roll out now." The Shrike had the Skyguard in its sights and its talons were now unfurled.

"Ten miles," cried Barry. "Nine, eight, standby, FIRE!"

Rod pushed the fire button and made the switch selection for the second Shrike. The second missile juddered loose and filled the cockpit with the enticing smell of cordite again.

I pulled my head out of the radar screen and glanced across at the radio altimeter. "Check height, 7,000 feet."

The RWR lit up like a Christmas tree. All hell had broken loose over the airfield and we bottomed out at 6,000 feet amidst a salvo of triple A from the Super Oerlikon guns. The sky pulsed with shards of light in the clouds all around us as Neil applied full power and recovered us to our sanctuary height of 12,000 feet. Barry counted down the time on the stopwatch as he had done on Black Buck 5. Twenty seconds had elapsed and the Skyguard was still active. And then, as if on cue after thirty seconds, total silence.

Twenty years after this event, Group Captain John Laycock forwarded to me an article from a South American publication that provided a historical account of our attacks from the perspective of Grupo de Artilleria Antiaerea 601 where the unit revealed that the TPS-43 had been temporarily damaged on Black Buck 5, and a Skyguard radar had been completely destroyed with the loss of four operators and a fifth injured on Black Buck 6. We had been fortunate on Black Buck 6. We believe that the Skyguard radar had probably been in standby mode but that its frequency modulators were probably still running and that is what the hyper-sensitive Shrike homing head had detected. As Gary Player the golfer once said: "The harder I practise, the luckier

I seem to get!" Up until this revelation by GAA 601, there was not one senior officer in Strike Command who was prepared to recognise or acknowledge the operational success of these two missions.

Our egress from the target area over East Falkland was uneventful apart from the odd spike on the RWR that had us thinking about the possibility of a Mirage combat air patrol in the area. But we had a true airspeed of 480 knots or eight miles per minute and so any adversary would probably need to go supersonic to catch us and that would almost certainly use up most of his fuel reserves. Again, we debated at length the chances of the Skyguard switching off after thirty seconds at the precise moment the missile was expected to impact.

As we approached our RV with the Victor for our final but most important refuel point, Chris and Brian exchanged positions once more. The whole rationale for bringing Brian along was for him to relieve Neil McDougall after thirteen hours in the air and assume responsibility for the final refuelling bracket. Controversially though, Neil elected to conduct the final AAR procedure himself rather than relinquish the task to the more refreshed and rested Brian Gardner.

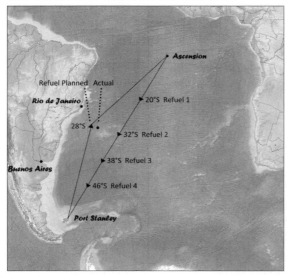

The Victor turned up on cue, assisted by a Nimrod for the RV, and Neil's attempt to connect with the basket on the first prod was rather abject. It was clear to us all that he was really fatigued but that was unsurprising. He began like a bull in a china shop.

"Let me have a go," suggested Chris as Brian was still not allowed into the right-hand seat. "No I'm fine," answered Neil but his second, third, fourth and fifth attempts were no better. On the sixth prod, disaster struck.

Black Buck 6 refuelling plan with location. Planned return refuelling 673 nautical miles to Rio. Actual nearly 800 nautical miles.

"Shit," muttered Neil with rather un-subtle understatement. With single-minded determination and stubbornness, his final attempt resulted in the probe penetrating the basket, damaging its spokes and sending splinters of aluminium down the engine intakes, damaging the inlet guide vanes of Nos 2 and 3 engines, and leaving the tip of the probe embedded in the basket!

The stark realisation of our predicament suddenly dawned on me. Without an uplift of fuel there was no way we would make Ascension Island. We were doomed. We had no diversions to fly to. Our rendezvous with the tanker had been further east than planned so that the Brazilian coast was almost 800 miles away and we only had sufficient fuel for about an hour and a half's endurance or 700 miles range. Our brief from the ops team back on Ascension was that if such an event occurred we should abandon aircraft and take to our dinghies. The thought of spending the remainder of the conflict bobbing about in a single-seat dinghy, miles from anywhere, waiting for some super tanker on the off chance to stumble across me did not really appeal!

Chris Lackman quickly totted up the fuel tanks and with only 13,500lbs remaining declared that we would not make land-fall. The only charts Barry and I had, with the exception of our targeting material and a quarter-million scale map of the Falklands, was a five-million scale chart that portrayed the whole of the South American coast from Panama in the north to Punta Arenas in Chile to the south, and the whole of the west coast of Africa from the Southern Cape to Morocco. We had no terminal approach charts (TAPs) or flight information publications (FLIPs) or diversion publications. All of those had been commandeered by the Victor and Nimrod crews on Ascension leaving us with a single photo-copied table of radio frequencies for Brazilian airspace. Yet it was they who were supposed to be supporting us not us them.

"Where is the nearest airfield navs?" enquired Neil.

"It's going to be Rio de Janeiro," Barry replied. I agreed and did a quick ready-reckon calculation to confirm our perilous fuel state.

"Bollocks," was one of the more printable exclamations from the combined rear crew. Neil eased back on the stick and commenced a cruise climb from 33,000ft to Flight Level 430.

"That should help eke out a few hundred more pounds of fuel," said Barry. "But will it be enough to make Rio?"

Unknown to us at this juncture XM597 had developed a fuel leak from the galley between the wing tanks and bomb-bay tank. Every attempt by Chris to re-balance the fuel tanks with the cross-feed cock resulted in us losing more fuel from a fractured fuel pipe. This was just not our day.

I placed my radar markers over the part of the Brazilian coastline that approximated to Rio de Janeiro and provided a rough steer through the flight director to the autopilot. The coast was still over 400 miles away. A further more detailed fuel check from Chris provided us with a little more optimism but it would still result in us having to bale out fifty to sixty miles short of Rio as the engines flamed out one by one.

"Hang on," exclaimed Rod. "If we do make it, what are we going to say about where we have come from and what we have been doing?"

"And what about the two remaining Shrikes?" added Barry. "There is no way we could claim to have been on a radar reconnaissance sortie with two ARM missiles slung under the wing."

"Best we jettison them," said Neil.

Rod reminded Neil that we had no safe jettison capability and that we would need to live fire the missiles off the rails.

"Nav radar, search ahead and check the sea for any surface vessels. We can't afford another major incident today."

Many fishing boats are equipped with radar for navigation and these often transmit in the I-band of the radar spectrum. As the Shrikes had to be launched with the warhead enabled, the last thing we needed was for one or both to guide and home in on a Brazilian trawler. That would have made us even less welcome in Rio if we were to make it to the bar that evening.

I switched on the H2S radar and to my horror there was what appeared to be a fishing fleet forty to fifty miles ahead of us on a westerly bearing. "We will need to come left by at least sixty degrees before we launch the Shrikes," I advised.

So for good measure Neil brought 597 hard left through ninety degrees onto a southerly heading. "OK, AEO," I said to Rod. "You are clear to live jettison," I added as I played with the tilt and gain of the radar.

"Firing in three, two, one…. That's one away. Firing the second in three, two one…." This time there was no judder or vibration. "I think we have a hang-up," called Rod.

He tried again and a third time, but either the firing pulse had failed or there was a problem with the launcher or missile, or both. Neil brought the aircraft back on to a westerly heading before we exacerbated our fuel predicament any further.

"We have another problem," said Barry. "What about all our planning material, charts, maps, H2S R88 radar film, crypto and codewords? If we do make Brazil, there is a potential intelligence windfall for their authorities there."

There was only one way of disposing all of the sensitive and classified material and that was by opening the escape hatch and throwing the lot out of the door. So we elected to de-pressurise the aircraft cabin and open the escape hatch in flight – at 43,000ft. Madness or what?

Now, to the best of my knowledge I don't think this had ever been tried in a Vulcan before at that height. Perhaps it had been attempted at a much lower altitude but the situation would then have most likely required the rear crew to abandon aircraft due to some life-threatening emergency such as an engine or airframe fire.

Neil had already gone to 'combat pressure'. "Standby," said Neil. "Toggles down and select 100% oxygen on your P masks. De-pressurising in three, two, one, now!"

There was a muffled bang instantly followed by a hazy mist in the cockpit that formed as water droplets condensed and cooled under reduced pressure. Our oxygen regulators immediately recognised the fall in pressure and commenced to force-feed 100% oxygen to our masks. The simple task of breathing and talking suddenly required a major effort on our part. Fortunately our aviation medicine training at North Luffenham had prepared us well; we had all previously experienced the effects of zero cabin pressure and the symptoms of hypoxia at altitude.

The mist had now cleared and I could see Barry and Rod again sitting alongside me in the rear cockpit – that was re-assuring. There was an eerie silence for a moment or two until Barry flicked the power switch under his plotter's table to open the escape hatch door. A roaring, ear-splitting noise filled the relative vacuum in the cockpit. Imagine driving down the M5 at seventy miles an hour and then opening all the car windows and sun roof and then attempting to hold an intelligent conversation with your partner. Increase that effect three-fold and you come somewhere near to appreciating the environment we now found ourselves in.

Brian Gardner had loaded all our classified planning material, photographic film and crypto into the aircrew ration box and added an undercarriage lock for extra weight. Brian and I then edged the ration box closer to the 'six by three foot' escape hatch and pushed it onto the lip of the door as we stared out into the South Atlantic abyss. One extra shove and the ration box slid down the door and disappeared out of sight.

"Clear to close," I screamed at Barry. Barry could not hear me over the maelstrom of noise. "Clear to close the hatch door," I screamed even louder, again to no avail. I prodded Barry on his shoulder and gave him a thumbs-up signal and a wave of the palm of my hand in an upwards motion to indicate that he could now close the hatch door. Barry flicked the switch under his table but nothing happened. Then I remembered. The manual operating handle will have now travelled into the locked-open detent position and would need to be un-locked manually. I was still out of my seat standing next to Brian who was by the sixth seat; we both had our parachutes on. I looked across at the escape hatch and at the expanse of ocean below and identified the door handle on the far side but realised I could not reach it without a crew ladder fixed onto the door. There was no space on this mission to stow a ladder in its usual stowage position in the nose section adjacent to the visual bomb aimer's position.

Brian immediately understood what was required. One of us would need to clamber down and straddle the escape hatch and attempt to reach the door handle and dislodge it from its locked detent position. One slip or stumble and it would be curtains. I doubt if either of us would have survived a parachute descent from 43,000ft. What followed was one of the scariest things I have ever done in my life. With my arms wrapped around Brian's waist we both edged closer to the door. The noise was incessant and we struggled to understand each other over the intercom. Sign language was required to reinforce each message. Brian straddled across the hatch and stretched his right arm forward in an attempt to reach the handle. He was about six inches short. I adjusted my anchor position at the top of the hatch and slid my grip lower down Brian's torso. The handle wouldn't budge. It was well and truly wedged into the locked-open position. I grabbed my aircrew knife and ripped it from its sheath and handed it to Brian. Brian used the knife to lever the handle out of its detent into the un-locked position. This time Barry's eyes were firmly fixed on mine and he knew instantly that he was now clear to close the hatch door. No need for a hand signal this time.

Whilst Brian and I had been practising aerobics on the cabin floor of the Vulcan, Rod had declared an emergency over the HF radio. He had eventually made contact with a Brazilian air traffic controller on VHF 121.5 but the controller struggled to understand fully our predicament and was proving rather un-cooperative. Eventually on UHF 243.0, a more cooperative controller engaged with us but we still did not have his permission to close in on Rio. We continued inbound nevertheless. We had been pressure breathing for a full thirty minutes, which made both internal and external communications nigh on impossible. My suggestion of "tell them we're from Huddersfield" in a Donald Duck accent gave us that little extra time to communicate with each other on intercom and to handle the in-flight emergency.

With the escape hatch now closed and locked we were able to re-pressurise and return to normality. But this was by no means a return to routine ops for us. We had insufficient fuel to make Rio, or had we? It was going to be touch and go.

Chris Lackman called out the fuel figures in turn from each of the fourteen fuel tanks. "1,000lbs, one and a half, two and a half, 2,000...." Barry totted the figures up and claimed we had clawed back an extra five or ten minutes duration or about forty to eighty miles of range. It looked as though the cruise climb to 43,000ft had helped but then the drag from the open door hatch wouldn't have assisted much either.

Now, unbeknown to us until well after we had landed, the Brazilian air defence commander had scrambled two Northrop F5s to intercept us. We never did learn what their intention was or what action they would have taken had they found us. Fortunately, the duty fighter controller vectored the pair to the wrong location and so the nearest they got to us was when we were short finals to land. To catch us up they had to turnabout and accelerate to Mach one plus, which resulted in one F5 delivering a supersonic boom over Copacabana beach and the bay of Rio.

Our voices were by now sounding a little more confident and the Brazilian controller had accepted that we were not going to turnabout and disappear out of his sector. We were now his problem for the day. Neil commenced a gentle cruise descent with about sixty miles to run and levelled off at 23,000ft. By now I had identified Rio International Galeão Airport on the H2S radar and provided an accurate steer to the flying pilot, Neil.

"We are not going any lower until I can see the runway threshold with my own eyes," exclaimed Neil.

Fortunately the visibility was superb that day and there was no cloud cover whatsoever. Provided the fuel held out we should be able to spiral down almost in the overhead with the throttles at idle. This was the plan. Were the engines to flame out now then we would still have a good chance of being rescued off the coast. The sea was fairly warm and so I could now dispense with my immersion suit.

We still did not have authority to land but we were going in anyway. We were talking to a controller and we were squawking emergency on the IFF. We had a radar service. The controller could provide safe separation and de-confliction for civil airliners in our vicinity. We crossed the coastline at 16,000ft and commenced a corkscrew descent, a full thirteen and a half hours after departing Ascension Island. The controller finally gave us permission to land on the duty runway but that would have required a risky, downwind over-flight of the city to reach the runway threshold. We could not afford the engines to flame out over a highly populated area. Neil elected to land on the reciprocal runway, downwind, rather than into a light, five to ten knot breeze.

"Let's get the gear down now," said Neil. We were now committed but Neil still needed to nail the approach parameters, and we were currently too 'hot' and too high at 10,000ft. The fuel gauges, according to Chris, were now indicating empty across all four groups. This was going to be close. Neil eased back on the throttles, extended the airbrake and bled the speed off. Chris pushed the gear 'down' button. One, two, three greens. That was a relief. Neil then stood the bomber on its port wing-tip and pulled it into a tighter two to three g turn with sixty-five degrees of bank. His concentration was now entirely focussed on making sure he would nail the parameters as he approached the high and low key positions from an approach that did not feature in the aircrew manual or flight reference cards. This was the only way Neil could trade off height against speed without exceeding the incipient stall. He needed to get the big bomber on to short finals with about 130-135 knots of airspeed. Neil was right on the money. A superb piece of skilful flying and airmanship ensured he was able to roll out on the extended centre line of the runway at 300 feet with about one mile to run.

The minimum landing fuel in peace-time after diversion for a Vulcan was 8,000lbs and for operational flying 4,000lbs; the fuel gauges were notoriously unreliable. A full visual circuit required 1,700lbs of fuel. We cleared the runway, stopped short and Rod slid out down the escape hatch door onto the taxiway to disable the Shrike missile, just in case. As we taxied onto a hard standing on the military side of Galeão airfield with only 1,500lbs of fuel remaining, one of the four Rolls-Royce Olympus 301 engines flamed out!

At Galeão we were greeted by forty to fifty armed guards along with their base commander, and were held under open arrest in the officers' mess for a period of seven days. We were well treated and cared for and were invited to a squadron BBQ and allowed to participate in a daily five-a-side football competition (which the Brazilians always won of course) but we were not allowed to leave. We each took it in turns to guard and watch over Vulcan XM597 for the whole time we were there. The remaining Shrike missile was confiscated by the Brazilian air force and taken to an armoury. We unloaded the missile ourselves using a hydraulic safety raiser with a mattress from the officers' mess laid on top, after making it safe with pylon pins and its own missile safety breaks. We were still a little concerned that a firing pulse may have travelled down the pylon and launcher unit and had initiated part of the missile launch sequence. Fortunately it hadn't.

The British air attaché from Sao Paulo took charge of our release negotiations but the Argentinians had already made a request via the Brazilian authorities for us to be handed over to them as prisoners of war. This request was politely refused. Eventually, diplomatic pressure was brought to bear but the real reason we were released, according to the Brazilian colonel who was assigned as our mentor and escort, was that the day after our eventual release on 11th July 1982, Pope John Paul ll was travelling to visit Buenos Aires. On his way to Argentina, arrangements were rapidly being made for him to fly into Rio Galeão airport where he was expected to say Mass to an invited congregation of nearly 100,000 followers. The altar for Mass was to be located on the hardstanding next to where our Vulcan bomber was parked. The base commander requested that we taxied 597 to the other side of the airfield so that it would be out of sight. We politely declined but suggested that if he filled our tanks to full with AVTUR we would get out of his hair and fly back to Ascension forthwith. Our request was granted, probably to save embarrassing the Pope or the president – or both.

That afternoon the Brazilian chief of air staff visited us to wish us well before our planned departure the following day. He asked what we thought of Rio but we replied that we had not been afforded the opportunity to taste or experience the delights it had to offer. He was shocked to hear this and immediately ordered the base commander to task one of his Super Pumas to take us on an aerial sight-seeing trip of Sugar Loaf Mountain and the beautiful coastline of Rio. He then ordered our colonel escort to

Galeão airport, Rio de Janeiro. From left, Barry Smith – nav plotter, Rod Trevaskus – AEO, Chris Lackman – co-pilot, Brian Gardner – third pilot, David Castle – nav radar, Neil McDougall – captain, assistant air attaché, and Rio base commander with family. (*Dave Castle*)

arrange for a taxi to take us down town to a cabaret show and a few farewell beers. We were aircrew. How could we possibly refuse his invitation? Neil our captain though correctly elected to stay with his bomber.

Without going into too much detail, we had a romping good time down town including being propositioned a few times along the strip between Copacabana and Ipanema beaches. Two girls in particular proved difficult to shrug off. One had an Australian accent but claimed to be Argentinian. We were naturally very suspicious and tried to keep her at arm's length. It wasn't until thirty years after this event that I learned who this girl and her colleague really were. When the Foreign Office had learned that the crew of Black Buck 6 was about to hit the town before being released back to Ascension Island, someone in the Ministry of Defence must have had a fit. He was probably ex-aircrew himself and knew of the potential pitfalls that could await unsuspecting aircrew after being incarcerated in an overseas mess for a whole week. After all this was a foreign country some 5,000 miles from the UK. Britain did not have any MI6 operatives in the area at the time and so a request was made to the CIA to put a tail on us, mainly for our own safety as who knows what could have happened to us that night as we sauntered around town from one cocktail bar to the next. There is one thing I can say and definitely vouch for though. Rio is a hell of a long way from Huddersfield.

On leaving the V Force, Wing Commander David Castle went on to realise his ambition by completing three tours on Buccaneers at RAF Lossiemouth. He became a qualified weapons instructor and was appointed the senior navigation instructor for 237 Operational Conversion Unit. He carried out seventeen missions during Gulf War 1 in the Pavespike laser designation role and retired from the RAF in 2005 after thirty-two years of service.

Chapter Fifteen

THE VULCAN K2 TANKER

John Laycock was station commander at Waddington as the operational life of the Vulcan drew to a close. He explains that as a final extension to its service life the Vulcan was converted to a tanker and had its fuel capacity increased by putting fuel tanks in the bomb bay. However, its total fuel load of just over 90,000lbs was still over 30,000lbs short of the '120,000lbs plus' fuel of the Victor K2. In fact John was in the co-pilot's seat of the Vulcan tanker being flown by Chris Lumb when the RAF Hercules took the picture of the aircraft refuelling another Vulcan being flown by Flight Lieutenant Trowbridge (see picture section).

By mid-April 1982 it had become clear that the RAF was desperately short of air-refuelling capacity. Any major air-refuelled operation in the South Atlantic would commit almost the entire Victor force and the capacity remaining in the UK would be very limited. Other refuelling tasks still had to be met, in particular support for the air defence aircraft in the UK Air Defence Region. At the very least, RAF tanker resources would need some short-term enhancement.

On 30th April a conference was held at British Aerospace, Woodford, to consider the possibility of converting some Vulcan B2 airframes to tankers. The initial engineering feasibility discussions concluded that if the hose drum unit, the giant cotton reel which held the 100-foot long refuelling hose, could be fitted into the aft fuselage below the fin, the entire bomb bay could be fitted with fuel tanks, adding some 21,000lbs of fuel to the internal fuel load of 72,000lbs. Also, with a fairly simple interconnecting system, all the fuel contents could be available for transfer in the air and all tanks could be filled to their maximum when receiving from another tanker. This configuration was approved on 4th May and six B2 aircraft were earmarked for conversion into single-point tankers, designated for the Vulcan B2(K), with the conversion work to be carried out at Woodford. The flying task was assigned to 50 Squadron, commanded by Wg Cdr Lumb, and thus began the extension of service of the squadron beyond 1st July 1982. Action was initiated to identify air and ground crew for the new unit and, suddenly, many more people at Waddington who so far had been excluded from the preparations for the Falkland action, were involved in a new and related activity.

One particular item of equipment now became the focus of attention for several reasons. All existing Vulcan refuelling probes were required, not just for Vulcan combat aircraft and the new tankers, but also for Nimrod maritime patrol aircraft, and VC10 and Hercules transport aircraft. Parties of engineers set off to recover refuelling probes from aircraft of the three Scampton squadrons and the Vulcan OCU, which had been disposed of either as scrap, relocated to other airfields in the UK and Mediterranean for fire and rescue training, or delivered to historical societies and museums. Probes were even recovered from aircraft previously gifted to locations in the USA and Canada. Goose Bay and Castle AFB in California were visited and their aircraft suitably modified, much to the surprise but willing cooperation of the new owners. All the recovered probes were refurbished and pressed back into service immediately.

The first Vulcan tanker was flight tested at Woodford on 18th June 1982 and delivered to 50 Squadron on 23rd June 1982 exactly fifty days after the plan was first conceived. Thus began a new phase of operational flying which was to last for two years and provide a much needed boost to the RAF's air-refuelling capacity.

> **Chris Lumb** was tasked with forming and running the first and only Vulcan K2 squadron. Here he paints a very comprehensive picture of the birth and operation of the squadron.

50 Squadron, RAF Waddington, 30th March 1984

The party's over and while the candles flicker, the memories of that day, nearly thirty years ago, when we disbanded the last Vulcan squadron, remain remarkably fresh. How could it be otherwise? I had joined the V Force as a wide-eyed co-pilot in 1965, never for a moment believing that I would sit in Jack Pembridge's old office (my first CO) and be there to command the last squadron. There was many a tear in the eye, a sad, disbelief that the mighty Vulcan's last operational role had come to an end. Disbelief that aircraft were destined for museums and gate-guards or lay like carcasses around the airfield being hit by wrecking balls before being bulldozed onto low-loaders and ferried ignominiously out of the main gates.

We shouldn't have been there, of course. We were scheduled to close, along with 44(R) and 101 Squadrons, a couple of years earlier but the Falklands War changed all that and gave us a last hurrah. We had all been posted and I was looking forward to my new job on exchange in Winnipeg, Canada, when news broke in May 1982 that six Vulcan bombers would be converted to tankers to relieve the pressure on the Victors which had served so bravely in the South Atlantic.

With my posting cancelled, my AOC, Mike Knight, told me I had ninety days to get the squadron operational. The crew room the following Monday morning resembled a club at the start of a new football season.

Players from all over the place were transferred in, and half my old squadron had gone. I knew all the faces but not all the names. Morale was good despite there being more questions than answers. We had three problems. We didn't know the first thing about air-to-air refuelling, we had no tanker aircraft and the line squadron, the best bunch of techies that I had ever served with, didn't know one end of a hose drum unit from the other. Solutions, however, were easy. Go to RAF Marham and learn all the theory you can from the tanker boys and await your aircraft. In the meantime, keep your hand in and fly the four bomber aircraft that we also owned.

We didn't wait long and I recall flying the first tanker, XH561, with Al McDicken out of Woodford on 23rd June 1982 and the rest followed quickly. The aircraft felt the same to fly despite the extra fuel tank and the bulbous HDU on the back, which would have made the rear end look uncannily like a Morris 1000 Traveller but for the set of traffic lights and the red markings aimed to help the receiver find the right azimuth.

On landing, we couldn't get that high, extravagant aerodynamic braking for fear of scraping the HDU that had a rather odd tail-scrape warning lever on it that my Flt Cdr Bill Burnett called the donkey's dick. Time to learn how to handle receiver aircraft on the towline and the procedures for multiple aircraft on trails overseas was short, and all the crews needed to become receiver qualified.

We were quickly in demand. The fighter boys were the bread and butter and we'd roar off to accommodate their needs, mostly over the North Sea. I spent most of my Vulcan bomber days avoiding going anywhere near a fighter and here we were welcoming them all like bees round the honey pot. How times change. The

The 'skip' with the warning probe underneath.
(*Mel James*)

First Vulcan tanker on delivery. From left,
Malcolm Muir (Avros), Flight Lieutenant Hill, Al McDicken (Avros),
Chris Lumb, Flight Lieutenant Billings. (*Chris Lumb*)

Falklands experience had shown the importance of AAR, and soon the Nimrod fleet and the C130 were added to our list of customers, teaching their crews by day and night. The C130 towline was flown at quite a slow speed for us and in a slow descent to meet both our needs.

Come the weekend, we would put two aircraft and crews on readiness to provide AAR for the alert fighters. Activity sometimes came unexpectedly and one weekend, after refuelling an F-3, we chased a Russian Bear to the north of Scotland. A Vulcan chasing a Bear!

I believe our time, as a tanker squadron, while brief, was highly valued. We got numerous aircraft and crews through their initial AAR training and saved the Victor Force a lot of flying hours. The Vulcan provides a very stable platform from which to give and receive fuel despite only having a single hose. Receiving fuel is the fun bit of the sortie and requires some initial practice because the high combing blocks out the view of the drogue, which sits below the pilot's vision.

'This brings on the warning light so watch it or you'll hit the bottom of the hose drum unit on the runway!' (*Chris Lumb*)

Chris Lumb's crew: Ken Denman, Bertie Newton, Chris Dent, Prince Michael, Chris Lumb and Geoff Wilson. (*Chris Lumb*)

As our own disbandment loomed on the horizon, there were many requests for a last flight and we were besieged by requests for displays. I had the honour to fly Prince Michael of Kent who sat through a most exciting hour as my main rudder drove itself fully starboard and locked there as we flew with full opposite aileron and full asymmetric power to stay level. The thing I most remember, after we had sorted it out, was arriving back at the crew room. There had been a ban on any form of drinking during the day and especially not on the squadron. Yet here was 50 Squadron, en masse, with pints of beer. "What the hell's going on?" I asked. "Ah," smiled Ken Denman my AEO, "we offered Prince Michael a cup of tea but he said he could murder a beer, so we ordered a couple of barrels!"

This was my busiest time; I can remember flying almost every day of the week, flying displays here or overseas or on standby to perform at the weekends. Life was very different from the bomber days. A bomber crew is like a chef. It is left to plan its own sortie, which usually lasted five hours with its own mix of ingredients and is re-

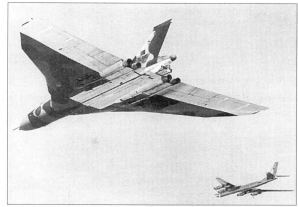

Vulcan tanker with Russian Bear.
(*Crown Copyright*)

sponsible for completing a matrix of training requirements over a six-month period. It is quite self-sufficient and inward looking in that its proficiency is rewarded by the success of its bombing and navigation scores. A tanker crew, by contrast, is tasked from an outside agency; its needs dictated by the needs of countless receivers. A sortie can be as short as a couple of hours because you give away more fuel than you burn. Its success is based on how flexibly it can meet the needs of the receiver crew. From chefs we became waiters.

On reflection, I'm proud that while there may have been the odd interesting moment, we suffered no major nasties and no one gave away so much fuel that they ran out themselves.

All credit to our engineers who kept turning us round and a splendid bunch of aircrews. Above all, none of this was possible without recognising what a versatile and magnificent operational beast the Vulcan was, serving our country in its new tanker role right to the end. Would I do it all again? You bet, because I wouldn't want anything else. When do I start?

Chris Lumb's account of the formation of 50 Squadron is excellent but I was fascinated by the story of the rudder going to full travel while he was in the right-hand seat. Apparently they were at 40,000ft; he must have been incredibly quick to have got the asymmetric power on before the aircraft rolled out of control. He knew he couldn't land like that but worked out how to switch off the main rudder motor and select the number two to get back to normality. As far as I know this was a unique event; certainly in all my years at Avros and subsequent connections I had never heard of a similar occurrence.

Chris finished flying after 50 Squadron but did an exchange tour with the 8th Air Force at Barksdale, was station commander at Brize Norton and finished his career as air attaché in Washington. He clearly found retirement difficult as he was the bursar at St Bedes' Eastbourne for nine years and then obtained an honours degree in sports journalism.

Anthony Wright was Vulcan tanker leader in Chris's squadron as he explains.

After the Falklands War it was clear that the number of Victor tankers would not be able to cope with all their current tanking tasks and, at the same time, support operations in the South Atlantic. As a short term measure, before VC10s and some Hercules were converted to tankers, it was decided to convert six Vulcan B2s into Vulcan K2s. The best aircraft were chosen from the Vulcan squadrons that were disbanding or had already been disbanded. All six K2s would operate on 50 Squadron alongside five remaining B2s.

Pulling out the drogue from the hose drum unit.
(Chris Lumb)

Pleasingly for me, XH558, the first B2 that entered RAF service and the first Vulcan that I flew in 1965, was one of those converted to a K2. Today it still survives, although converted back into a B2, as the only flying Vulcan display aircraft.

British Aerospace at Woodford was given the task of conversion and quickly came up with a solution. There was to be a single refuelling point under the fuselage at the rear of the Vulcan from which the ninety feet of hose with its basket would trail out from what was effectively a 'wooden box' behind which was housed the Mk17 hose drum unit in the space vacated by the electronic counter measures equipment. A small set of traffic lights was positioned either side of the box for receiver aircraft to refuel at night. Finally, a third bomb-bay fuel tank was also installed. As the nav radars on 50 Squadron were going to be the aircrew operating this tanking equipment, the refuelling panel was positioned with the relevant switches, indicators and fuel flow gauges near the bombing panel at the nav radar's position.

The colour scheme underneath the Vulcan was changed to include a broad white-painted area which stretched from the front of the bomb-bay doors to the rear, wide enough to reach the inboard engines on either side. Two red alignment lines from front to back in the white area were also added and another block of white was painted across the underside of the wings at the trailing edge.

Inevitably, all of we nav radars had to go to RAF Marham for a few days to complete a tailor-made crash course on everything about tanking. A Victor tanker instructor was allotted solely to us and we used the Marham tanker refuelling panel simulator and classroom to learn the relevant skills. Once the Vulcan K2s were fitted out, our instructor came to RAF Waddington and flew with us, occupying the sixth seat in the Vulcan to ensure our competency in the air. Thus, we all became tanker operators and as nav radar leader I had become the only Vulcan tanker leader.

All this happened in just a few weeks with the bombers converted to tankers; pilots had to be trained to fly the K2 in a manner so that they didn't damage the so-called 'skip' under the tail on take-off or landing, and the nav radars trained to dispense fuel via the HDU. The crews practised tanking procedures and pilots, not trained to receive fuel, were also taught the air-to-air refuelling flying techniques involved. My first K2 sortie was on 30th June 1982.

Once word spread that Vulcans were tanking, all pilots of aircraft that could receive fuel wanted to have a go with this 'new' tanker. So I've refuelled our squadron Vulcans, Buccaneers, RAF Harriers and Sea Harriers, Hercules, Jaguars, Lightnings, Nimrods, Phantoms, Tornados and Victors. The greatest number of successive prods that I took part in during one sortie was thirty in total, twenty-eight dry and two wet, and that included a Hercules.

Vulcan tanker's eye view of a Phantom customer and a Russian Bear.

My record amount of fuel that I offloaded on one sortie was 53.5K (fuel in lbs) to seven Phantoms and two Lightnings. The areas most frequented to offload fuel were on towlines, designated areas which were generally long oblong boxes, mainly up and down the North Sea, where we were directed to refuel aircraft or just fly up and down within one of the areas waiting for trade.

We also took on the role of Operation Tansor which consisted of two crews, primary and secondary, whose job it was to be on call twenty-four hours a day, on the ground at different readiness times, to get airborne and refuel; for example, quick readiness alert Phantoms shadowing Russian Bears up in the Faeroes Gap around sixty-five degrees north, which was a regular occurrence. If the primary crew got airborne then the secondary took its place. Sometimes we would operate as a Tansor Mobile, where we were already airborne and ready to respond.

We also completed a number of trails. This was where we tanked aircraft across long distances where they didn't have the range to complete the journey but could do so after receiving fuel from us. I did the first Vulcan trail across the Atlantic, while others included one with Tornados to RCAF Goose Bay and return, and another with Jaguars to Bardufoss, Norway. The Vulcan tankers also took part in a number of different types of exercises. Those that appear in my logbook are namely: Bombay Duck, Coffee Charlie, Coffee Delta, Cold Cape, Elder Forest, Erica, Granular, Hawk Trail, JMC's, Mallet

Blow, Maulstick, Northern Wedding, Ossex, Priory, Roebuck, Scotadex, Scotex, Shout, Snow Goose, Storm Trail, Tankex, Teamwork and Westaxe. Although these seemed to be often obscure names, the component parts of who was operating with whom, the areas of operation and the tasks and aircraft involved, with Royal Navy ships at times, were well known to all those who took part. The occasional flypast at the nearby RAF Swinderby for their passing out parades was also tailored into a sortie whenever tasks permitted.

One story I remember from our tanking days involves the HDU and the hose and what we had been taught about them at Marham. The words of our instructor I recall were "there are only two places where the hose is safe, fully in or fully out". Therefore, when it was anywhere in between there was always a chance of the hose parting company with the HDU. One day one of the nav radars was flying the towline up north. Anticipating a request from a receiver aircraft, which had not quite arrived, he flicked the switch to trail the hose. Not really paying too much attention he went back to whatever he was doing. A short time later the receiver came up behind the Vulcan and asked for the hose to be trailed. The nav radar, now ready for action, stated that it was. The receiver pilot replied that it wasn't! After a quick check the embarrassed nav radar conceded that the pilot was correct. While the panel indicated that the hose was fully trailed, looking through the AEO's periscope it was nowhere to be seen. Somewhere, at some time, over Scotland, whilst the hose was trailing out, but not fully extended, it had dropped off! We never heard anything from the public. However, if anyone walking or climbing in the Scottish mountains or hills finds a large diameter, ninety-foot hose with a large thing looking like a shuttlecock on the end it belongs to the Royal Air Force.

Despite our heavy workload of tasks with the K2s, the Vulcan B2s were still being used. With 27 Squadron disbanded the B2s also undertook some maritime radar re-

50 Squadron Crest.
(*Anthony Wright*)

connaissance (MRR) work of which our crew flew five sorties; in addition they were also employed to train pilots in the role of receiving from a tanker. Furthermore they were still used to train co-pilots on their intermediate captains' course (ICC). One such time was when I was the detachment commander and we flew out Vulcan B2s to Akrotiri, Cyprus for the ICC of two of our co-pilots; they subsequently became captains on Victors.

On 12th October 1982 three of our Vulcan B2s took part in the Falklands War Victory Parade flypast over the City of London. I was in the lead aircraft, captained by Roger Dunsford one of the flight commanders.

The last month of 50 Squadron, March 1984, was quite hectic both from the flying carried out and the preparations for a disbandment parade with the various social activities that followed. To illustrate just a few of our sorties: all crews flew a number of exercises and we, along with another crew, took part in a photographic day for the press. In the morning the press flew in a Hercules, with its loading ramp down, taking photographs of our aircraft over the North Sea. Roger Dunsford and I flew in XH560, a Vulcan K2, and refuelled another Vulcan captained by Bill Burnett, the other flight commander. Indeed, this picture is often seen in aviation books and magazines.

During the same sortie we also refuelled Tornados, Jaguars, Buccaneers and a Phantom. Finally, we refuelled from another Vulcan. After the press had finished their airborne photography we all landed ready for the afternoon's event. This time four Vulcans were involved in a take-off for the media. It was to be the last ever scramble of Vulcans. Our crew was again to take part flying the same aircraft along with two other K2s and one B2.

On 23rd March our crew was on Tansor and we were called out to refuel Phantoms as far as sixty-three degrees north, Saxa Vord, and Unst. By pure chance it turned out to be the last call out for a Vulcan operational tasking. Finally, on 27th March I flew in the last Vulcan four-ship formation. As you would expect, one of the places which we flew over was Woodford, the home of Avro. Our squadron, the last Vulcan squadron, disbanded on Saturday 31st March 1984. On the Monday I arrived at the Ministry of Defence, Whitehall to start my next post – flying a desk.

Falklands celebration flypast 12th October 1982.

Chapter Sixteen

THOSE THAT ARE LEFT

There are three Vulcans which are still operating, thirty years after the aircraft went out of service. XH558 based at Doncaster is still flying and plans to do so until 2015; XM665 is based at Wellesbourne Mountford and is also civil registered but does not fly though it taxies every year; and XL426 based at Southend Airport used to taxi and hopefully will be taxiing again soon.

To keep these aircraft operating requires an enormous effort, almost entirely by volunteers, though Vulcan to the Sky, superbly managed by Robert Pleming, has a few employees to keep it airworthy. This book would not be complete without documenting what is involved to keep these aircraft going and the write-ups clearly show that there are Vulcan Boys who are still very current.

Charles Brimson manages the Vulcan that lives at Wellesbourne Mountford. He explains what it takes to keep this aircraft in operational condition so that the engines can be safely run and the aircraft taxied. As a regular visitor to the annual open day I never cease to be impressed by the professionalism of the small team and their continual achievement.

Vulcan B2 XM655 at Wellesbourne Mountford

XM655 is an Avro Vulcan B2, and the youngest Vulcan in existence (the third to last produced, XM656 and XM657 having both been scrapped). Delivered to IX Squadron at RAF Cottesmore in November 1964, she moved with the squadron to the Waddington wing in January 1968. She then served with 101 and 44 (Rhodesia) squadrons, and was with 50 Squadron when she was put up for disposal in late 1983. She was bought by businessman Roy Jacobsen who had hopes to fly her on the air show circuit.

XM655 was the first Vulcan 'civilianised' and was flown in to Wellesbourne Mountford about a week after a Cat 3 check, on 11th February 1984. Hundreds of people were there to watch her arrive. She had flown only 5,744 hours, making her a very viable proposition for taking to the air once more. However, the Civil Aviation Authority made it clear that the aircraft would not be flying again without stringent conditions being satisfied. While efforts at funding the work necessary were begun and the aircraft was put on the civil register as G-VULC, little real progress was made. A plan to fly the aircraft in America got as far as registering it on the American civil register as N655AV but no further. After two years Roy Jacobsen lost interest in XM655 and bought another Vulcan (XL426) which was delivered to Southend. Unpaid parking fees were mounting at Wellesbourne and after a number of years the airfield owners took Jacobsen to court to recover them. The result was that the ownership of the aircraft passed to Wellesbourne airfield.

XM655 had stood without attention for so long that she was in quite poor condition. Ten years of neglect had finally put paid to any lingering hopes of her ever flying

204

Vulcan XM655 volunteer team: Tim Deeley (engineer), Avril Magill (MaPS membership secretary and Wings & Wheels classic vehicles organiser), David McCulloch (air cadets instructor and engineer), Tanya Skelton (air cadets instructor), Ian Skelton (air cadets instructor and rigger), Bob Jackson (engineer), Charles Brimson (MaPS chairman and AEO), Bryan Hull (engineer, Wings & Wheels organiser and web store), Malcolm Campbell-Ritchie (engineer), Eric Ranshaw (chief engineer and MaPS treasurer), Sarah Oddy (MaPS secretary), Roger Bowen (MaPS vice chairman and engineer), Isabel Jackson (engineer), Len Hewitt (engineer and MaPS webmaster), Damaris Tapp (visitor manager and Wings & Wheels events organiser) and Ben Tapp (engineer). (*Charles Brimson*)

again. At one stage she had been broken into, the cockpit instrumentation vandalised and the co-pilot's control column removed with a hacksaw. The wing-tip panels were also damaged at some point. However, once the ownership had been transferred the future for the aircraft began looking brighter.

The Delta Engineering Association was formed to look after XM655 and it was made clear from the outset that the intention was to get it into ground-running condition only. The aircraft was gradually brought back to life; all the hydraulics were overhauled, the damage to the cockpit was repaired and a number of engine runs undertaken.

Delta Engineering moved from Wellesbourne to Kemble in March 1996 and, after the brief and unhappy existence and demise of the XM655 Association, the volunteers remaining at Wellesbourne decided that the best way forward would be a properly constituted membership organisation to look after XM655. As a result the 655 Maintenance and Preservation Society (655 MaPS) was formed in late 1998 with the clearly stated aims of 'maintaining and preserving AVRO Vulcan XM655 as a live and working example for the benefit of all' and 'providing a great example of Royal Air Force and British aviation heritage in order to further advance the education of the public about the history and purpose of the Vulcan in its RAF service'. The membership of MaPS comprises several hundred loyal folk whose generosity goes a long way towards funding the fuel, oils, and other consumables required to keep the complex aircraft operationally alive, although not airworthy.

The MaPS engineering team consists of a group of less than ten volunteers who spend every Saturday looking after the Vulcan. Their backgrounds include ex-RAF engineering, civilian turbine propulsion and other non-aviation related backgrounds – their common link being a love of all things Vulcan. They have to be 'jacks of all trades' as a typical day at Wellesbourne might include subjects as diverse as fault-finding a troublesome electrical problem amongst the aircraft's two electrical systems, carrying out routine maintenance on one of the ten powered flying control units, removing corrosion and painting the magnesium alloy airframe, giving guided tours of the Vulcan to visitors, or dreaming up fund-raising events to provide the finance to keep the whole show going!

Thanks to the generosity of Wellesbourne airfield and with funds provided by the society's members and other donors, 655MaPS have been able to assemble an impressive collection of workshops, storage units and ground equipment to support and service XM655. The engineering team have built up a library of original air publications and servicing publications to which they can refer when carrying out any work on the aircraft. MaPS also keep in close working contact with the Vulcan to the Sky Trust (VTST) at Hinckley and Finningley and the Vulcan Restoration Trust (VRT) at Southend Airport, sharing resources and knowledge to the joint benefit of all three Vulcans.

Although the Wellesbourne group is unencumbered by the necessarily high standards of maintaining an airworthy aircraft, they are nonetheless determined to maintain the Vulcan to a very high standard both from the safety aspect and also as a tribute to the people who designed, built and operated these aircraft during the days of the Cold War in the RAF. The aircraft is always crewed by an experienced Vulcan aircrew when it is taxied; fortunately there is no shortage of willing pilots and AEOs when the call goes out each year.

XM655 is virtually complete in terms of installed equipment, with the H2S radar, the terrain following radar (TFR) and identification friend or foe (IFF) systems all still in place, as well as the complete suite of electronic counter measures equipment. The only notable item missing when XM655 left RAF service was the in-flight refuelling probe; not surprising considering the worldwide hunt for serviceable probes which had occurred during the Falklands conflict a couple of years earlier. Eventually, a replacement probe was obtained and installed, and XM655 regained her familiar profile.

An even more recent addition ensures that the aircraft looks like a bomber – mounted within the cavernous bomb bay now is a 'Vulcan Seven Store Carrier' which is the piece of kit from which were suspended seven 1,000lb conventional HE bombs. This has been provided on long-term loan from the RAF Museum. MaPS volunteers have fabricated seven very realistic fibreglass replicas of 1,000lb HE bombs (complete with genuine arming vanes), the visual impact of which stuns visitors to the aircraft when the bomb doors are opened.

The rear spar has been inspected and found to be in excellent condition. XM655 now has fuel in her tanks at all times to keep the system and the seals 'wet'. All the aircraft electrical and hydraulic systems are powered up and exercised regularly.

The Vulcan has been repainted several times to keep the inevitable corrosion of the almost fifty-year-old structure under control, the flying control surfaces (elevons and rudder) have been re-skinned, the jet pipe end caps have been replaced and the two engines with the longest running hours have been removed, opened, inspected and re-installed. The engineering team have recently embarked on a programme to fabricate replacement frames and re-skin the trailing edge of the four inboard elevons. Parts of the 'spine' of the airframe skin have also had to be replaced with modern aluminium as well. The MaPS team are also taking advantage of the situation where several original equipment manufacturers (OEMs) are once again manufacturing Vulcan parts to keep XH558 airworthy: this being the case MaPS is buying whatever consumables they can both afford and need such as new tyres and braking system parts until they once again become unavailable.

Engine ground runs (EGRs) are carried out approximately every three months, together with slow taxi runs to ensure the steering and braking systems are functional. Once each year, usually in June, XM655 is the star of the show at Wellesbourne Wings & Wheels, which is MaPS' major public event of the year. The highlight is for the crowd to witness the awesome spectacle of four mighty Olympus 301 turbojets, between them generating 80,000lbs of static thrust, very rapidly accelerating the Vulcan to about 90kts in a matter of a few seconds, followed by closing the throttles, extending the airbrakes and pulling back on the 'stick' to raise the nose-wheel briefly into the air. This last action ensures that the great delta wing becomes a very effective aerodynamic brake, as the end of the 3,000ft runway at Wellesbourne rapidly fills the view from the pilots' seats! The fuel used during this brief demonstration is enormous; with the throttles fully open for no more than eight seconds, the four engines burn something like 3,000 litres of Jet A-1 from start-up to close-down.

The responsibility for organising Wings & Wheels each year also lies with the small body of hard-working volunteers (several of whom have full-time jobs as well), the sub-committee meeting for the first time a month or so after the previous year's show has happened. The aim of the Wings & Wheels committee sounds simple; it is to put on a great show, spending as little as possible in order to make as much money for XM655 as possible. When it comes to the show, the small MaPS team receives very welcome support from the local (and not so local) air cadet squadrons who help with crowd control and parking organisation, Wellesbourne airfield management and air traffic control and other volunteers drafted in for the day.

Raising funds is a never-ending challenge – Wings & Wheels is an annual show, so the MaPS team have set up a shop selling branded XM655 merchandise both at the airfield as well as via their website. The website also brings in leads for organised visits of interested societies and clubs, for whom MaPS will happily put on a special show, in return for cash!

As well as tending to the needs of the Vulcan, efforts have to be made to keep the ground equipment serviceable as well. MaPS has a growing collection of kit, most of it all former RAF V Force equipment, such as the Tugmaster Sentinel aircraft tug, the Houchin ground power diesel generator, a Palouste low-pressure turbine air starter, a hydraulically powered armament lifter and, most recently added, a standard airfield bomb transporter.

What drives the MaPS team on is the knowledge that they are the custodians of the only Olympus 301-powered Vulcan in the world still capable of moving under its own power, and that their unique operation of having the aircraft accessible to the public and yet as close to its original guise as a nuclear-armed bomber as possible, makes all the hard work seem very worthwhile indeed.

> A splendid description of what it takes to keep 655 going. In my opinion a visit to Wellesbourne on the open day is a great experience – the enthusiasm of all the helpers is obvious and a pleasure to experience not to mention seeing the Vulcan perform at really close quarters.
>
> **Mike Pollitt** taxis 655 and he gives an operator's perspective of demonstrating the aircraft.

As I move the throttle levers forward in their central quadrant between the two pilots the characteristic howl of four Olympus 301 series engines, each capable of producing 20,000lbs of thrust, rises above the usual piston-engine noise from the active flying clubs at Wellesbourne. I note the crowds of onlookers cover their ears, those that haven't already that is, as the noise outside the cockpit is tremendous. With the thrust now building toward 80,000lbs and her usual weight being less than 120,000lbs, I begin to appreciate how a pebble might feel just prior to being released from a catapult! A check of the engines as they momentarily align around 80% rpm, brakes released and straight up to 100%.

I have ridden powerful motorcycles and flown single-seat jets (although not Lightnings) for many hundreds of hours but there is nothing in my experience to compare with a low-fuelled Vulcan out of the blocks. Four seconds later and her speed is powering through 90 knots at full power and just a second later as the first airspeed indicator passes 110 knots we close the throttles, select high drag airbrake and pull the stick back. The nose-wheel rises to the classic Vulcan high nose, high drag, braking attitude that unfortunately, we cannot maintain for very long on Wellesbourne's very short main runway of 917m (3,008ft). A warning light illuminates to demonstrate that the warning lever on the aircraft's tail is in contact with the ground – a second light illuminates to show that the warning lever is depressed more than half way, the tail is literally now only an inch or so above the runway. Before we lose all lift, the nose is lowered and the brakes applied and another ground run has ended – all too quickly.

It is the end of a long weekend's preparation for the crew but the culmination of twelve months of love and careful maintenance provided by Charles Brimson and the enthusiastic 655 ground crew volunteers, who devote so many of their weekends throughout the year to keeping this brilliant aircraft in such fine condition. Her paintwork is immaculate and the engines and flying controls feel really taut and I'm always amazed at the way her systems come to life even though she remains outside throughout the winter. David Thomas, John Laycock, Barry Masefield (our AEO) and I come down on the day prior to the fast ground run to start her up and give her a short taxi to check her systems. It's like coming home climbing up the entry ladder, smelling the characteristic Vulcan cockpit odour and hearing Barry's voice reading out the checklist. But she comes alive with an R/T call to Wellesbourne ATC, "Vulcan request engine start, four people on board".

We usually run up the engines, after engine start, in pairs No 1 & 4 and then 2 & 3 to check condition and instrumentation. On ground-run day we park on the east side of the airfield on R/W 23; generating sufficient power to begin taxiing alone can create a lot of dust and has moved fifty-gallon oil drums at 200 metres in past years, so we take great care to ensure that there are no loose objects behind her. Generally, the run is conducted on Father's Day at the Wellesbourne Wings & Wheels Air Day and it is usually accompanied by a classic car rally and hopefully a few flypasts by other classic aircraft too. We are so grateful to the local ATC squadron (1368) who provide a valiant service as show marshals for us on the day.

"Vulcan request taxi four people on board" – Frankie in the tower replies, "Vulcan clear taxi and hold prior to entering 36/18". Forward on the throttles to about 60-65% and 655 moves majestically forward prior to an initial brake and steering check. "Vulcan clear enter runway and backtrack for ground run." If we go to the north end of the airfield for the run in a southerly direction we have a volunteer on the road outside to prevent the odd caravan passing immediately behind as we run up to take-off power. In turning to line up for the run two years ago, I blew two people over as we turned and the engines were only just above idle. "Vulcan clear run...."

> Though I operated most of the Vulcans that Avros built I never had to do what Mike did. It is a tricky manoeuvre carrying out an accelerate stop on a short 3,000ft runway and great care has to be taken, not only to stop but also not to overheat the brakes. I particularly noticed Mike commenting on the tail bumper warning light illuminating since when landing the aircraft normally, even very slowly. I never saw it come on but it clearly comes in very useful at Waddington.

> **Mike Pollitt** was also very much involved with XH558 in a managerial capacity until it moved north from Bruntingthorpe. He explains, amongst other things, what is involved in arranging all the displays.

Vulcan Mk2 XH558 Based at Doncaster Airport — the Operations Director Perspective
Eventually, after almost seven years refurbishment and £7.5m investment on 18th October 2007 Al McDicken (captain and test pilot), David Thomas (first pilot) and Barry Masefield (AEO) entered the cockpit of 558 and started her engines. In front of a number of aviation journalists, a couple of broadcast companies and a small crowd of well wishers, including two CAA representatives, XH558 returned to the sky for the first time since David Thomas had landed her at Bruntingthorpe in Leicestershire fourteen years earlier. It was an emotional moment for all of us involved with the Vulcan to the

Sky project and it marked what we hoped at the time would be the culmination of a tremendous engineering achievement to restore her to flying condition and the moment when we would begin to attract major financial sponsorship.

There followed a series of flight tests flown with Iain Young, chief test pilot for Marshalls Aerospace, David Thomas, Barry Masefield and Andy Marsden, navigator. Finally, with all the required paperwork at last in place and on the day before the Waddington Air Show, which we all so desperately wanted to make, the CAA presented me with the permit to fly on 3rd July 2008. I should add that the CAA had been supportive of the project throughout and had helped David and I publish the organisational control manual, the vast majority of which David tirelessly produced that laid down the training, currency and display requirements and limitations. It took David and me a couple of years to make the transition from the military procedures we knew so well to the CAA methodology. This did lead to frustration on both sides – why were we using military maps and publications still when we were supposed to be a civilian organisation? Eventually a more pragmatic approach evolved and we successfully passed our next CAA inspection. Anyway, back to 3rd July 2008. Having gained our permit to fly we now had to gain our display authorisation, which meant three public displays in front of a CAA examiner.

David Evans had kindly agreed to travel up from CAA HQ at Gatwick to position at RAF Waddington in the hope that we might gain our permit that day. At 1530 with David Thomas as captain, Martin Withers as co-pilot and with Barry Masefield and his trainee AEO Phil Davies also on board, XH558 departed Bruntingthorpe for RAF Waddington. Pam Thomas, David's wife joined me in the car for a dash up the A46 from

Vulcan XH558 still flying. (*Laurens van de Craafs – www.airtoair.nl*)

Bruntingthorpe to Waddington. We arrived as David completed his third display and David Evans awarded him his display authorisation. We were fit for display at Waddington on 5th July 2008! David Thomas was at the helm, and had been the display pilot on the Vulcan Display Flight with the RAF in the 1980s and early 1990s. Together with Barry Masefield as AEO and Martin Withers as the co-pilot, XH558 was back on the display circuit.

Vulcan XH558 celebrating six years since the first flight as G-VLCN.
(*Charles Toop*)

My role as operations director began soon after. It was my responsibility to ensure that we had sufficient aircrew for the displays we intended to perform and that they were trained in accordance with the syllabus agreed with the CAA and maintained currency as aircrew and display aircrew in line with CAA regulations. I also liaised with the display venues to see if they would like the Vulcan to appear at their show and negotiated the display fee with the show organisers. In those early years we charged £10,000 for a display but £5,000 for a flypast. This might appear to be a large sum for what was an eight-minute display. However, if I could arrange to do a couple of displays on the same day then I had more room for negotiation and we could hope to meet our operating costs. The bomber was costing Vulcan to the Sky £20,000 for each flying hour. If we could agree the fee then we would do our utmost to appear.

Weather was our worry. We had gained a permit to fly, which restricted us to visual meteorological conditions (VMC) that meant, basically, we had to remain clear of cloud. Way before we commenced flying in early 2007 we had submitted to the CAA a case for us to be granted an elementary IMC clearance that would allow us to enter cloud with the intention of climbing through it to gain VMC on top. By remaining clear of cloud we were flying the aircraft like all general aviation traffic and dicing with small aircraft, gliders and microlights in uncontrolled airspace in the lower altitudes. Looking out of the Vulcan was not the easiest occupation — it has been described as akin to sitting in a post box and trying to spot other flying objects by peering through the slot. We did have a couple of minor air misses but eventually in 2013, the CAA granted our request to fly under instrument flying rules with strictly limited IMC procedures.

Initially, David Thomas, Al McDicken, Martin Withers and Kevin Rumens (who was an ex-Tornado GR4 pilot, now with Virgin Atlantic but had previously flown the Vulcan as a co-pilot during the Vulcan Display Flight years) were our initial pilot pool with Barry Masefield and Phil Davies as our AEOs. Later Bill Perrins, Phil O'Dell and Bill Ramsey joined the pilot team. We were also fortunate to be joined each year by Paul Mulcahy (CAA chief test pilot) who conducted the annual air test and even attended our annual refresher ground school. Last but by no means least Andy Marson, navigator, often flies with the crew and kindly hosts the annual refresher ground school. Very recently Barry announced his intention to retire at the end of the 2013 season and they have trained Jonathan Lazzari to replace him. I think I can remember Jonathan was on 44 Squadron – and very young in the late 1970s! I retired in December 2010 just before the move to Doncaster and Martin Withers took on the role of operations director as well as chief pilot.

The biggest headache for me during my time as operations director was the continual lack of funding for the project. It was extremely frustrating never to know if you would have the financial resources to continue and therefore you could never guarantee being able to meet a display venue commitment. This caused a degree of friction between ourselves and some air show organisers but most understood the situation and appreciated our predicament. As you know Dr Robert Pleming and his team are now endeavouring to maintain XH558 in flight until the end of the 2015 season. I wish them all well.

Mike has explained how the flying operation of 558 is planned in every detail from the ground training, to the practice displays and then to the displays themselves. All this has to be carried out in what is clearly a very careful and demanding financial climate which is overseen by Robert Pleming and the trustees of Vulcan to the Sky. A triumph to all concerned. On a personal note I regard 558 in a fatherly way having tested and delivered it to the RAF and so it was a great moment for me, as well as for everyone else, to watch 558 fly again from Bruntingthorpe; it was also a slightly surprising moment since a few years earlier when I was on the board of the Civil Aviation Authority the last thing we wanted was to have military aircraft on the civil register!

David Griffiths has been involved as a trustee of the Vulcan Restoration Trust and XL426 for many years. He explains the current status and the forecast for commencing taxiing again.

Vulcan XL426 at Southend Airport: The Vulcan Restoration Trust
Vulcan B2 XL426 at Southend Airport is one of the proud members of the exclusive club of three 'live' Vulcans. Retired from the RAF in 1986, her ownership transferred to

what is now the Vulcan Restoration Trust in 1993. In 1995 she taxied for the first time after her arrival at the airport and in 1997 she performed her first speed run. Performing regular speed runs each year, she was eventually withdrawn from regular taxiing in 2006 for some extensive engineering work to ensure that she be capable of taxiing for at least a further twenty years. Taxiing the aircraft at least three times a year for nearly ten years had taken its toll on the aircraft systems and was putting the volunteer engineering support team under huge pressure as they fixed minor problems, all of which could do with some serious 'down time' to develop more robust engineering solutions. Financing this engineering programme was a fund-raising scheme called 'Return to Power' which has been well supported by not only members of the VRT but also by the public. In the closing months of 2013, XL426 is emerging from this long period of restoration as a far better airframe than she was when she began her sabbatical.

Vulcan Mk2 XL426 with some of the volunteers who are bringing the aircraft back to life. Front row: Kevin Packard, Tony Kitson, Andy Vass. Back row: Matt Chester, Matt Lawrence (chief engineer), Colin Cockerton, Andy Wagstaff (lead engineer), Steven Harvey, Peter Rainey, Pablo Martinez Perez. (*David Griffiths*)

Since 2006, two elevons have been substantially rebuilt, a job which has included remanufacture of some major structural components; the braking and associated hydraulic system has been overhauled and a substantial section replaced; all the wheels and brake units, including spares have been overhauled by Rotable Repairs Ltd and a brand new set of tyres acquired for the aircraft. The list of other jobs carried out includes a complete overhaul of the powered flight control units, the undercarriage legs and even the crew seats – in fact everything needed for a taxiing Vulcan. Most visible to the public has been a recent repaint which will be completed during the winter of 2013-14 and sees the aircraft honouring two squadrons with which it served, 617 and 50, each insignia being applied to opposite sides of the huge tail fin.

Public access to XL426 is a challenge but one that has been overcome with the

Refitting the XL426 rebuilt elevons. (*David Griffiths*)

programme of highly popular 'Visit the Vulcan' days which take place on four Sundays during the spring and summer months. The need to keep XL426 on the 'live' side of the airport necessarily restricts public access and more so recently as London Southend Airport has been transformed from a sleepy backwater to a bustling regional airport. Nevertheless, the airport management have been most accommodating and access, whilst more tightly controlled than in the past, has proved no problem for the public open days.

Matt Lawrence and the engineering team have grown steadily over the last ten years but the skills have grown exponentially with far more ambitious technical projects being well within the capability of the team. The rapid growth of London Southend saw the demolition of the VRT's main engineering and spares storage facility on the airport but, necessity being the mother of invention, a far superior workshop and spares store has been created a few miles away.

The VRT is a wholly volunteer operation and continues to be largely funded from its membership subscriptions with additional support from its trading arm, VRT Enterprises Ltd which operates an on-line shop on the website (www.avrovulcan.com).

The relationship with Vulcan To The Sky and 655 MaPS has been invaluable as all three groups are able to share spares and expertise and the VRT has been delighted with several flying visits from XH558 over the past few years. The Vulcan Restoration Trust is dedicated to keeping XL426 as a living breathing airframe for many years to come and her return to taxiing status in late 2013 will be the beginning of another leg in quite a rollercoaster ride since the organisation formed in 1990. The VRT intends XL426 to remain a fully paid-up member of the Live Vulcan Club for a good few years yet!

I am so pleased to be able to have in this book these accounts of managing and servicing the three Vulcans that are left because it is important for people who love watching them to realise how much money and voluntary effort is needed to keep them operating. We are indeed fortunate to have so many dedicated enthusiasts so that we can see these splendid aircraft still performing.

EPILOGUE

It is a challenge to know how to end this book with such splendid accounts of the Vulcan from almost the day it was created to the present day, when it is enjoying an afterlife. The aircraft was born to defend the United Kingdom from nuclear attack during the Cold War and there can be no doubt that it did this most successfully. It is difficult now, almost seventy years after it was conceived, to appreciate all the decisions and compromises that had to be made so that the aircraft could be produced in the required time frame.

One has to admire the confidence and ambition of the engineers in the UK aircraft and engine industries at that time to undertake to produce an aircraft like the Vulcan, with no guarantee that its aerodynamics would be acceptable or that the engines would be available to propel it to the required level of performance. In fact it took the combined skills of Avros, the Royal Aircraft Establishment and a little firm called Newmarks to make the aircraft usable; and the combined skills of Armstrong Siddeley, Bristol Engine Company and Rolls-Royce to produce the amazing Olympus engine, the forerunner of today's superb military and civil engines. It should be remembered that by the time the 21,000lb thrust engine was available together with the Mk2 airframe, the aircraft pretty well met all the original 1946 specifications, with the bonus of the delta design being able to provide the UK's ultimate deterrent at low level.

For many years the Royal Air Force had aircraft loaded with atomic bombs ready for immediate take-off, kept ready by the ground crews with the aircrews at instant readiness. No flying hours went into the aircraft manuals or the aircrews' log books but the ensuing years of peace were due in no small part to these crews' dedication.

And then came the entirely last-minute extension of the useful life of the aircraft with the Falklands campaign. It took the imagination of the chief of the Air Staff, Sir Michael Beetham, a one-time Valiant pilot, to realise what the Vulcan might be able to do and with the blessing of Mrs Thatcher he instigated the Black Buck raids; still they were only made possible by incredibly hard and dedicated work from hundreds if not thousands of people, somehow fitting the Vulcan out with the necessary tools and equipment and then training the crews, Victor as well as Vulcan, to make the hazardous journey 3,885 miles from Ascension Island just south of the equator to the stormy southern oceans in the Roaring Forties and then to make it back.

However, the story is not yet over for the Vulcan, thanks to the imagination of volunteers who prevented three aircraft going to the scrap yard. These aircraft thrill people in the UK and beyond and show what can be done with sufficient determination. Let us hope that there are many youngsters who are inspired by these aircraft, study aerospace engineering and take on the mantle of Roy Chadwick and Frank Whittle.

Tony Blackman
December 2013

APPENDIX 1
ACRONYMS & EXPLANATIONS

A&AEE	Aircraft and Armament Experimental Establishment
AAM	Anti-Aircraft Missile
AAPP	Auxiliary Airborne Power Plant
AAR	Air-to-Air Refuelling
AC	Air Conditioning
AEO	Air Electronics Officer
AFB	United States Air Force Base
AGL	Above Ground Level
AID	Aeronautical Inspection Department
AOC	Air Officer Commanding Group
ARM	Anti-radiation missile
AVS	Air Ventilate Suits
BTR	Basic Training Requirements
CFS	Central Flying School
DCF	Duty Commander Flying
'Doppler Effect'	Change of frequency due to relative movement
DSSS	Direct-sequence spread spectrum communication system
DTTF	Double Top Training Flight
ECM	Electronic Counter Measures
ETPS	Empire Test Pilot School
FRC	Flight Reference Cards
FTE	Flight Test Engineer
F700	Servicing Record book for each aircraft
F/S	Fire/Security (PanAm Ascension)
GPI Mk 6	Ground Position Indicator
'Green Satin'	Doppler drift and ground speed computer
H2S	Early radar fitted to the V Force
HDU	Hose Drum Unit
HTP	High Test Peroxide
IFF	Identification Friend or Foe
ILS	Instrument Landing System
IMC	Instrument Meteorological Conditions
IMN	Indicated Mach Number
INS	Inertial Navigator
IRT	Instrument Rating Test
ITP	Instruction to Proceed
JSTU	Joint Services Trial Unit
LGB	Laser Guided Bombs
MaPS	Vulcan 655 Maintenance and Preservation Society
MFS	Smiths Military Flight System
MHQ	Maritime Headquarters
MOD	Ministry of Defence
MOD(PE)	Ministry of Defence Procurement Executive
MPA	Marine Patrol Aircraft
MRR	Maritime Radar Reconnaissance
NATO	North Atlantic Treaty Organisation
NBC	Nuclear Biological Chemical suit
NBS	Navigation and Bombing System
NOTAMs	Notices to Airmen (or Not to worry about the next morning NOT AM!)
NTP	Navigation Termination Point
OCU	Operational Conversion Unit
ORP	Operational Readiness Platform
PAWS	Pan American World Service
PEC	Position Error Correction
PEs	Position Error Measurements
PFC/ PFCU	Powered Flying Control Units
PFTS	Production Flight Test Schedule
PK	Probability of kill
QFI	Qualified Flying Instructor
QRA	Quick Reaction Alert
RAE	Royal Aircraft Establishment
RAM	Reconnaissance Air Meet
RAT	Ram Air Turbine
RBSU	Radar Bomb Scoring Units
Red Steer	Tail Warning Radar
'Red Shrimp'	ECM Jammer
RSnn	Readiness State nn minutes
RTB	Return to Base
RV	Rendezvous Point
RWR	Radar Warning Receiver
SAC	Strategic Air Command
SBAC	Society of British Aerospace Constructors
SEAD	Suppression of enemy air defences
SOP	Standard Operating Procedure
SSA	Supplementary Storage Area where nuclear stores were kept
STS	Structural Test Specimen
TACAN	Tactical Air Navigation System
TANSOR	Tanker Sortie defence UK
TFR	Terrain Following Radar
TRU	Transformer Rectifier Unit
VMC	Visual Meteorological Conditions
VRT	Vulcan Restoration Trust
WRE	Weapons Research Establishment, Woomera, Australia

APPENDIX 2
BLACK BUCK RAIDS ON FALKLANDS ISLANDS BY VULCANS, 1982

Operation Corporate: Black Buck Raids on Falkland Islands by Vulcans, 1982

Black Buck 1	21 x 1,000lb	30th April	XM607	Martin Withers
Black Buck 2	21 x 1,000lb	3rd May	XM607	John Reeve
Black Buck 3	Martels/ Bombs	16th May	XM607	
Black Buck 4	Shrikes. Failed due HDU fault	28th May	XM597	Neil McDougall
Black Buck 5	3 Shrikes	30th May	XM697	Neil McDougall
Black Buck 6	2 Shrikes	2nd June	XM597	Neil McDougall
Black Buck 7	21 x 1,000lb	11th June	XM607	Martin Withers

Crew Compositions

Martin Withers, Peter Taylor, Bob Wright, Gordon Graham, Hugh Prior, plus Dick Russell (6th seat Victor air-to-air refueling instructor [AARI])

John Reeve, Don Dibbens, Mick Cooper, Jim Vinales, Barry Masefield, plus Pete Standing (6th seat Victor AARI)

Neil McDougall, Chris Lackman, Dave Castle, Barry Smith, Rod Trevaskus, plus Vulcan Captain Brian Gardner (6th seat)

Monty Montgomery, Bill Perrins, Dave Stenhouse, Dick Arnott, John Hathaway with Ian Clifford/Pete Ford/Flight Lieutenant Parker

Black Buck 3 proved to be an interesting non-event which up to now has not been fully described. The Vulcans arrived in Ascension with Martels fitted and the sortie was being prepared with full Victor support. However, almost at the last moment, a message was received at Widewake operations from Waddington via HQ 1 Group to remove the Martels and pylons; the reason for this is now officially given as to avoid collateral damage but it might also have been associated with a crew concern that the airframe drag with the Martels had increased considerably. The removal instruction was not carried out immediately for some reason and 1 Group had to get on to Mel James directly to corroborate the instruction. His team was working at full stretch and decided it was quicker to remove the whole port pylon rather than separate the Martel and its attachment from the Pye pylon beam; Mel covered the gaps left by the removal of the pylon with speed tape. The aircraft were then prepared to carry 21 x 1000lb bombs but by now time was running short for the planned sortie date of 16th May and so Northwood took the decision to cancel the mission giving bad weather as the reason.

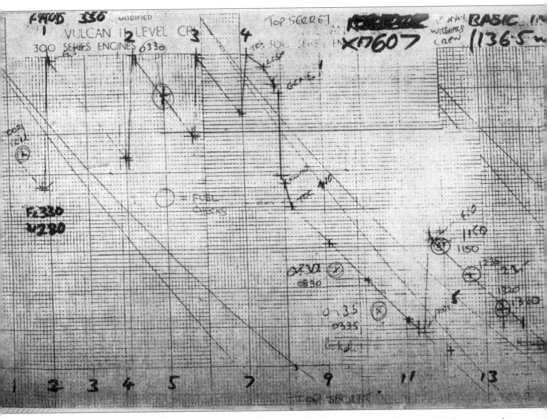

This fuel planning chart is the original fuel plan for Black Buck 1; 'Withers crew' can be seen written on the top of the page and a similar sheet would have been given to John Reeve and his crew who were the prime crew for Black Buck 1. This plan was changed to improve the fuel usage for Black Buck 2.

The fuel planning chart shown above has the weight on the left-hand side and the time on the bottom; each big square represents 10,000lbs. The take-off weight was 136,500lbs plus 72,000lbs of fuel totalling 208,500lbs, 4,500lbs above the certificated maximum take-off weight. Four refuellings were planned outbound and there is a circled cross between refuellings two and three drawn by Dick Russell in the right-hand seat showing that the actual fuel was as the plan. The vertical line after refuelling number four shows where the bombs are dropped and therefore represent a weight loss of 21,000lbs. The planned top of climb at 41,000lbs can be seen, marked TOC and the line descends steadily to the final refuel. The significant points are the five circled crosses representing the actual fuel against the planned fuel. The first two are below the planned line by about 7,000lbs but after the refuel the next three circled crosses are on the fuel plan. Not surprisingly when 'superfuse' was called Martin asked for an extra 10,000lbs which he clearly obtained.

INDEX

1

101 Squadron 38, 47, 51, 66, 105, 111, 129,
135, 137, 140, 141, 146, 172, 196, 204
148 Squadron 52

4

44 (Rhodesia) Squadron 38, 39, 66, 68,
70, 71, 72, 74, 75, 84, 97, 98, 109, 111,
129, 136-139, 140-142, 162, 168, 169,
172, 175, 196, 204, 212

6

617 Squadron 17, 89, 92, 102, 103, 109,
121, 213

8

83 Squadron 89, 91

A

Akrotiri 54, 65, 70, 71, 75, 76, 77, 78, 120,
122, 202
Arnott, Dick 62, 114, 217
Ascension 114, 128, 132, 133, 135, 136,
140, 141, 143, 146-169, 172, 173, 176,
177, 181, 182, 184, 187, 192, 193, 194,
215, 217

B

Barksdale 101-104, 106, 109, 199
Big Flight 59, 62, 63, 64, 101
Blackman, Tony 9, 10, 14-17, 28, 29, 156,
166
Blue Danube 15
Blue Steel 17, 24, 25, 34, 89-94, 100, 102
Boscombe 14, 15, 24, 35, 51, 135, 175, 185
Bourne, David 9, 100, 102, 115
Brimson, Charles 9, 204, 205, 208
Broadhurst, Harry 15, 18

C

Calder, Jock 17
Candlish, Ed 108
Castle, David 9, 10, 160, 171, 194, 217
Concorde 33-35
Cuban missile crisis 49, 51, 81

D

D'Arcy, Mike 39, 41, 68, 70, 71, 76, 78
Dee, Tony 107
Dobson, Roy 28

E

ECM 42, 128-131, 138, 145, 152, 178, 216

F

Falk, Leysa 29
Falk, Roly 14-16, 28, 29
Filton 25, 33, 35, 36
Finningley 23, 38, 39, 41, 42, 53, 68, 74, 80, 84, 126, 171, 172, 206

G

Giant Voice 10, 59, 63, 65, 100, 101-105, 108, 115, 161, 164
Goose Bay 63, 64, 72, 82, 86, 100, 101, 102, 111, 115, 116, 117, 119, 196, 201
Griffiths, David 9, 212

H

Haddock, Jack 12, 24
Harrison, Jimmy 12, 14-18, 24, 28
Hartley, Ted 9, 11-13, 26-28, 30, 31
Hathaway, John 114, 145, 217
Hawkins, Ossie 17, 23, 24
HDU 135, 149, 196, 197, 201, 202, 216, 217
Hinge, Colin 107, 108
Hoskins, Peter 107
Howard, Podge 15-18
HTP 91, 92, 216

J

James, Mel 9, 95, 98, 135, 140, 146, 217

K

Kendrick, Ken 9, 136

L

Laycock, John 9, 95, 96, 100, 127, 135, 152, 157, 162, 174, 176, 177, 184, 186, 195, 209
Leach, Ray 9, 95
Leckenby, Phil 9, 38, 68, 74, 78
Leconfield 22, 31
Lumb, Chris 9, 195-200

M

MaPS 205-208, 214, 216
Marham 52, 53, 119, 129, 131, 138, 143, 152, 154, 158, 169, 196, 200, 202
Marmont, Ted 9, 39, 67, 73, 76
Martin, Dickie 17, 23, 24, 30

Mayes, Wg Cdr 111, 114
McDougall, Neil 129, 132, 133, 135, 154, 160, 162, 173, 174, 187, 217
MFS 43, 45, 74, 216
Montgomery, Monty 9, 102, 111, 129, 132, 142, 148, 151, 164, 217
Muharraq 54, 90

N

Nellis 101, 110-113, 119

O

Offutt Air Force Base 63, 74, 82, 86, 100-102, 111, 115-117, 119, 120, 123-125, 162
Oil burner 60, 100, 123

P

Perrins, Bill 9, 114, 160, 212, 217
Pleming, Robert 10, 125, 204, 212
Pogson, Bob 9, 11, 20, 27-29
Pollitt, Harry 9, 24, 25, 33
Pollitt, Mike 9, 208, 209
Port Stanley 10, 131-133, 148, 151-170, 171, 173, 179, 184
Proudlove, Dickie 20, 31
Pye, Chris 136

Q

QRA 45-47, 49, 50, 52, 53, 55, 63, 76, 92, 216

R

Red Flag 10, 66, 100, 101, 102, 110-114, 119, 129, 148, 154
Reeve, John 9, 112, 129, 132, 144, 145, 162, 163, 166, 174, 217, 218
Reid, Chris 9, 89
Rio de Janeiro 10, 138, 139, 149, 171, 172, 188, 190-194
Rolls-Royce 25, 33, 34, 49, 125, 130, 137, 182, 192, 215

S

Salisbury 70-72
Scampton 14, 65, 85, 86, 89, 91, 92, 93, 102, 103, 110, 111, 120, 140, 143, 161, 172

Sextant 68, 74, 78, 104-108, 173

Shrike 10, 130, 133-135, 137, 138, 149, 152, 160, 167, 171, 175-179, 182-186, 188, 192, 193, 217

Skybolt 14, 43-45, 128, 130, 133, 135, 136, 141, 152, 174, 178

Sumner, Adrian 9, 115, 120

T

Taceval 95-97, 98, 99

Tapestry 65, 85

TFR 44, 111, 131, 180, 206, 216

Tornado 8, 35, 36, 111, 127, 131, 168, 201, 203, 212

TSR2 36, 82

V

Vinales, Jim 9, 100, 104, 161, 217

W

Waddington 16, 17, 19, 23, 30, 31, 38, 41, 45, 46, 63, 66, 68-70, 73-75, 76, 78, 84, 96-99, 103, 110, 111, 114, 119, 120, 123, 125, 127, 128, 129-142, 146-149, 152-154, 157, 158, 162, 163, 164, 172-174, 184, 195, 196, 200, 204, 209, 210, 211, 217

West, Peter 9, 80

Wideawake 141-143, 146, 147, 151-170, 177, 178, 182, 183

Withers, Martin 8, 9, 102, 111, 114, 129, 132, 133, 145, 148, 150-153, 163-165, 210-212, 217

Woodford 7, 12, 14-18, 21-31, 33, 34, 140, 195, 196, 200, 203

Wright, Anthony 9, 52, 59, 100, 110, 114, 147, 200

X

XA903   17, 24, 34

XL361   102

XL573   102, 124

XM603   23,

XM605   102, 123, 124

OTHER TITLES BY TONY BLACKMAN CURRENTLY AVAILABLE

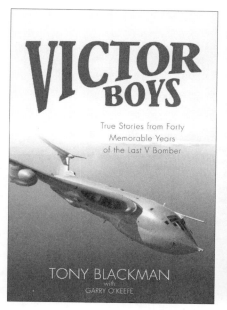

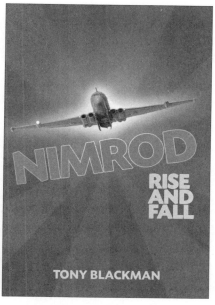

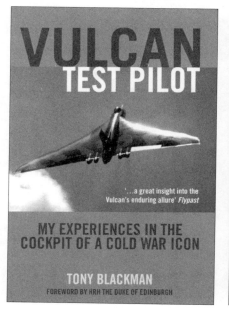

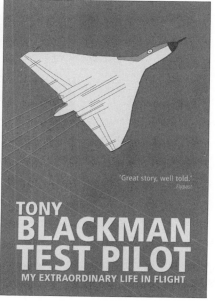